Enter The Dragon

Melbourne House

First Published in the United Kingdom
by Melbourne House

This Remastered Edition
Published in 2022 by
Acorn Books
acornbooks.uk

Publisher's Note

The Dragon 32 heralds a new direction in affordable computers - a computer that is well-built, robust, attractive and has ample memory!

This makes working and playing on the Dragon 32 a joy, and Melbourne House is very pleased to be involved in programming and developing new frontiers on the Dragon 32.

The programs in this book are the result of many people's work, and are intended to show you the scope of this microcomputer. The programs themselves range from simpler programs to programs that stretch the limits of the computer.

All are intended to stir your imagination and spur you on to write your own exciting programs. So if you have a program or article about the Dragon 32 that you think would be of interest to other owners, please write to us. We will give you a prompt assessment and reply whether the material is something we could use. In this way, you will also be helping us to provide Dragon 32 users with more and better material!

In the meantime, happy computing.

ALFRED MILGROM
PUBLISHER

P.S Don't forget to fill in the registration card at the back of this book, so that we may keep you informed of development about the Dragon 32.

Contents

THE DRAGON KEYBOARD

As you may know the INKEY$ function of the DRAGON computer does not allow for the keys to repeat (i.e to get INKEY$ to recognize a key more than once you must release the key and press it again). This is not very useful for games where you are trying to move and fire your ship (or whatever). To overcome this the following method allows you to scan the keyboard directly and see which keys have been pressed.

It is based on the fact that the DRAGON computer has a set of eight memory locations that are a copy of exactly what is being pressed at the keyboard. Because these exist we can use PEEK to check the keyboard and thus have repeating keys for games etc.

To find out which key has been pressed from these locations is quite simple and the following table will give you the information you need.

location	254	253	251	247	239	223	191
338	0	8	@	H	P	X	ENTER
339	1	9	A	I	Q	Y	CLEAR
340	2	:	B	J	R	Z	
341	3	;	C	K	S	UP	
342	4	,	D	L	T	DOWN	
343	5	-	E	M	U	LEFT	
344	6	.	F	N	V	RIGHT	
345	7	/	G	O	W	SPACE	

(UP, DOWN, LEFT and RIGHT are the arrow keys on the keyboard).

The left hand column is the address of the location to be PEEKed to check the keys in the given row: i.e PEEK(342) will check keys "4 , D L T DOWN"

The top row of numbers is the value that will be returned if the key in the column above is pressed: e.g if the key L is pressed then PEEK(342) will give 247.

Note that this method only tells you what key has been pressed, it does not recognize the SHIFT or BREAK keys so that you cannot get some of the punctuation marks or lower case letters.

Lastly a different value will be returned if more than one key has been pressed. Since most programs require that only one key be pressed at a time this is not a problem.

A NOTE ON THE USE OF 'PCLEAR'

In many of the programs in this book you will see that very near the start of the program a PCLEAR is done to allocate enough graphic pages for the program. Because doing a PCLEAR may involve moving the program in the computer's memory you may find that the first time you run the program it will not work correctly. Do not worry about this just run it again and all will be well (If it still misbehaves then there is probably a mistake in what you have typed in).

Alternatively you can do a PCLEAR before you run the programs - just make sure you use the right value when you do it.

MAKING IT ALL GO FASTER

The standard DRAGON is designed to run at a clock speed of 0.9 MHz (this is the speed of the 6809 microprocessor inside the machine). However it is possible to make it go faster by changing some memory locations.

By using the following POKEs we can get a speed increase of about 1.35 times normal. However there are some disadvantages. Firstly we cannot use the cassette recorder to load or save programs when the machine is in the high speed mode. Secondly if you try to use a printer it will not work correctly.

If these issues do not effect your program (and for most of the programs in this book they do not matter) then you can make the program run faster by typing the following before you run the program:

```
POKE 65495,0
```

This will put the machine in the faster mode. To get back to normal speed the statement

POKE 65494,0

will return the machine to normal mode.

Please note you will need to do this in order to load any new games, and so on. Turning the machine off also returns it to normal mode

If you wish your program to run faster for part of it and at normal speed for the other part, you can insert the POKEs into the appropriate places in your program.

React

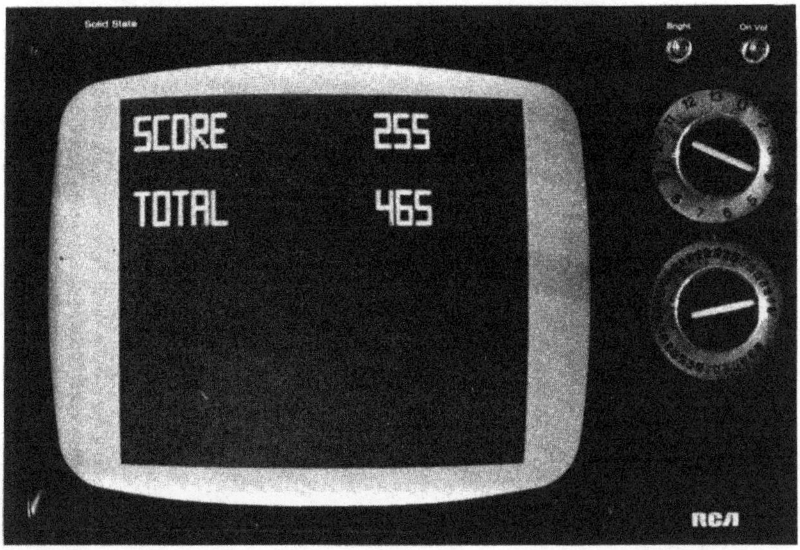

This program will allow you to see how fast you can react. The computer will flash a single digit somewhere on the screen. Your job is to press the key with the same number on it as fast as possible. As well as getting different digits they may be of different sizes so you must keep your wits about you.

Each time you manage to press the right key your score will be increased but the longer you take the less you get. How fast are you ??

Program structure

10 - 220	initialization
230 - 260	main loop
270 - 280	end/restart game
500 - 710	draw a digit
1000 - 1090	time the player until the right key is pressed
10000 - 10240	draw score

Variables

A$,B$,C$,D$	Arrays for digits
X,Y	Random position of digit
SC	Random scale factor to change size of digit

REACT

```
 20 DIM BL(5)
 30 SL=500
 40 A$="U8"
 50 B$="L4U4R4U4L4"
 60 C$="NL4U8L4D4R4"
 70 D$="U8L4D8R4"
 80 PMODE 1,1:COLOR 2,3:PCLS:SCREEN 1,0
 90 GET(1,1)-(12,20),BL,G
100 DRAW"BM10,10;NR8D8R8D8L8"
110 DRAW"BM+12,+0;NR8U16R8"
120 DRAW"BM+4,0;D16R8U16L8"
130 DRAW"BM+12,+0;ND16R8D8L8F8"
140 DRAW"BM+4,+0;NR8U8NR6U8R8"
150 DRAW"BM10,50;R4ND16R4"
160 DRAW"BM+4,+0;D16R8U16NL8"
170 DRAW"BM+4,+0;R4ND16R4"
180 DRAW"BM+4,+0;ND16R8D8NL8D8"
190 DRAW"BM+4,+0;NR8U16"
200 S=0:T=0
210 J=S:CJ=2:SJ=4:XJ=100:YJ=10:GOSUB10000
220 J=T:XJ=100:YJ=50:GOSUB10000
230 FOR N=1 TO 25
240 GOSUB500
250 GOSUB1000
260 NEXT N
270 DRAW"BM100,150;NR8D8NR6D8R8;BM+8,+0;
      U16F16U16;BM+8,+0;R4F4D8G4L4U16"
280 I$=INKEY$:IF I$="S" GOTO 80 ELSE GOTO 280
500 ' DRAW A SYMBOL
510 B=RND(4):IF B=2 GOTO 510
520 PMODE 1,3:COLOR 2,B:PCLS(B)
530 X=RND(230)+20:Y=RND(160)+30
540 SC=3+RND(9)
550 E$="BM"+STR$(X)+","+STR$(Y)+";S"+STR$(SC)+";"
560 DRAW E$
570 J=RND(200):IF J>4 GOTO 570
580 ON J GOTO 590,600,610,620
590 SI$="1":DRAW A$:GOTO 630
600 SI$="2":DRAW B$:GOTO 630
610 SI$="9":DRAW C$:GOTO630
620 SI$="0":DRAW D$
630 IS=0:SCREEN 1,0
640 I$=INKEY$
650 IF I$=SI$ GOTO670
660 IS=IS+5:IF IS<SL GOTO 640
670 PMODE 1,1:SCREEN1,0
680 S=SL-IS
690 IF S<0 THEN S=0
700 T=T+S
710 RETURN
1000 PMODE 1,1
1010 FOR Y=10 TO 50 STEP40
1020 FOR X=100 TO 190 STEP10
```

```
1030 PUT(X,Y)-(X+11,Y+19),BL,PSET
1040 NEXT X
1050 NEXT Y
1060 J=S:SJ=4:CJ=2:XJ=100:YJ=10:GOSUB10000
1070 J=T:XJ=100:YJ=50:GOSUB10000
1080 FOR I=1 TO 200:NEXT I
1090 RETURN
10000 ' DRAW NUMBER
10010 J$=STR$(J)
10020 LJ=LEN(J$)
10030 XC=XJ+(8-LJ)*12:YC=YJ
10040 FOR IL=2 TO LJ
10050 IJ=VAL(MID$(J$,IL,1))
10060 XC=XC+12
10070 GOSUB 10100
10080 NEXT IL
10090 RETURN
10100 ' DRAW DIGIT
10110 TJ$="BM"+STR$(XC)+","+STR$(YC)+";C"
      +STR$(CJ)+";S"+STR$(SJ)+";"
10120 DRAW TJ$
10130 ON IJ+1 GOTO 10140,10150,10160,10170,10180,
      10190,10200,10210,10220,10230
10140 DRAW"D16R8U16L8":RETURN
10150 DRAW"BM+8,+0;D16":RETURN
10160 DRAW"R8D8L8D8R8":RETURN
10170 DRAW"R8D8NL8D8L8":RETURN
10180 DRAW"D8R8NU8D8":RETURN
10190 DRAW"NR8D8R8D8L8":RETURN
10200 DRAW"NR8D16R8U8L8":RETURN
10210 DRAW"R8D16":RETURN
10220 DRAW"D16R8U8NL8U8L8":RETURN
10230 DRAW"ND8R8D8NL8D8L8":RETURN
10240 RETURN
32000 END
```

Number Scrunch

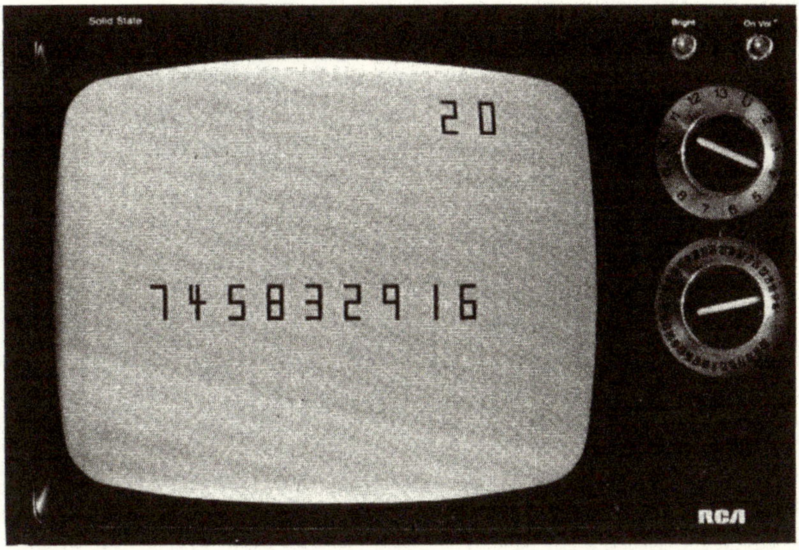

In this very addictive game the computer will scramble the digits from 1 to 9. You must re-arrange them as quickly as possible. You must re-shuffle the numbers by reversing a group of them i.e you pick a group of digits and the computer will reverse them.

You pick a group of digits by pressing a number from to 9 (your group always starts at the left end of the list). There are a number of systems for ordering the digits in the smallest number of moves, see if you can find the best one.

An example may make things clearer:
suppose the list of numbers is
    6 4 7 1 5 3 9 8 2
and you press the number '4'
then the computer will revers the first 4 digits
to give you
    1 7 4 6 5 3 9 8 2

Program structure

10 - 130	initailization
500 - 570	main loop (returns to top from line 660)
680 - 690	restart by returning to line 60
1000 - 1180	shuffle digits
2000 - 2160	display score by takin digits from main display

Variables

R(),S()	Temporary stores for moving drawings of digits
P()	Current permutation of the digits
C1,C2	Count of moves made by player

NUMBER SCRUNCH

```
10 CLS:PRINT @226,"PUT THE NUMBERS IN SEQUENCE"
20 PRINT @290,"PRESSING A '6' REVERSES
     THE          FIRST SIX DIGITS";
30 PRINT @418,"PRESS 'S' TO START"
40 I$=INKEY$:IF I$<>"S" GOTO40
45 PMODE 1,1:PCLS:SCREEN 1,0
50 A$="BM24,100;D16;BM+24,+0;L8U8R8U8L8;BM+24,+0;
     R8D8NL8D8L8;BM+24,-16;D8R4ND8NU8R4;BM+24,-8;"
60 DRAW A$
70 A$="L8D8R8D8L8;BM+32,-16;L8D16R8U8L8;
     BM+24,-8;R8D16;BM+24,+0;U8NL8U8L8D16R8;
     BM+24,+0;U16L8D8R8"
80 DRAW A$
90 Y1=100:Y2=116
95 GOSUB 500
100 I$=INKEY$:IF I$="" GOTO 100
110 I=VAL(I$):IF I=0 GOTO 100
130 J=INT(I/2):I2=I+1
140 FOR N=1 TO J
150 X1=24*N-8:X2=X1+16:X3=(I2-N)*24-8:X4=X3+16
160 GET(X1,Y1)-(X2,Y2),R,G
165 T=P(N)
170 GET(X3,Y1)-(X4,Y2),S,G
180 PUT(X1,Y1)-(X2,Y2),S,PSET
185 P(N)=P(I2-N)
190 PUT(X3,Y1)-(X4,Y2),R,PSET
195 P(I2-N)=T
200 NEXT N
220 GOSUB 700
230 SOUND 200,2
400 FOR N=1 TO 9
410 IF P(N)<>N GOTO 100
420 NEXT N
430 FOR N=1 TO 5:SOUND 180+N,1:NEXT N
440 GOTO 40
500 FOR N=1 TO 9:P(N)=N:NEXT N
510 FOR N=1 TO 9
512 J=RND(9)
515 X1=24*N-8:X2=X1+16:X3=J*24-8:X4=X3+16
525 GET(X1,Y1)-(X2,Y2),R,G
530 T=P(N)
535 GET(X3,Y1)-(X4,Y2),S,G
540 P(N)=P(J)
545 PUT(X1,Y1)-(X2,Y2),S,PSET
550 P(J)=T
555 PUT(X3,Y1)-(X4,Y2),R,PSET
560 NEXT N
565 SOUND 190,1:SOUND 170,2
570 A$="BM200,5;R8D8L8D8R8;"
580 B$="BM+24,+0;U16L8D16R8"
590 DRAW A$+B$
595 C1=2:C2=0
600 RETURN
```

```
 700 C2=C2-1
 710 IF C2>0 GOTO800
 720 IF C2=0 GOTO770
 730 C2=9
 740 GET(1;1)-(17,17),R,G:PUT(200,5)-(216,21),R,PSET:
         PUT(224,5)-(240,21),R,PSET
 750 IF C1=2 THEN C1=1:DRAW"BM208,5;D16":GOTO 800
 755 C1=0:DRAW"BM208,5;D16L8U16R8":GOTO800
 770 DRAW"BM232,5;L8D16R8"
 780 IF C1=1 THEN RETURN
 790 FOR N=1 TO 3:SOUND 150,2:SOUND 100,3:NEXT N:
         GOTO40
 800 FOR T=1 TO 9
 810 IF P(T)=C2 GOTO 830
 820 NEXT T
 830 X1=24*T-8:X2=X1+16
 840 GET(X1,Y1)-(X2,Y2),R,G
 850 PUT(224,5)-(240,21),R,PSET
 860 RETURN
2000 END
```

Leapfrog

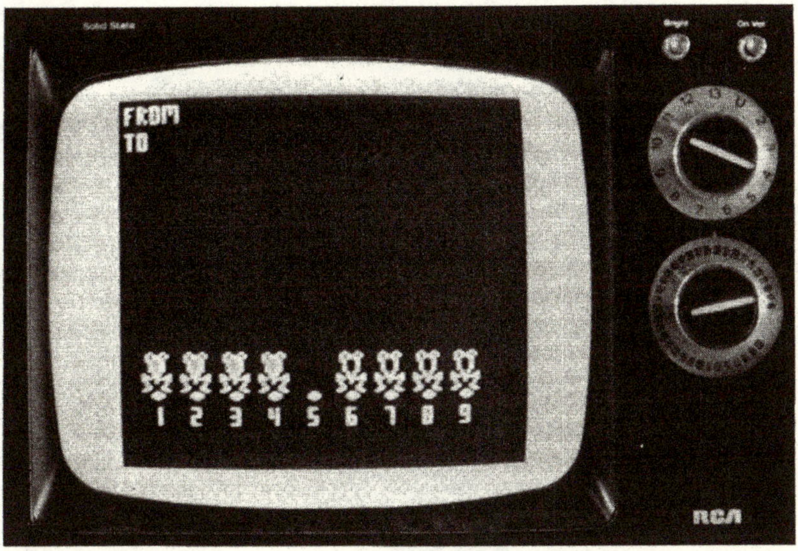

How many moves will it take you to swap all the frogs? You must move all the frogs on the left the right and all those on the right to the left. However you can only jump a frog if the stone next to him is empty or if there is only one other frog between him and an empty stone. For example some valid first moves would be:

move the frog from stone 4 to stone 5

or move the frog from stone 7 to stone 5

To move your frogs just hit the number of the stone you want to move from and then hit the number of the stone you want to move the frog to. If you try to do an illegal move the computer will tell you. Good luck, and you may be suprised at how few moves it takes.

Program structure

10 - 460	define frog shapes and perform other initialization
500 - 840	main loop: input and check move then do it if it is ok. Also checks for end of game
1000 - 1110	sets up for a jump then does the jump and then tidys up
2000 - 2140	does a left jump
3000 - 3140	does a right jump
4000 - 4070	print the number of moves taken

Variables used

BL	Blank screen rectangle used to erase frogs
F1,F2,F3	Pictures for the frogs
ST()	Status for each of the stones 0 = no frog 1 = green frog 2 = red frog
N1,N2	Start and finish jump positions
Z	Temporary store for transferring digits to the score

LEAP FROG

```
  10 CLEAR 200:PCLEAR4:PCLS:PMODE3,1
  20 COLOR2,3
  30 SCREEN1,0
  40 DIM F1(12),F2(12),BL(12),F3(12),Z(3),Z0(3)
  50 A$="BM2,2;R4D8L4U8"
  60 DRAW A$
  70 GET(0,0)-(8,12),Z0,G
  80 PCLS
  90 GET(1,1)-(24,20),BL,G
 100 A$="BM0,15;R3U5R3F2R2F4U3E4R1E1R2U3;BM14,17;
        G1L1G2R4;BM16,10;U4NR2L2NU2L4U5R2;BM8,7;D2L4"
 110 DRAW A$
 120 GET(1,1)-(24,20),F3,G
 130 PCLS
 140 A$="BM23,15;L3U5L3G2L2G4U3H4L1H1L1U3;BM10,17;
        F1R1F2L4;BM8,10;U4NL2R2NU2R4U5L2;BM16,7;D2R4":
        ' FROG F2
 150 DRAW A$
 160 GET(1,1)-(24,20),F2,G
 170 PCLS
 200 C=0:PCLS
 210 A$="BM22,152;G1D1F1R3E1U1H1G2R1U1":' STONE
 220 DRAW A$
 230 GET(20,152)-(43,171),F1,G
 240 FOR I=1 TO 8
 250 X1=20+24*I:X2=X1+23:PUT(X1,152)-(X2,171),F1,PSET
 260 NEXT I
 270 A$="BM25,160;D8;BM+24,+0;L4U4R4U4L4;BM+24,+0;
        R4D4NL4D4L4;BM+24,-8;D4R4NU4D4;BM+24,-8;
        L4D4R4D4L4;BM+28,-8;L4D8R4U4L4;BM+24,-4;
        R4D8;BM+24,+0;U8L4D4NR4D4R4;BM+20,+0;
        R4U8L4D4R4":' DIGITS
 280 DRAW A$
 290 A$="BM17,136;U3E1R1F1D2G1D5F2D1F1ND2R1E2U1
        E1U5R1E2H2L1G2NL2F1BM19,145;L2H1L2NU1D2F4
        L1G1L2BM25,145;R3E1R2NU1D2G4R1F1R2":
        ' FROG F1
 300 DRAW A$
 310 GET(12,132)-(35,151),F1,G
 320 PAINT(22,138),1,2
 330 FOR I=1 TO 8
 340 IF I=4 GOTO 400
 350 X1=12+I*24:X2=X1+23
 360 X3=X1+10
 370 PUT(X1,132)-(X2,151),F1,PSET
 380 IF I<4 THEN PT=1 ELSE PT=4
 390 PAINT(X3,138),PT,2
 400 NEXT I
 410 A$="BM4,4;NR4D4NR2D4;BM+8,+0;U8R2F2G2L2F4;
        BM+4,+0;U8R4D8L4;BM+8,+0;U8R4ND4R4D8"
 420 DRAW A$
 430 A$="BM4,18;R2ND8R2;BM+4,+0;D8R4U8L4"
 440 DRAW A$
```

```
450 FOR I=1 TO 4:ST(I)=+1:ST(I+5)=-1:NEXT I
460 ST(5)=0
500 I$=INKEY$:IF I$="" GOTO 500
510 N1=VAL(I$):IF N1=0 GOTO 590
520 IF ST(N1)=0 GOTO 590
530 GET(N1*24-5,158)-(N1*24+3,170),Z,G
540 PUT(51,1)-(59,13),Z,PSET
550 PUT(51,19)-(74,38),BL,PSET
560 I$=INKEY$:IF I$="" GOTO 560
570 N2=VAL(I$):IF N2=0 GOTO 590
580 IF ST(N2)=0 GOTO 700
590 CLS:PRINT@295,"ERROR, TRY AGAIN"
600 FOR I=1 TO 3:SOUND190,1:SOUND240,1:NEXTI:
        FOR I=1 TO 400:NEXT I
610 PRINT @295,"SO, GIVING UP ? "
620 SCREEN 1,0
630 GOTO 500
700 IF ABS(N1-N2)>2 GOTO 590
710 GET(N2*24-5,158)-(N2*24+3,170),Z,G
720 PUT(51,18)-(59,31),Z,PSET
730 GOSUB 1000
740 IF C>99 THEN CLS:
        PRINT @224,"YOU'RE HOPELESS,";:
        PRINT @270,"START AGAIN.";:
        FOR I=1TO1200:NEXTI:SCREEN1,0:GOTO200
750 FOR I=1 TO 4
760 IF ST(I)<>-1 GOTO 500
770 IF ST(I+5)<>1 GOTO 500
780 NEXT I
790 FOR I=1 TO 6:SOUND190,3:SOUND180,3:NEXT I
800 CLS
810 PRINT @224,"CONGRATULATIONS,":
        PRINT @289,"YOU DID IT IN ";C;" MOVES.":
        PRINT @490,"PRESS S TO RESTART."
820 FOR I=1 TO 1380:NEXT I
830 SCREEN 1,0
840 I$=INKEY$:IF I$="S" THEN GOTO 200 ELSE GOTO 840
1000 X1=24*N1-11
1010 PUT(X1,132)-(X1+23,151),BL,PSET
1020 SOUND 250,1
1030 IF N1>N2 GOSUB 2000 ELSE GOSUB 3000
1040 X1=24*N2-9
1050 PUT(X1,132)-(X1+23,151),F1,PSET
1060 SOUND 100,1
1070 IF ST(N1)>0 THEN PT=1 ELSE PT=4
1080 PAINT(X1+10,138),PT,2
1090 ST(N2)=ST(N1):ST(N1)=0:C=C+1
1100 GOSUB4000
1110 RETURN
2000 DX=(N2-N1)*6
2010 X1=X1+DX
2020 IF ST(N1)>0 THEN PT=1 ELSE PT=4
2030 PUT(X1,110)-(X1+23,129),F2,PSET
2040 PAINT(X1+11,119),PT,2
2050 X2=X1+DX
2060 PUT(X1,110)-(X1+23,129),BL,PSET
```

```
2070 PUT(X2,108)-(X2+23,127),F1,PSET
2080 PAINT(X2+11,117),PT,2
2090 X1=X2+DX
2100 PUT(X2,108)-(X2+23,127),BL,PSET
2110 PUT(X1,110)-(X1+23,129),F3,PSET
2120 PAINT(X1+11,119),PT,2
2130 PUT(X1,110)-(X1+23,129),BL,PSET
2140 RETURN
3000 DX=(N2-N1)*6
3010 X1=X1+DX
3020 IF ST(N1)>0 THEN PT=1 ELSE PT=4
3030 PUT(X1,110)-(X1+23,129),F3,PSET
3040 PAINT(X1+11,119),PT,2
3050 X2=X1+DX
3060 PUT(X1,110)-(X1+23,129),BL,PSET
3070 PUT(X2,108)-(X2+23,127),F1,PSET
3080 PAINT(X2+10,114),PT,2
3090 X1=X2+DX
3100 PUT(X2,108)-(X2+23,127),BL,PSET
3110 PUT(X1,110)-(X1+23,129),F2,PSET
3120 PAINT(X1+11,119),PT,2
3130 PUT(X1,110)-(X1+23,129),BL,PSET
3140 RETURN
4000 D1=INT(C/10):D2=C-10*D1
4010 IF D1=0 GOTO 4040
4020 GET(D1*24-5,158)-(D1*24+3,170),Z,G
4030 PUT(230,10)-(238,22),Z,PSET
4040 IF D2=0 THEN PUT(240,10)-(248,22),Z0,PSET:RETURN
4050 GET(D2*24-5,158)-(D2*24+3,170),Z,G
4060 PUT(240,10)-(248,22),Z,PSET
4070 RETURN
5000 END
```

3-D Treasure Hunt

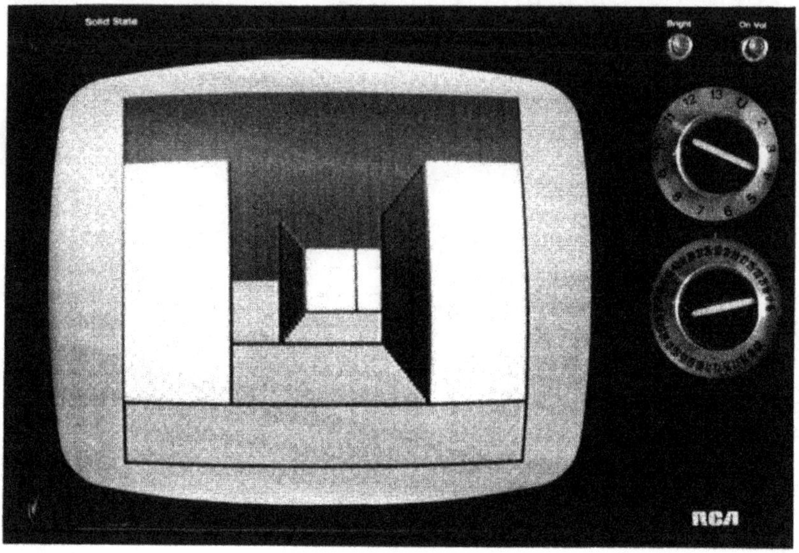

Copyright (c) Colin Carter

Can you find the treasure hidden in the maze or will you become hopelessly lost and confused? This amazing 3-D game gives you an actual perspective view of the maze you are searching, plus you can have a map of the maze to help you (the map shows the location of the treasure but unfortunately it doesn't show you where you are).

Your three dimensional view shows the walls in front of you and beside you in different colours, as well as the grass and sky. In some places you will see the grass and sky meeting between a gap in the walls - this means that you should perhaps take a closer look to see what is really out there.

The computer will display an instruction page for you and you can return to this page at any time by pressing the '0' key.

Program structure

10 - 690	initialization and map
1000 - 1110	main loop
2000 - 4730	prepare to draw the view
4740 - 4800	end/restart game
5000 - 5170	ensure walls have similar status
5500 - 5610	display options
6000 - 6070	move forward
6080 - 6160	disclose position on map

Variables

X,Y	Position on map
ST(W)	Status of wall W Walls are numbered 1 to 480 Each position on the map has walls numbered: W = Top wall, W+1 = Bottom wall, W+2 = Left wall, W+3 = Right wall, where W is given W=40*y+4*x-43 for position X,Y.
L(),R()	Status for left and right walls in the view.

Note the logic which builds the random maze allows impossible mazes to be produced. If this happens don't worry just give up and try another one.

3-D TREASURE HUNT

```
 20 PCLEAR 6
 30 PMODE 1,1:PCLS:PMODE1,3:PCLS:PMODE 1,5:PCLS
 40 DIM ST(280),BX(4,4),M(2,4),L(4),R(4)
 50 CLS:PRINT @37,"YOU ARE IN A MAZE,"
 70 PRINT @78,"FIND THE GOLD."
 80 GOSUB 5500
 90 PRINT @480,"YOU MAY GET AN IMPOSSIBLE MAZE."
100 I$=INKEY$:IF I$<>"S" GOTO 100
110 CLS:PRINT @170,"PLEASE WAIT"
120 P=30
125 RESTORE
126 EN=-1
130 'SET SOME WALLS AT RANDOM
140 FOR W=1 TO 280
150 IF P<RND(100) THEN ST(W)=-1 ELSE ST(W)=+1
160 NEXT W
170 'CLOSE SIDE WALLS
180 FOR W=40 TO 280 STEP 40
190 ST(W)=+1:ST(W-37)=+1
200 NEXT W
210 FOR W=1 TO 37 STEP 4
220 ST(W)=+1:ST(W+241)=+1
230 NEXT W
240 GOSUB5010
250 PMODE 1,1:COLOR 3,1:PCLS:CLS
260 FOR X=1 TO 9
270 FOR Y=1 TO 6
280 T=40*Y+4*X
290 IF ST(T-40)>0 GOTO 380
300 IF ST(T-42)>0 GOTO 380
310 IF ST(T+3)>0 GOTO 380
320 IF ST(T+1)>0 GOTO 380
330 ON RND(4) GOTO 340,350,360,370
340 ST(T-40)=+1:ST(T-37)=+1:GOTO380
350 ST(T-42)=+1:ST(T-3)=+1:GOTO380
360 ST(T+3)=+1:ST(T)=+1:GOTO380
370 ST(T+1)=+1:ST(T-38)=+1
380 NEXT Y
390 NEXT X
400 SCREEN 1,0
410 LINE(1,1)-(251,176),PSET,B:'FRAME
420 'DRAW MAP
430 FOR X=1 TO 10
440 X2=X*25+1
450 FOR Y= 1 TO 7
460 Y2=Y*25+1
470 W=40*Y+4*X-40
480 IF ST(W)>0 THEN LINE(X2,Y2-25)-(X2,Y2),PSET
490 W=W-2
500 IF ST(W)>0 THEN LINE(X2,Y2)-(X2-25,Y2),PSET
510 NEXT Y
520 NEXT X
530 'PLACE THE GOLD
```

```
540 XG=RND(10):YG=RND(7)
550 X=XG*25-24:Y=YG*25-24
560 A$="BM"+STR$(X)+","+STR$(Y)+";BM+17,+8;
      U4L8D16R8U4L4"
570 DRAW A$
580 X=RND(10):Y=RND(7):VW=RND(4)
590 CH$="BM+4,+0;H2U2L6D5F2R6U3L6ND3H2R6"
600 FOR D=0 TO 4:FOR C=1 TO 4:READ BX(D,C):NEXT C:
      NEXT D
610 DATA 66,34,190,158,96,64,160,128,112,80,144,
      112,122,90,134,102,124,92,132,102
620 FOR I=1 TO 4:FOR C=1 TO 2:READ M(C,I):NEXT C:
      NEXT I
630 DATA 3,4,4,3,2,1,1,2
640 FOR I=1 TO 4:READ QR(I):NEXT I
650 DATA 4,3,1,2
660 FOR I=1 TO 4:READ QL(I):NEXT I
670 DATA 3,4,2,1
680 FOR I=1 TO 4:READ QA(I):NEXT I
690 DATA 2,1,4,3
1000 I$=INKEY$:IF I$="" GOTO 1000
1010 I=ASC(I$)
1020 IF I=70 GOTO 6000:'F
1030 IF I=82 THEN VW=QR(VW):GOTO2000:'R
1040 IF I=76 THEN VW=QL(VW): GOTO 2000:'L
1050 IF I=65 THEN VW=QA(VW): GOTO 2000:'A
1060 IF I=77 THEN PMODE 1,1:SCREEN 1,0:GOTO 1000:'M
1070 IF I=86 GOTO 2000:'V
1080 IF I=79 THEN GOSUB 5500: GOTO 1000:'O
1090 IF I=69 GOTO 6080:'E
1100 IF I=83 GOTO 110 :'S
1110 GOTO 1000
2000 D=0:C=40*Y+4*X+VW-44:S5=+1:M1=M(1,VW):M2=M(2,VW)
2010 SOUND 200,1
2020 IF VW<3 GOTO2160
2030 IF VW=3 THEN DX=-1 ELSE DX=+1
2040 W=C+4*D
2050 DI=ABS(D)
2060 IF DI=5 GOTO 2280
2070 L(DI)=ST(W-VW+M1):R(DI)=ST(W-VW+M2)
2080 IF L(DI)>0GOTO2100
2090 SL(DI)=ST(W-40*DX)
2100 IF R(DI)>0 GOTO 2120
2110 SR(DI)=ST(W+40*DX)
2120 IF ST(W)>0 GOTO 3010
2130 D=D+DX
2140 GOTO2040
2150 '
2160 IF VW=1 THEN DY=-1 ELSE DY=+1
2170 W=C+40*D
2180 DI=ABS(D)
2190 IF DI=5 GOTO 2280
2200 L(DI)=ST(W-VW+M1):R(DI)=ST(W-VW+M2)
2210 IF L(DI)>0GOTO2230
2220 SL(DI)=ST(W+4*DY)
2230 IF R(DI)>0GOTO2250
```

```
4030 FOR C=0 TO D
4040 IF L(C)>0 THEN PT=4 ELSE PT=2
4050 PAINT(BX(C,1)-2,96),PT,3
4060 IF R(C)>0 THEN PT=4 ELSE PT=2
4070 PAINT(BX(C,3)+4,96),PT,3
4080 NEXT C
4090 IF D<4 THEN PAINT(128,96),2,3
4100 FOR C=0 TO D:
        LINE(BX(C,1),BX(C,2))-
        (BX(C,3),BX(C,4)),PSET,B:NEXT C
4110 FOR C=0 TO D
4120 IF L(C)>0GOTO4180
4130 IF SL(C)>0GOTO4180
4140 IF C=0 THEN LINE(0,96)-(BX(0,1),96),PSET:
        GOTO4160
4150 LINE(BX(C,1),96)-(BX(C-1,1),96),PSET
4160 PAINT(BX(C,1)-2,98),1,3
4170 PAINT(BX(C,1)-2,94),3,3
4180 IF R(C)>0 GOTO 4240
4190 IF SR(C)>0 GOTO 4240
4200 IF C=0 THEN LINE(255,96)-(BX(0,3),96),PSET:
        GOTO4220
4210 LINE(BX(C,3),96)-(BX(C-1,3),96),PSET
4220 PAINT(BX(C,3)+2,98),1,3
4230 PAINT(BX(C,3)+2,94),3,3
4240 NEXT C
4500 SCREEN 1,0:PCOPY 3 TO 5:PCOPY 4 TO 6:PMODE 1,5:
        SCREEN 1,0
4510 DX=0:DY=0:ON VW GOTO 4520,4530,4540,4550
4520 DY=-1:GOTO 4560
4530 DY=+1:GOTO 4560
4540 DX=-1:GOTO 4560
4550 DX=+1
4560 C=0:IF D=0 GOTO 4640
4570 FOR C=0 TO D
4580 X2=X+C*DX:Y2=Y+C*DY
4590 IF X2<>XG GOTO4620
4600 IF Y2<>YG GOTO 4620
4610 EN=+1:C7=C
4620 NEXT C
4630 IF EN>0 THEN GOTO 4680 ELSE GOTO 1000
4640 IF X<>XG GOTO 1000
4650 IF Y<>YG GOTO 1000
4660 DRAW"BM128,165;S24;"+CH$+";S4;"
4670 GOTO 4710
4680 SC=4*(6-C7):Y2=BX(C7,4)+2
4690 DRAW"BM128,"+STR$(Y2)+";S"+STR$(SC)+";"+CH$
4700 DRAW"S4"
4710 FOR I=1 TO 7:SOUND 180+I,1:NEXT I
4720 IF X<>XG GOTO 1000
4730 IF Y<>YG GOTO 1000
4740 FOR I=1 TO 50
4750 NEXT I
4760 SOUND 180,3
4770 FOR I=1 TO 8
4780 SOUND 200,1
```

```
2240 SR(DI)=ST(W-4*DY)
2250 IF ST(W)>0 GOTO 3010
2260 D=D+DY
2270 GOTO 2170
2280 IF ST(W)<0 THEN S5=-1
2290 D=4
3000 '
3010 REM: VERTICAL LINES
3030 PMODE 1,3:COLOR 3,1:PCLS
3040 SCREEN 1,0
3050 LINE(0,1)-(252,196),PSET,B:'FRAME
3060 D=ABS(D)
3070 C=0
3080 IF C=D GOTO 3110
3090 LINE(BX(C,1),BX(C,2))-(BX(C,1),BX(C,4)),PSET
3100 C=C+1:GOTO3080
3110 IF L(C)>0 THEN
        LINE(BX(C,1),BX(C,2))-(BX(C,1),BX(C,4)),PSET
3120 C=0
3130 IF C=D GOTO 3160
3140 LINE(BX(C,3),BX(C,2))-(BX(C,3),BX(C,4)),PSET
3150 C=C+1:GOTO3130
3160 IF R(C)>0 THEN
        LINE(BX(C,3),BX(C,2))-(BX(C,3),BX(C,4)),PSET
3170 REM ANGLE/HORIZ LINES
3180 IF L(0)>0 GOTO 3210
3190 LINE(0,158)-(66,158),PSET
3200 LINE(0,34)-(66,34),PSET:GOTO 3230
3210 LINE(32,192)-(66,158),PSET
3220 LINE(31,1)-(66,34),PSET
3230 IF R(0)>0 GOTO 3260
3240 LINE(190,158)-(251,158),PSET
3250 LINE(190,34)-(251,34),PSET:GOTO3280
3260 LINE(190,158)-(224,192),PSET
3270 LINE(190,34)-(223,1),PSET
3280 LINE(BX(D,1),BX(D,2))-(BX(D,3),BX(D,2)),PSET
3290 LINE(BX(D,1),BX(D,4))-(BX(D,3),BX(D,4)),PSET
3300 C=1
3310 IF C>D GOTO 3380
3320 IF L(C)>0 THEN DC=1 ELSE DC=0
3330 X1=BX(C,1):X2=BX(C-1,1)
3340 FOR I=2 TO 4 STEP 2
3350 LINE(X1,BX(C,I))-(X2,BX(C-DC,I)),PSET
3360 NEXT I
3370 C=C+1: GOTO 3310
3380 C=1
3390 IF C>D GOTO 4000
3400 IF R(C)>0 THEN DC=1 ELSE DC=0
3410 X1=BX(C,3):X2=BX(C-1,3)
3420 FOR I=2 TO 4 STEP 2
3430 LINE(X1,BX(C,I))-(X2,BX(C-DC,I)),PSET
3440 NEXT I
3450 C=C+1:GOTO 3390
4000 'COLOR IT
4010 PAINT(128,30),3,3
4020 PAINT(128,165),1,3
```

```
4790 NEXT I
4800 I$=INKEY$:IF I$="S" THEN GOTO 110 :
        ELSE GOTO 4800
5000 ' ENSURE COMMON WALLS HAVE SAME STATUS
5010 FOR Y=1 TO 7
5020 C=40*Y-41
5030 FOR X=2 TO 10
5040 W2=C+4*X
5050 W1=W2-3
5060 ST(W2)=ST(W1)
5070 NEXT X
5080 NEXT Y
5090 FOR X=1 TO 10
5100 C=4*X-43
5110 FOR Y=2 TO 7
5120 W2=C+40*Y
5130 W1=W2-39
5140 ST(W2)=ST(W1)
5150 NEXT Y
5160 NEXT X
5170 RETURN
5500 PRINT @97,"ACTIONS YOU CAN DO ARE ANY OF"
5510 PRINT @131,"THE OPTIONS:"
5520 PRINT @165,"S - START/RESTART"
5530 PRINT @197,"O - OPTIONS LIST"
5540 PRINT @229,"M - MAP DISPLAY"
5550 PRINT @261,"V - VIEW DISPLAY"
5560 PRINT @293,"F - FORWARD ONE SQUARE"
5570 PRINT @325,"R - RIGHT TURN"
5580 PRINT @357,"L - LEFT TURN"
5590 PRINT @389,"A - ABOUT TURN"
5600 PRINT @421,"E - EXIT-I GIVE UP"
5610 RETURN
6000 W=40*Y+4*X+VW-44
6010 IF ST(W)>0 GOTO 2000
6020 ON VW GOTO 6030,6040,6050,6060
6030 Y=Y-1:GOTO6070
6040 Y=Y+1:GOTO6070
6050 X=X-1:GOTO6070
6060 X=X+1
6070 GOTO 2000
6080 ON VW GOTO 6090,6100,6110,6120
6090 A$="BM+12,+5;NG5ND15NF5":GOTO6130
6100 A$="BM+12,+20;NH5NU15NE5":GOTO 6130
6110 A$="BM+5,+12;NE5NR15NF5":GOTO 6130
6120 A$="BM+5,+12;R15NH5NG5"
6130 XE=X*25-24:YE=Y*25-24:A$="BM"+STR$(XE)+","
        +STR$(YE)+";"+A$
6140 PMODE 1,1:SCREEN 1,0
6150 DRAW A$
6160 I$=INKEY$:IF I$="S" GOTO 110 ELSE GOTO 6160
7000 END
```

Simulation

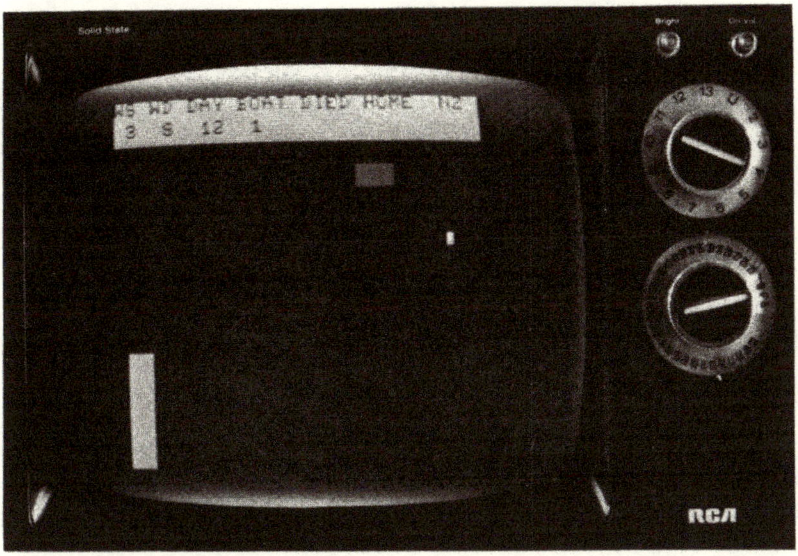

Copyright (c) Colin Carter

This is a type of program known as a simulation. It is used to model a physical situation in a way that would be very hard to do in real life. Computers are very good for simulations because of their ability to keep track of large numbers of variables without getting confused.

This simulation is a simplified version of a study undertaken to investigate the theory that polynesian fishing fleets may have been blown off course and landed in New Zealand. The factors involved are very complex ranging from the prevailing wind conditions to the sea currents and the availabilty of food if the fleet gets lost.

Because we do not have access to all the data about these factors the program uses a very simple system. The wind conditions are random with a table of probabilities for different geographical positions, while the probabilities of finding food and surviving are basically random. What this program shows you is one way to approach a simulation and maybe it will help you write one of your own on a subject that interests you.

This program uses the random number generator described elsewhere in the book so you can change things by using a different number in line 160.

As given in the listing the program was run for 800 trips: out of these 598 died at sea, 195 were blown home and 7 reached New Zealand. See what sort of results you can get with your own random numbers.

```
100 DIM WS(2,32),WD(3,32)
110 CLS
120 PRINT @293,"HOW MANY TRIPS";
130 INPUT NT
140 CLS(0)
150 PS=95:'PROB SURVIVE TODAY
160 U=0.466387284633::
      REM ANY SILLY NUMBER BETWEEN 0 AND 1
170 ' READ WIND SPEED PROBS'
180 FOR J=1 TO 32
190 FOR I=1 TO 2
200 READ WS(I,J)
210 NEXT I
220 NEXT J
230 DATA 5,3,3,4,3,3,2,3,2,3,2,2,1,2,1,2,3,3,3,2,2,
      2,2,2,2,1,1,2,1,2,1,1,2,3,2,2,2,2,2,2,2,2,
      1,3,1,3,1,2,1,4,2,3,3,3,3,3,3,3,3,3,2,3,1,4
240 ' READ WIND DIRECTION PROBS
250 FOR J=1 TO 32
260 FOR I=1 TO 3
270 READ WD(I,J)
280 NEXT I
290 NEXT J
300 DATA 1,3,4,1,2,4,1,2,4,1,2,3,0,1,4,1,2,4,1,
      2,3,1,2,2,1,2,4,1,2,4,0,1,4,1,2,4,1,2,4,
      1,2,3,1,1,2,2,1,1,1,3,3,1,2,4,1,2,4,1,
      2,3,1,2,3,1,2,2,2,1,2,2,1,1,1,3,4,1,2,3,
      1,2,2,2,1,1,2,1,1,2,2,1,2,2,1,3,1,1
310 PRINT @115,CHR$(191)+CHR$(191)+CHR$(191);::
      REM DRAW ISLAND
320 FOR X=2 TO 5: FOR Y=22 TO 31:SET(X,Y,1):NEXT Y:
      NEXT X:' DRAW N.Z.
330 PRINT @0,"WS WD DAY BOAT DIED HOME  NZ ";
340 PRINT @32,STRING$(29,CHR$(143));
400 B=0:F=0:H=0:DS=0:NZ=0:SZ=0
410 ' SZ IS SUM OF DAYS SURVIVED'
500 ' START (SELECT POSITION)'
510 SZ=SZ+Z
520 Z=0
530 NL=10:GOSUB2000:X=35+NU:NL=6:GOSUB2000:Y=3+NU
540 IF POINT(X,Y)=4 GOTO 530
550 SET(X,Y,5):SOUND 250,1
560 Y2=Y:X2=X
570 B=B+1
580 PRINT @42,B;
600 ' CHOSE RANDOM NOS FOR WS & D
610 NL=10:GOSUB2000:S=NU:GOSUB2000:D=NU
620 ' FIND PLACE IN WS & D TABLES
630 J1=INT(X/8)+1:J2=INT(Y/8)+1
640 J=(J2-1)*8+J1
650 ' LOOKUP WS TABLE'
660 IF S<=WS(1,J) THEN S=1:GOTO 700
670 IF S<=WS(1,J)+WS(2,J) THEN S=2:GOTO700
```

```
 680 S=3
 690 ' LOOKUP D TABLE'
 700 IF D<=WD(1,J) THEN D=1:D$="N ":GOTO 740
 710 IF D<=WD(1,J)+WD(2,J) THEN D=2:D$="E ":GOTO 740
 720 IF D<=WD(1,J)+WD(2,J)+WD(3,J) THEN D=3:D$="W ":
       GOTO740
 730 D=4:D$="S "
 740 PRINT @32,S;" ";D$;" ";
 800 ' MOVE IT'
 810 IF D=1 THEN Y2=Y-S: IF Y2<0 THEN GOTO 1300 :
       ELSE GOTO 850
 820 IF D=2 THEN X2=X+S:IF X2>63 THEN GOTO1300 :
       ELSE GOTO 850
 830 IF D=3 THEN X2=X-S:IF X2<0 THEN GOTO 1300 :
       ELSE GOTO 850
 840 Y2=Y+S:IF Y2>31 THEN GOTO 1300
 850 IF Y2<4 THEN GOTO 600 ELSE
       IF Y2>31 THEN GOTO 600 ELSE
       IF X2<0 THEN GOTO 600 ELSE IF X2>63 GOTO 600
 900 C=POINT(X2,Y2)
 910 ' SURVIVE ANOTHER DAY ?'
 920 NL=100:GOSUB2000:IF NU>PS GOTO 1300
 930 Z=Z+1
 940 PRINT @38,Z;
 950 IF C=4 GOTO 1100
 960 IF C=1 GOTO 1200
 970 SET(X2,Y2,5)
 980 FOR I=1 TO 20:NEXT I
 990 RESET(X,Y)
1000 X=X2:Y=Y2
1010 GOTO600
1100 H=H+1
1110 RESET(X,Y)
1120 SOUND 220,1:SOUND 240,1
1130 PRINT @51,H;
1140 GOTO1400
1200 NZ=NZ+1
1210 PRINT @57,NZ;
1220 FOR I=1 TO 3:SOUND 150,1:SOUND180,1:NEXT I
1230 RESET(X,Y)
1240 GOTO 1400
1300 RESET(X,Y):' HE DIES HERE'
1310 PLAY"T50;O1;V31;L5;1;L255;1;"
1320 SET(X,Y,5)
1330 PLAY"T50;O1;V31;L5;1;L255;1"
1340 ' WAIT A RESPECTABLE TIME'
1350 FOR I=1 TO 1000:NEXT I
1360 RESET(X,Y)
1370 DS=DS+1
1380 PRINT @46,DS;
1400 ' MORE ?
1410 IF B<NT GOTO 500
1420 PRINT @115,CHR$(128)+CHR$(128)+CHR$(128);
1430 FOR X=2 TO 5:FOR Y=22TO31:RESET(X,Y):NEXT Y:
       NEXT X
1440 PRINT @416,"AVE TRIP:    ";INT(SZ/B);" DAYS";
```

```
1450 PRINT @160,"SET OUT:     ";B;
1460 PRINT @224,"DIED AT SEA:";DS;
1470 PRINT @288,"FOUND HOME: ";H;
1480 PRINT @352,"ARRIVED SAFE";NZ;
1490 PRINT @490,"ANY KEY TO START.";
1500 I$=INKEY$:IF I$=""GOTO1500
1510 CLS:PRINT @293,"HOW MANY TRIPS";
1520 INPUT NT
1530 CLS(0):GOTO310
2000 ' RANDOM NUMBER GENERATOR'
2010 U=997*U
2020 U=U-FIX(U)
2030 IF NL=1 THEN RETURN
2040 NU=FIX(NL*U+1)
2050 RETURN
2060 END
```

Guess

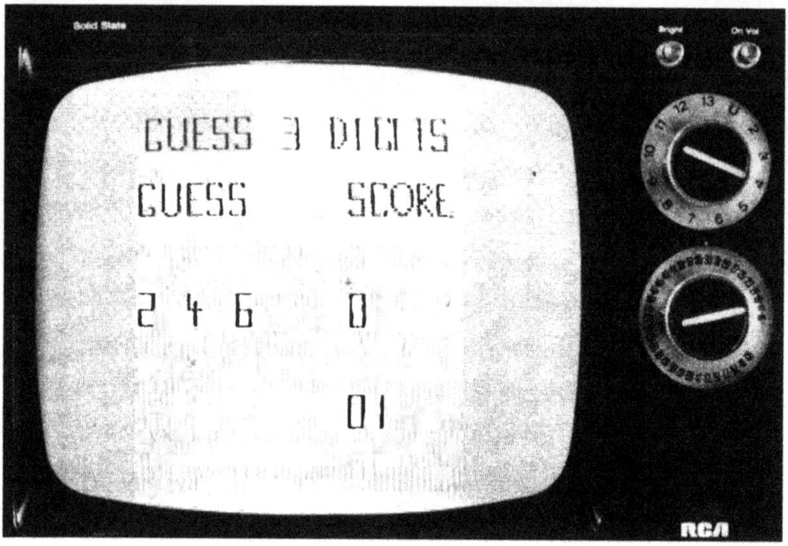

No you don't have to guess the name of the program, just the three numbers that the computer is thinking of. You input your guess as three digits and the computer will give you a clue as to how many of your digits are correct. See how many moves it will take you to get the computer's number.

To input your guess just press the keys corresponding to the digits you want in the order that you want them.

The computer will then look at what you gave it and print a number as a clue for you.

This number is made up as follows:

For each digit that is correct and in the right position add 2 to the clue.

For each digit that is correct but in the wrong position add 1 to the clue.

Note each digit may be counted more than once when the computer is working out the clue.

For example:

Suppose the computers number is 1 2 3
and you type 4 1 3
then the computer will print 3 as the clue
that is 1 for the '1' in the second position
and 2 for the '3' in the third position

or if you type 2 1 1
then the computer will print 3 again
since it has 1 for the '2'
and 1 for the '1' in the second position
and 1 for the '1' in the third position

Get the idea?

Program structure

10 - 170	initialization
520 - 1250	main loop
520 - 640	subloop to input players guess
1500 - 1590	Display clue
1600 - 1630	Blank out old screen images
2000 - 2120	initial set up of screen format
2500 - 2620	draw a digit
3000 - 3110	end/restart game

Variables

X,Y	Position indicators for placement of screen images
P()	Computers number
J()	Players guess
N,N1,N2,N3	Indices for P() and J()

GUESS

```
  20 DIM BL(9,17),J(3),P(3)
  30 CLS:PRINT @34,"FIGURE OUT MY THREE DIGITS"
  40 PRINT @96,"SCORING POINTS:";
  50 PRINT @130,"1 - RIGHT DIGIT/WRONG POSITION"
  60 PRINT @162,"2 - RIGHT DIGIT/RIGHT POSITION"
  70 PRINT @226,"ONLY THE TOTAL WILL BE GIVEN"
  80 PRINT @290,"DIGITS MAY APPEAR IN MULTIPLES";
  90 PRINT @454,"PRESS 'S' TO START/RESTART"
 100 I$=INKEY$:IF I$<>"S" GOTO 100
 110 CLS
 120 GOSUB 2000
 130 FOR N=1 TO 3:P(N)=RND(10)-1:NEXT N
 140 D0=-1:D1=0:GOSUB 1510
 150 X1=20:Y1=100:GOSUB 1610
 160 X1=50:GOSUB 1610
 170 X1=80:GOSUB 1610
 500 ' ACCEPT DIGITS
 510 N=1
 520 I$=INKEY$:IF I$="" GOTO 520
 530 J(N)=ASC(I$)-48
 540 IF J(N)>9 GOTO 570
 550 IF J(N)<0GOTO570
 560 GOTO580
 570 PLAY"T5;O1;A;A":GOTO 520
 580 SOUND 200,1
 590 ON N GOTO 600,610,620
 600 DRAW"BM20,100;":GOTO 630
 610 DRAW"BM50,100;":GOTO 630
 620 DRAW"BM80,100;"
 630 ID=J(N):GOSUB 2510
 640 N=N+1:IF N<4 GOTO 520
1000 ' SCORE
1010 PT=0
1020 FOR N=1 TO 3
1030 IF J(N)=P(N) THEN PT=PT+2:J(N)=-1
1040 NEXT N
1050 N1=1:N2=2:N3=3:GOTO1080
1060 N1=2:N2=3:N3=1:GOTO1080
1070 N1=3:N2=1:N3=2
1080 IF J(N2)<0 THEN GOTO 1100
1090 IF J(N1)=P(N2) GOTO 1130
1100 IF J(N3)<0 GOTO 1140
1110 IF J(N1)=P(N3) GOTO 1130
1120 GOTO 1140
1130 PT=PT+1
1140 ON N1 GOTO 1060,1070,1150
1150 DRAW"BM150,100;"
1160 X1=150:GOSUB 1610
1170 SOUND 240,1
1180 ID=PT:GOSUB 2510
1190 GOSUB 1510
1200 IF PT=6 GOTO 3010
1210 I$=INKEY$:IF I$="" GOTO 1210
```

```
1220 N=1
1230 X1=20:Y1=100:GOSUB1610
1240 X1=50:GOSUB1610
1250 X1=80:GOSUB1610
1260 GOTO 530
1500 ' DISPLAY SCORE
1510 D0=D0+1
1520 IF D0=10 THEN D0=0:D1=D1+1
1530 X1=166:Y1=150:GOSUB 1610
1540 DRAW"BM166,150;"
1550 ID=D0:GOSUB 2510
1560 X1=150:GOSUB 1610
1570 DRAW"BM150,150;"
1580 ID=D1:GOSUB 2510
1590 IF D1=2 GOTO 3010 ELSE RETURN
1600 ' BLANK OUT
1610 X2=X1+9:Y2=Y1+17
1620 PUT(X1,Y1)-(X2,Y2),BL,PSET
1630 RETURN
2000 ' SET UP SCREEN
2010 PMODE 3,1:PCLS:SCREEN 1,0
2020 GET(1,1)-(10,18),BL,G
2030 A$="BM+8,+2;U2L8D16R8U4L2;BM+8,-12;
     D14F2R6E2U14;BM+14,+0;L8D8NR4D8R8;
     BM+12,-14;U2L8D8R8D8L8U2;BM+22,-12;
     U2L8D8R8D8L8U2;"
2040 B$="BM+30,-14;R8D8NL8D8L8;BM+30,+0;
     NU16R4E4U8H4L4;BM+14,+0;R2NR2D16NL2R2;
     BM+14,-14;"
2050 C$="U2L8D16R8U4L2;BM+8,-12;R2NR2D16NL2R2;
     BM+12,+0;U16NL4R4;BM+12,+2;U2L8D8R8D8L8U2"
2060 DRAW"BM25,10;"+A$
2070 DRAW B$
2080 DRAW C$
2090 DRAW"BM20,44;"+A$
2100 B$="BM+8,+2;U2L8D8R8D8L8U2;BM+22,-12;
     U2L8D16R8U2;BM+16,-2;U8H4L4G4D8F4R4E4;
     BM+4,-12;ND16R4F4G4L4F8;BM+4,+0;NR8U8NR4U8R4"
2110 DRAW"BM150,44;"+B$
2120 RETURN
2500 ' DRAW DIGITS
2510 ON (ID+1) GOTO 2520,2530,2540,2550,2560,2570,
     2580,2590,2600,2610
2520 A$="R8D16L8U16":GOTO 2620
2530 A$="BM+4,+0;D16":GOTO 2620
2540 A$="R8D8L8D8R8":GOTO2620
2550 A$="R8D8NL4D8L8":GOTO2620
2560 A$="D8R4NU4ND8R4":GOTO 2620
2570 A$="NR8D8R8D8L8":GOTO 2620
2580 A$="NR8D16R8U8L8":GOTO2620
2590 A$="R8D16":GOTO2620
2600 A$="D16R8U8NL8U8L8":GOTO2620
2610 A$="ND8R8D8NL8D8"
2620 DRAW A$:RETURN
3000 ' END THIS GAME
3010 X1=150:Y1=100:GOSUB 1610
```

```
3020 A$="U14E2R4F2D6NL8D8;BM+4,+0;U16D4F8D4U16;
     BM+12,+2;U2L8D8R8D8L8U2"
3030 DRAW"BM150,116;"+A$
3040 DRAW"BM20,100;"
3050 X1=20:GOSUB 1610:X1=50:GOSUB 1610:X1=80:
     GOSUB 1610
3060 ID=P(1):GOSUB 2510
3070 DRAW"BM50,100;":ID=P(2):GOSUB 2510
3080 DRAW"BM80,100;":ID=P(3):GOSUB 2510
3090 I$=INKEY$:IF I$<>"S" GOTO 3090
3100 X1=150:GOSUB 1610:X1=162:GOSUB 1610:X1=174:
     GOSUB 1610
3110 GOTO 130
```

Random Numbers

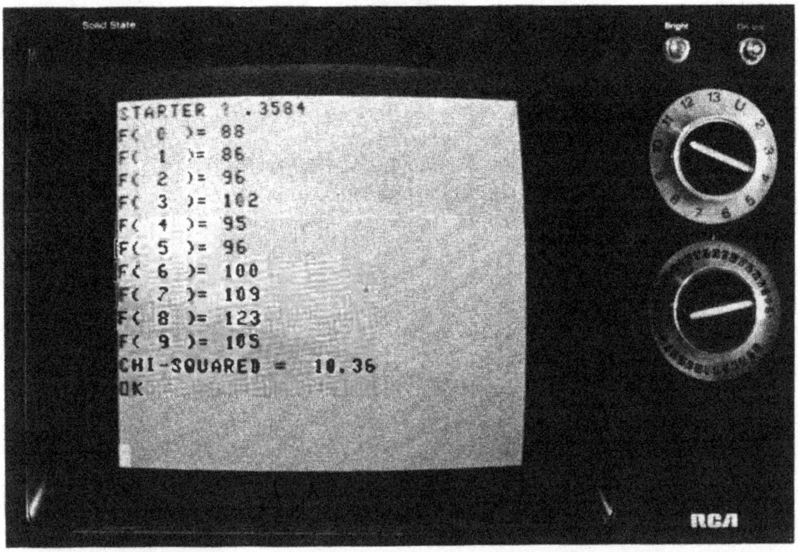

This short program shows you one method of generating random numbers without using the built in RND function. It is really quite simple: a starting value for the generator is input (U1) and then each time a random number is required it is computed from 997*U1 and this value is put back into U1 for the next one.

As well the program computes a value called Chi-squared for a set of random numbers produced by this generator. This is a measure of how random the numbers really are.

The Chi-squared value (X2) is found by generating a set of random numbers (1000 in this case) and counting how many of each number occurs. In this example the generator produces values between 0 and 1 and this is scaled to produce integer values between 0 and 9, so we have an array (F(9)) to hold the counts for each value.

Once we have produced our 1000 numbers we can calculate X2. It it obtained by taking the difference between the count for each number and the count we would have expected to get (with 1000 numbers each of which can be 1 of 10 values we would expect 100 of each value to appear). These differences are then squared and added together. The smaller the result the better the random numbers: a value of less than 16.9 is about right, if it much larger than this the generator is biased towards some numbers rather than others. If however it is less than 3 then you really have a random number generator that is too good to be true.

You should try experimenting with different values of U1 and see how good a generator you can produce.

You may also be interested in writing a similar program yourselves that uses the DRAGONS's inbuilt RND function and see how good a value of Chi-squared you can obtain.

```
100 'RANDOM NUMBER GENERATOR
110 INPUT "STARTER "; U1
130 DIM F(9)
140 FOR I=0 TO 9:F(I)=0:NEXT I
150 N=0
160 U2=997*U1
170 U2=U2-FIX(U2)
180 N=N+1
190 I=FIX(10*U2)
200 F(I)=F(I)+1
210 U1=U2
220 IF N<1000 GOTO 160
230 FOR I=0 TO 9
240 PRINT "F(";I;")=";F(I)
250 NEXT I
260 'CHI-SQUARED SECTION
270 X2=0
280 FOR I=0 TO 9
290 X2=X2+(F(I)-100)*(F(I)-100)
300 NEXT I
310 X2=X2/100
320 PRINT "CHI-SQUARED = ";X2
330 END
```

Jackpot

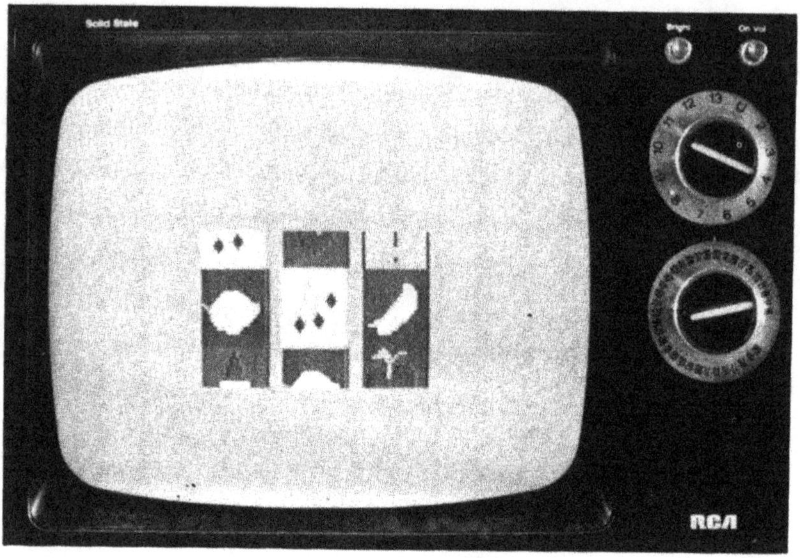

Now you can have a gambling casino on your DRAGON with this poker machine. Put in your money and watch the wheels spin. Will you be lucky and win a fortune - or will you lose your shirt?

The good thing about this game is that you don't lose any money if you are unlucky (on the other hand you don't win any either).

Program structure

10 - 630	initialize variables and define the pictures for the wheels.
1000 - 1090	main loop
2000 - 2400	spin the wheels
2500 - 2600	calculate the winnings
3000 - 3180	Display amount of money left
3190 - 3210	end game

Variables

F1()-F9()	Arrays for drawings
I1,I2,I3	Start positions for wheels
L1,L2,L3	Turn limits for wheels
C	Drum turns count
ST	Number of drums still turning
M	Money remaining
X,Y	Position of drawing
K	Defines which wheel is being used

JACKPOT

```
 20 PCLEAR 8
 30 PMODE 3,1:PCLS(3)
 40 DIM F1(42),F2(42),F3(42),F4(42),F5(42),F6(42),
      F7(42),F8(42),F9(42)
 50 DIM BL(74)
 60 CLS(1):PRINT@266,"PLEASE WAIT.";
 70 A$="BM4,28;C2;R4U2R4E14U4R2F4D8G6L2G4L2G2L6U4"
 80 DRAW A$
 90 PAINT(20,25),2,2
100 GET(0,0)-(40,40),F1,G
110 A$="BM16,14;C4;H4L4G4D8F10R10E8U12H4L4G6L2"
120 PCLS(3):DRAW A$
130 PAINT(20,20),4,4
140 A$="C1;U6E2H6G4NL2R4F2R4E4R4"
150 DRAW A$
160 PAINT(12,2),1,1
170 GET(0,0)-(40,40),F2,G
180 A$="BM12,18;C2;G4D6F4R6E4U6H4L6"
190 PCLS(3):DRAW A$
200 PAINT(16,25),2,2
210 A$="C1;H6R4U4F4U6F2D4E6D4G4R4G4L6"
220 DRAW A$
230 PAINT(15,17),1,1
240 GET(0,0)-(40,40),F3,G
250 PCLS(3):CIRCLE(20,20),12,4
260 PAINT(20,20),4,4
270 CIRCLE(22,18),4,1
280 PAINT(22,18),1,1
290 GET(0,0)-(40,40),F4,G
300 A$="BM14,6;C1;D12G6;BM14,6;F6D12;BM14,6;R6F10"
310 PCLS(2):DRAW A$
320 CIRCLE(10,28),5,4
330 CIRCLE(22,26),5,4
340 CIRCLE(30,16),5,4
350 PAINT(10,28),4,4
360 PAINT(22,26),4,4
370 PAINT(30,16),4,4
380 GET(0,0)-(40,40),F5,G
390 A$="BM6,20;C2;E8R8F2R2F4R4D4G6L2G4L6H2L4H4U6"
400 PCLS(4):DRAW A$
410 PAINT(20,20),2,2
420 DRAW"BM0,18;C1;F4R4"
430 GET(0,0)-(40,40),F6,G
440 PCLS(3):CIRCLE(20,22),10,2
450 PAINT(20,22),2,2
460 A$="BM20,2;C4;D2G2D2G2D4G2R12H2U4H2U2H2"
470 DRAW A$
480 PAINT(20,10),4,4
490 A$="BM14,22;C4;R2;BM24,22;R2;BM14,26;
      F2R8E2;BM20,22;D2"
500 DRAW A$
510 GET(0,0)-(40,40),F7,G
520 A$="BM18,4;C3;D24;BM24,10;H2L8G2D4F2R8F2D4G2L8H2"
```

```
 530 PCLS(2):DRAW A$
 540 GET(0,0)-(40,40),F8,G
 550 A$="BM10,14;C4;U2E6R6F6D2G6L2D8;BM20,34;D2"
 560 PCLS(1):DRAW A$
 570 DRAW"BM0,0;D40R40U40L40"
 580 GET(0,0)-(40,40),F9,G
 590 PCLS(1):GET(0,0)-(140,20),BL,G
 600 A$="A;A#;A-;"
 610 A$=A$+A$+A$+A$+A$
 620 PG=1:I1=RND(9):I2=RND(9):I3=RND(9):M=500
 630 CLS(1)
1000 ' SPIN
1010 L1=4+RND(3):L2=7+RND(3):L3=10+RND(3)
1020 C=0
1030 ST=0
1040 M=M-50
1050 IF M<0 GOTO 3190
1060 GOSUB 2000
1070 GOSUB 2500
1080 GOSUB 3000
1090 IF PEEK(345)=223 THEN GOTO 1000 ELSE GOTO 1090
2000 IF PG=1 THEN PG=5 ELSE PG=1
2010 PMODE 3,PG:PCLS(1):J=0:K=0:I=I1
2020 X=50+K*50:Y=50+J*40
2030 IJ=0
2040 ON K+1 GOTO 2050,2060,2070
2050 IF C<L1 THEN Y=Y+ST*20:GOTO2080 ELSE IJ=-ST:
      GOTO 2080
2060 IF C<L2 THEN Y=Y+ST*20:GOTO2080 ELSE IJ=-ST:
      GOTO 2080
2070 IF C<L3 THEN Y=Y+ST*20 ELSE IJ=-ST
2080 P=X+40:Q=Y+40:IJ=IJ+I+J+ST:IF IJ>9 THEN IJ=IJ-9
2090 ON IJ GOTO 2100,2110,2120,2130,2140,2150,
      2160,2170,2180
2100 PUT(X,Y)-(P,Q),F1,PSET:GOTO2190
2110 PUT(X,Y)-(P,Q),F2,PSET:GOTO2190
2120 PUT(X,Y)-(P,Q),F3,PSET:GOTO2190
2130 PUT(X,Y)-(P,Q),F4,PSET:GOTO2190
2140 PUT(X,Y)-(P,Q),F5,PSET:GOTO2190
2150 PUT(X,Y)-(P,Q),F6,PSET:GOTO2190
2160 PUT(X,Y)-(P,Q),F7,PSET:GOTO2190
2170 PUT(X,Y)-(P,Q),F8,PSET:GOTO2190
2180 PUT(X,Y)-(P,Q),F9,PSET
2190 ON K+1 GOTO 2200,2210,2220
2200 IF C<L1 THEN GOTO 2230 ELSE J=J+1:
      IF J<3 THEN GOTO 2020 ELSE GOTO 2240
2210 IF C<L2 THEN GOTO 2230 ELSE J=J+1:
      IF J<3 THEN GOTO 2020 ELSE GOTO 2240
2220 IF C<L3 THEN GOTO 2230 ELSE J=J+1:
      IF J<3 THEN GOTO 2020 ELSE GOTO 2240
2230 J=J+1:IF J<3-ST GOTO 2020
2240 J=0:K=K+1:IF K=1 THEN I=I2:GOTO2020
2250 IF K=2 THEN I=I3:GOTO2020
2260 PUT(50,50)-(190,70),BL,PSET
2270 PUT(50,150)-(190,170),BL,PSET
2280 SCREEN 1,0
```

```
2290 IF C<L1 THEN SOUND 200,1
2300 IF C<L2 THEN SOUND 190,1
2310 IF C<L3 THEN SOUND 180,1
2320 IF ST=1 THEN ST=0 ELSE ST=1:GOTO2000
2330 C=C+1
2340 IF C<=L1 THEN I1=I1+1
2350 IF C<=L2 THEN I2=I2+1
2360 IF C<=L3 THEN I3=I3+1
2370 IF I1>9 THEN I1=I1-9
2380 IF I2>9 THEN I2=I2-9
2390 IF I3>9 THEN I3=I3-9
2400 IF C<=L3 THEN GOTO 2000 ELSE RETURN
2500 IF I1<>I2 GOTO 2570
2510 IF I1<>I3 GOTO2600
2520 PLAY A$
2530 M=M+1000
2540 IF I1=8 THEN M=M+9000:PLAY"XA$;XA$;"
2550 IF I1=9 THEN M=M-980
2560 RETURN
2570 IF I1=I2 GOTO 2600
2580 IF I1=I3 GOTO 2600
2590 IF I2<>I3 THEN RETURN
2600 PLAY"C;O3;C;"
2610 M=M+100
2620 IF I1=8 GOTO 2640
2630 IF I2=8 GOTO 2660 ELSE GOTO 2680
2640 IF I2=8 GOTO 2670
2650 IF I3=8 THEN GOTO 2670 ELSE RETURN
2660 IF I3=8 GOTO 2670 ELSE RETURN
2670 M=M+400
2680 RETURN
3000 ST=-1:II=100000:M2=M:
       DRAW"BM64,34;D30;BM+6,-20;H2L8G2D4F2R8
       F2D4G2L8H2;BM76,42;"
3010 NN=INT(M2/II)
3020 IF II=10 THEN DRAW"BM+0,+8;R2;BM+4,-8;"
3030 IF NN<>0 THEN ST=+1: GOTO3050
3040 IF ST<0 THEN DRAW"BM+16,+0;":GOTO 3160
3050 ON NN+1 GOTO 3060,3070,3080,3090,3100,3110,3120,
       3130,3140,3150
3060 DRAW"D16R8U16L6;BM+16,+0;":GOTO3160
3070 DRAW"BM+6,+0;D16;BM+10,-16;":GOTO3160
3080 DRAW"R8D8L8D8R8;BM+8,-16;":GOTO3160
3090 DRAW"R8D8NL8D8L8;BM+16,-16;":GOTO3160
3100 DRAW"D8R4NU4ND8R4;BM+8,-8;":GOTO3160
3110 DRAW"NR8D8R8D8L8;BM+16,-16;":GOTO3160
3120 DRAW"NR8D16R8U8L8;BM+16,-8;":GOTO3160
3130 DRAW"R8D16;BM+8,-16;":GOTO3160
3140 DRAW"D16R8U8NL8U8L8;BM+16,+0":GOTO3160
3150 DRAW"ND8R8D8NL8D8L8;BM+16,-16;"
3160 M2=M2-NN*II
3170 II=II/10:IF II>=1 GOTO 3010
3180 RETURN
3190 CLS(0)
3200 PRINT @160,"COME BACK WITH SOME MORE MONEY ?";
3210 I$=INKEY$:IF I$="S" GOTO 620 ELSE GOTO 3210
4000 END
```

Black Jack

The DRAGON CASINO is back in business with this traditional card game. Up to two can play against the computer (who is the dealer), each player starting with a bank balance of $200.

The rules of the house are:

- after the first card has been dealt to all players (and the computer but you can't see what his card is yet), each player in turn must input his bet for the round.
  Note the casino does not extend credit.
- each player (and the computer) are dealt a second card, one by one the players must either draw an extra card or sit with what they have

The computer wins if it has an equal or higher total than you (provided it does not go over 21). You win the amount you have bet unless you have blackjack (an ace and a 10,J,Q or K), or unless you have 5 cards totalling less than or equal to 21. In these cases the computer pays double your original bet.

To play run the program and use the following keys:

- If the computer has displayed the message 'CUT' then it wants you to cut the cards. Press the 'C' key
- To input your bet just type in the digits followed by ENTER
- When the computer has displayed the message 'HIT' it is waiting for you to decide what to do :
  - Press 'H' to take another card (HIT)
  - Press 'S' to stay with what you have (SIT)
  - Press 'D' to double your bet

Program structure

10 - 160	initialization
170 - 180	pre-loop call for a new deck
500 - 570	main loop
580 - 740	cut and shuffle deck
1000 - 1280	deal a card to all players
1500 - 1790	accept bets
1800 - 1810	end/restart game
2000 - 2260	handle 'hit' requests
2270 - 2290	print blank cards
2300 - 2840	score
3000 - 3260	allocate funds
3270 - 3430	display a digit
3440 - 3650	print 'BET', 'HIT', 'CUT'
3660 - 3870	display a coloured digit
3880 - 4100	display a card
4110 - 4330	display black digits on white cards
5000 - 5180	deal second cards

Variables

M()	Remaining money for each player
N()	Number of cards each player has
B()	players bets
T()	Total card points for each player
TD	Dealers points
CD()	Deck of cards
C()	Cards used already
DC()	Dealers cards
K	Number of cards used

```
 20 DIM CD(52),C(2,10),D(10)
 30 CLS
 40 PRINT @200,"HOW MANY PLAYERS ?";
 50 I$=INKEY$:IF I$="" GOTO 50
 60 NP=VAL(I$):IF NP=1 GOTO 80
 70 IF NP<>2 GOTO 50
 80 CLS(0)
 90 M(1)=200:M(2)=200:N(1)=0:N(2)=0:B(1)=0:
      B(2)=0:T(1)=0:T(2)=0:TD=0
 100 IF NP=1 THEN M(2)=0
 110 PW=14
 120 YJ=13:C=3
 130 FOR N=1 TO NP
 140 XJ=(N-1)*17:J=M(N)
 150 GOSUB 3270
 160 NEXT N
 170 GOSUB 3600:'PRINT"CUT"
 180 GOSUB 580:'CUT'
 500 GOSUB 1000:'DEAL'
 510 GOSUB 1500:'BET'
 520 GOSUB5000:'SECOND CARD'
 530 GOSUB 2000:'HIT'
 540 GOSUB2500:'TALLY BETS'
 550 GOSUB 3000
 560 FOR I=1 TO 1500:NEXT I
 570 GOTO500
 580 GOSUB 3600
 590 I$=INKEY$:IF I$<>"C" GOTO 590
 600 SOUND 200,1
 610 FOR I=0 TO 3
 620 I2=I*13
 630 FOR J=1 TO 13
 640 CD(I2+J)=J
 650 NEXT J
 660 NEXT I
 670 FOR I=1 TO 52
 680 J=RND(52)
 690 TM=CD(J)
 700 CD(J)=CD(I)
 710 CD(I)=TM
 720 NEXT I
 730 K=1
 740 RETURN
1000 'DEAL  CARDS
1010 XB=256:GOSUB 2280
1020 XB=272:GOSUB 2280
1030 N=1:XC=0:YC=9:XD=4
1040 FOR M=1 TO NP
1050 IF M(M)>0 GOTO 1070
1060 IF M(1)+M(2)=0 THEN GOTO 1800 ELSE GOTO 1110
1070 K=K+1:IF K>52 THEN GOSUB 580
1080 C(M,N)=CD(K)
1090 IC=CD(K)
```

```
1100 GOSUB3880
1110 XC=XC+17
1120 NEXT M
1130 YC=1:XD=XD+3:XC=XD
1140 PRINT @XD,CHR$(207)+CHR$(207)+CHR$(207);
1150 SOUND 100,1
1160 PRINT @XD+32,CHR$(207)+CHR$(207)+CHR$(207);
1170 PRINT @XD+64,CHR$(207)+CHR$(207)+CHR$(207);
1180 PRINT @XD+96,CHR$(204)+CHR$(204)+CHR$(204);
1190 XB=XD+3:GOSUB 2280
1200 K=K+1:IF K>52 THEN GOSUB 580
1210 DC(N)=CD(K)
1220 X1=3:X2=18:XD=8:N(1)=1:N(2)=1:ND=1
1230 K2=1
1240 FOR MN=1 TO 2
1250 T(MN)=0
1260 IF C(MN,K2)<10 THEN T(MN)=T(MN)+C(MN,K2) :
        ELSE T(MN)=T(MN)+10
1270 NEXT MN
1280 RETURN
1290 'PRINT"BET" & ACCEPT SAME'
1500 GOSUB 3480
1510 XB=128:GOSUB 2280
1520 XB=144:GOSUB2280
1530 C=4:YJ=5
1540 FOR MN=1 TO NP
1550 IF M(MN)<>0 GOTO1570
1560 IF M(1)+M(2)=0 THEN GOTO 1800 ELSE B(MN)=-1:
        GOTO 1780
1570 PF=64+(MN-1)*30
1580 B(MN)=0: XJ=(MN-1)*16
1590 PRINT @PF,CHR$(255)+CHR$(255);
1600 I$=INKEY$
1610 PRINT @PF,CHR$(128)+CHR$(128);
1620 IF PEEK(338)=191 GOTO 1690
1630 IF I$="" GOTO 1590
1640 I=ASC(I$):IF I=32 GOTO 1690
1650 I=VAL(I$)
1660 B(MN)=B(MN)*10+I:J=B(MN)
1670 GOSUB 3270
1680 GOTO1590
1690 IF M(MN)>=B(MN) GOTO 1720
1700 XB=XJ+128:GOSUB 2280
1710 J=0:B(MN)=0:GOTO 1590
1720 GOSUB 3270
1730 M(MN)=M(MN)-B(MN)
1740 J=M(MN):YJ=13
1750 XB=(YJ-1)*32+XJ:GOSUB2280
1760 C=3:GOSUB 3270:C=4
1770 YJ=5
1780 NEXT MN
1790 RETURN
1800 CLS:PRINT @259,"COME BACK TOMORROW ?";
1810 I$=INKEY$:IF I$="S" THEN GOTO 30 ELSE GOTO 1810
1820 'PRINT"HIT"& ACCEPT SAME'
2000 GOSUB 3540
```

```
2010 YC=9
2020 FOR MN=1 TO NP
2030 IF M(MN)>0 GOTO2050
2040 IF B(MN)<0 GOTO 2230
2050 PF=64+(MN-1)*30
2060 PRINT @PF,CHR$(255)+CHR$(255);:I$=INKEY$
2070 PRINT @PF,CHR$(128)+CHR$(128);
2080 IF I$="H" GOTO 2180
2090 IF I$="S" GOTO 2250
2100 IF I$="D" GOTO 2120
2110 GOTO 2060
2120 IF B(MN)>M(MN) GOTO 2060
2130 M(MN)=M(MN)-B(MN):B(MN)=2*B(MN)
2140 XJ=(MN-1)*16
2145 YJ=5: XB=128+XJ: GOSUB2280
2150 C=4:J=B(MN):GOSUB 3270
2160 YJ=13:XB=384+XJ:GOSUB 2280
2170 C=3:J=M(MN):GOSUB 3270
2180 IF N(MN)>=5 GOTO 2250 ELSE K=K+1:
        IF K>52 THEN GOSUB 580:GOSUB3540:GOTO2060
2190 N(MN)=N(MN)+1:C(MN,N(MN))=CD(K)
2200 IC=CD(K):XC=(MN-1)*17+(N(MN)-1)*3:YC=9:
        GOSUB 3880
2210 IF CD(K)<10 THEN V=CD(K) ELSE V=10
2220 T(MN)=T(MN)+V:IF T(MN)<22 GOTO 2060
2230 XB=128+(MN-1)*16:GOSUB2280
2240 B(MN)=-1
2250 NEXT MN
2260 RETURN
2270 'PRINT BLANKS'
2280 FOR I8=0 TO 96 STEP 32:PRINT
        @XB+I8,STRING$(15,CHR$(128));:NEXT I8
2290 RETURN
2300 'TALLY BETS'
2500 XB=14:GOSUB2280:FOR MN=1 TO NP
2510 IF B(MN)>=0 GOTO 2540
2520 NEXT MN
2530 RETURN
2540 XC=7:YC=1:IC=DC(1):GOSUB 3880
2550 FOR MN=1 TO NP
2560 T(MN)=0
2570 FOR NC=1 TO N(MN)
2580 IF C(MN,NC)<10 THEN T(MN)=T(MN)+C(MN,NC) :
        ELSE T(MN)=T(MN)+10
2590 NEXT NC
2600 FOR NC=1 TO N(MN)
2610 IF C(MN,NC)>1 GOTO 2630
2620 IF T(MN)<12 THEN T(MN)=T(MN)+10
2630 NEXT NC
2640 NEXT MN
2650 TD=0:AC=0
2660 IF DC(1)<10 THEN TD=TD+DC(1) ELSE TD=TD+10
2670 IF DC(1)=1 THEN AC=AC+1
2680 IF AC>0 GOTO 2760
2690 IF TD>16 GOTO 2760
2700 K=K+1:IF K>52 THEN GOSUB 580:GOSUB 3540
```

```
2710 ND=ND+1:DC(ND)=CD(K):XC=XC+3:IC=CD(K)
2720 GOSUB 3880
2730 IF DC(ND)<10 THEN TD=TD+DC(ND) ELSE TD=TD+10
2740 IF DC(ND)=1 THEN AC=AC+1
2750 GOTO 2680
2760 IF TD>16 THEN RETURN
2770 IF TD>21 THEN RETURN
2780 IF AC=0 GOTO 2830
2790 IF TD+10>21 GOTO 2830
2800 IF TD>B(1) THEN RETURN
2810 IF NP=1 GOTO 2830
2820 IF TD>B(2) THEN RETURN
2830 GOTO 2700
2840 RETURN
3000 FOR MN=1 TO NP
3010 IF B(MN)<0 GOTO 3040
3020 IF N(MN)<5 GOTO 3040
3030 M(MN)=M(MN)+4*B(MN):B(MN)=-1
3040 NEXT MN
3050 FOR MN=1 TO NP
3060 IF B(MN)<0 GOTO 3100
3070 IF N(MN)>2 GOTO 3100
3080 IF T(MN)<21 GOTO 3100
3090 M(MN)=M(MN)+3*B(MN):B(MN)=-1
3100 NEXT MN
3110 IF TD<22 GOTO 3160
3120 FOR MN=1 TO NP
3130 IF B(MN)<0 GOTO 3150
3140 M(MN)=M(MN)+2*B(MN):B(MN)=-1
3150 NEXT MN
3160 FOR MN=1 TO NP
3170 IF B(MN)<0 GOTO 3190
3180 IF T(MN)>TD THEN M(MN)=M(MN)+2*B(MN)
3190 NEXT MN
3200 FOR MN=1 TO NP
3210 J=M(MN): YJ=13: XJ=(MN-1)*16
3220 XB=384+XJ:GOSUB 2280
3230 C=3:GOSUB 3270:C=4
3240 IF M(MN)=0 THEN B(MN)=-1
3250 NEXT MN
3260 RETURN
3270 'DISP A NUMBER J AT XJ,YJ
3280 I1=INT(J/1000)
3290 XD=XJ:YD=YJ
3300 IF I1=0 GOTO3330
3310 IC=I1:GOSUB 3660
3320 XD=XD+3
3330 I2=INT((J-1000*I1)/100)
3340 IF I1+I2=0 GOTO 3370
3350 IC=I2:GOSUB 3660
3360 XD=XD+3
3370 I3=INT((J-1000*I1-100*I2)/10)
3380 IF I1+I2+I3=0 GOTO 3410
3390 IC=I3:GOSUB 3660
3400 XD=XD+3
3410 IC=J-(1000*I1+100*I2+10*I3)
```

```
3420 GOSUB 3660
3430 RETURN
3440 'PRINT T,BE,HI,CU
3450 'T
3460 PRINT @PW+7,CHR$(131)+CHR$(131)+CHR$(130);:
        PRINT @PW+40,CHR$(138);:
        PRINT @PW+72,CHR$(138);
3470 RETURN
3480 'BE
3490 PRINT @PW,CHR$(129)+CHR$(131)+CHR$(131)+
       CHR$(128)+CHR$(131)+CHR$(131)+CHR$(130);
3500 PRINT @PW+32,CHR$(128)+CHR$(139)+CHR$(135)
       +CHR$(128)+CHR$(139)+CHR$(131)+CHR$(128);
3510 PRINT @PW+64,CHR$(129)+CHR$(139)+CHR$(135)
       +CHR$(128)+CHR$(139)+CHR$(131)+CHR$(130);
3520 GOSUB 3440
3530 RETURN
3540 'HI
3550 PRINT @PW,CHR$(129)+CHR$(128)+CHR$(129)
       +CHR$(128)+CHR$(129)+CHR$(131)+CHR$(128);
3560 PRINT @PW+32,CHR$(133)+CHR$(131)+CHR$(135)
       +CHR$(128)+CHR$(128)+CHR$(138)+CHR$(128);
3570 PRINT @PW+64,CHR$(133)+CHR$(128)+CHR$(133)
       +CHR$(128)+CHR$(129)+CHR$(139)+CHR$(128);
3580 GOSUB 3440
3590 RETURN
3600 'CU
3610 PRINT @PW,CHR$(129)+CHR$(131)+CHR$(131)
       +CHR$(128)+CHR$(130)+CHR$(128)+CHR$(130);
3620 PRINT @PW+32,CHR$(133)+CHR$(128)+CHR$(128)
       +CHR$(128)+CHR$(138)+CHR$(128)+CHR$(138);
3630 PRINT @PW+64,CHR$(133)+CHR$(131)+CHR$(131)
       +CHR$(128)+CHR$(139)+CHR$(131)+CHR$(138);
3640 GOSUB 3440
3650 RETURN
3660 'DISP DIGIT IC AT XD,YD IN COLOR C
3670 C2=(C-1)*16:JD=(YD-1)*32+XD
3680 IF IC=2 GOTO 3730
3690 PRINT @JD+34,CHR$(130+C2);:
       PRINT @JD+66,CHR$(138+C2);
3700 IF IC=0 GOTO 3730
3710 IF IC=6 GOTO 3730
3720 IF IC<>8 GOTO 3740
3730 PRINT @JD+32,CHR$(129+C2);:
       PRINT @JD+64,CHR$(133+C2);
3740 IF IC=6 GOTO 3790
3750 IF IC=5 GOTO3790
3760 PRINT @JD+34,CHR$(138+C2);:
       PRINT @(JD+2),CHR$(130+C2);
3770 IF IC=1 THEN RETURN
3780 IF IC=4 GOTO 3840
3790 PRINT @JD,CHR$(129+C2)+CHR$(131+C2)+CHR$(130+C2);
3800 IF IC=7 THEN RETURN
3810 IF IC=2*INT(IC/2) THEN
       PRINT @JD+64,CHR$(133+C2)+CHR$(131+C2); :
       ELSE PRINT @JD+64,CHR$(129+C2)+CHR$(131+C2);
```

```
3820 IF IC=2 THEN PRINT @JD+66,CHR$(130+C2);
3830 IF IC=0 GOTO 3860
3840 PRINT @JD+33, CHR$(131+C2);
3850 IF IC<4 THEN RETURN
3860 PRINT @JD,CHR$(129+C2);:
        PRINT @JD+32,CHR$(133+C2);
3870 RETURN
3880 'DISP CD(K),AS IC, AT XC,YC
3890 SOUND 100,1
3900 JC=(YC-1)*32+XC
3910 IF IC=1 GOTO 3940
3920 IF IC<10 THEN GOSUB 4110:GOTO4080
3930 ON (IC-9)GOTO 3970,4000,4030,4060
3940 'ACE
3950 PRINT @JC,CHR$(206)+CHR$(204)+CHR$(205);:
        PRINT @JC+32,CHR$(202)+CHR$(204)+CHR$(197);:
        PRINT @JC+64,CHR$(203)+CHR$(207)+CHR$(199);
3960 GOTO 4080
3970 '10
3980 PRINT @JC,CHR$(206)+CHR$(206)+CHR$(204)+CHR$(207)
        ;:PRINT @JC+32,CHR$(202)+CHR$(202)+CHR$(202)
        +CHR$(207);:PRINT @JC+64,CHR$(203)+CHR$(203)
        +CHR$(195)+CHR$(207);
3990 GOTO 4080
4000 'JACK
4010 PRINT @JC,CHR$(207)+CHR$(207)+CHR$(205);:
        PRINT @JC+32,CHR$(206)+CHR$(207)+CHR$(197);:
        PRINT @JC+64,CHR$(203)+CHR$(195)+CHR$(199);
4020 GOTO 4080
4030 'QUEEN
4040 PRINT @JC,CHR$(206)+CHR$(204)+CHR$(205);:
        PRINT @JC+32,CHR$(202)+CHR$(206)+CHR$(197);:
        PRINT @JC+64,CHR$(203)+CHR$(195)+CHR$(199);
4050 GOTO 4080
4060 'KING
4070 PRINT @JC,CHR$(206)+CHR$(206)+CHR$(207);:
        PRINT @JC+32,CHR$(202)+CHR$(196)+CHR$(207);:
        PRINT @JC+64,CHR$(203)+CHR$(207)+CHR$(199);
4080 PRINT @JC+96,CHR$(204)+CHR$(204)+CHR$(204);
4090 IF IC=10 THEN PRINT @JC+99,CHR$(204);
4100 RETURN
4110 'DISP DIGITS ON WHITE
4120 FOR J7=0 TO 64 STEP 32:PRINT
        @JC+J7,CHR$(207)+CHR$(207)+CHR$(207);:NEXT J7
4130 IF IC=2 GOTO 4180
4140 PRINT @JC+34,CHR$(205);:PRINT @JC+66,CHR$(197);
4150 IF IC=0 GOTO 4180
4160 IF IC=6 GOTO 4180
4170 IF IC<>8 GOTO 4190
4180 PRINT @JC+32,CHR$(206);:PRINT @JC+64,CHR$(202);
4190 IF IC=6 GOTO 4240
4200 IF IC=5 GOTO 4240
4210 PRINT @JC+34,CHR$(197);
4220 IF IC=1 THEN RETURN
4230 IF IC=4 GOTO4290
4240 PRINT @JC,CHR$(206)+CHR$(204)+CHR$(205);
```

```
4250 IF IC=7 THEN RETURN
4260 IF IC=2*INT(IC/2) THEN
     PRINT @JC+64,CHR$(202)+CHR$(204); :
     ELSE PRINT @JC+64,CHR$(206)+CHR$(204);
4270 IF IC=2 THEN PRINT @JC+66,CHR$(205);
4280 IF IC=0 GOTO 4310
4290 PRINT @JC+33,CHR$(204);
4300 IF IC<4 THEN RETURN
4310 PRINT @JC+32,CHR$(202);
4320 IF IC<>4 THEN RETURN
4330 PRINT @JC,CHR$(206)+CHR$(207)+CHR$(205);:RETURN
4340 'SECOND CARD EACH
5000 FOR MN=1 TO NP
5010 IF B(MN)<0 GOTO 5080
5020 K=K+1:IF K>52 THEN GOSUB 580:GOSUB 3540:
     GOSUB2060
5030 N(MN)=N(MN)+1:C(MN,N(MN))=CD(K)
5040 IC=CD(K):XC=(MN-1)*17+(N(MN)-1)*3:YC=9:GOSUB3880
5050 IF CD(K)<10 THEN V=CD(K) ELSE V=10
5060 T(MN)=T(MN)+V
5070 XB=128+(MN-1)*16
5080 GOSUB 2280: NEXT MN
5090 YC=1:XD=9:XC=XD
5100 PRINT @XD,CHR$(207)+CHR$(207)+CHR$(207);
5110 SOUND 100,1
5120 PRINT @XD+32,CHR$(207)+CHR$(207)+CHR$(207);
5130 PRINT @XD+64,CHR$(207)+CHR$(207)+CHR$(207);
5140 PRINT @XD+96,CHR$(204)+CHR$(204)+CHR$(204);
5150 XB=XD+3:GOSUB2280
5160 K=K+1:IF K>52 THEN GOSUB580
5170 N(1)=2:N(2)=2:ND=2
5180 RETURN
```

Bubble Sort

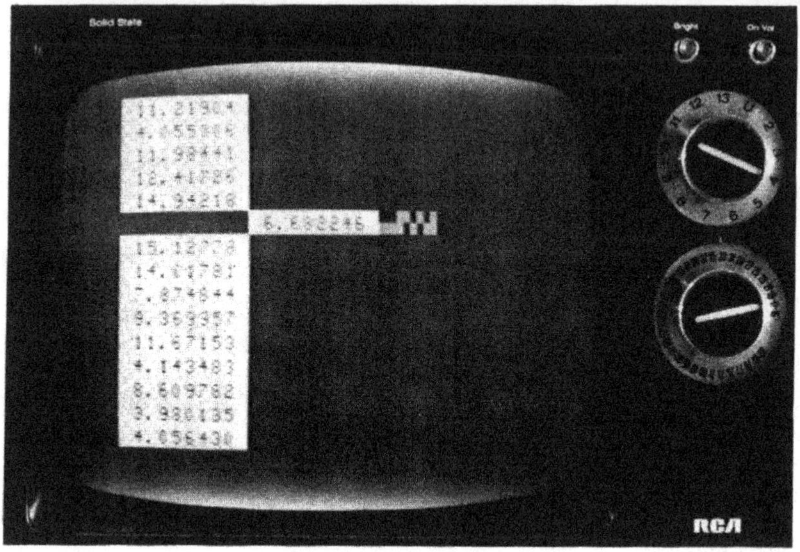

There are all sorts of people interested in computing, but in mathematics the word 'sort' has a different meaning. There are indeed many different sorts of sorts.

A sort is a process by which you can create order out of chaos, and usually the sorting process is applied to a large number of names or an array of numbers.

The program given here serves as both a demonstration of the processes involved in the sorting process, as well as being the basis for a compact subroutine you can use in your own programs - for example to sort a list of names and addresses, or to sort a hand of cards in a bridge game.

The demonstration of these sorts given here is graphically very enjoyable as well as being slow enough to allow a good understanding of the sorting process.

The bubble sort:

The first program given here is a traditional bubble sort. What the program does is that it compares two numbers adjacent in a list: if the numbers are the wrong way round (in other words the larger number comes before the smaller number) then it swaps them around.

If you run this program, you will soon realise why it is called a bubble sort - the larger numbers appear to bubble toward the bottom as the process continues.

The first program will keep on swapping adjacent numbers, over and over again, each time getting the list of numbers a little bit more sorted than before until finally there is no more sorting to be done. Average sorting time for 15 randomly ordered numbers will be around one minute.

The program is very cute in its execution, and you can see how hard the dumper truck has to work to sort the mess out. You will soon realise that there must be a better way to sort things.

Modified bubble sort:

The second program listing is a modified bubble sort. Now the program is no longer concerned to swap merely adjacent numbers - it is prepared to roam much further afield.

This cuts the number of swaps to be done to about half those on a traditional bubble sort. Sorting of 15 numbers will also take an average of about one minute, but obviously most of the time is spent in showing you the numbers being swapped.

You will find that the second program though is similar to the first one for the input part, because the swapping vicinity is no longer limited to adjacent numbers, the dumper needs to actually carry the move the numbers around. ie lines 1120-1130, lines 1210-1230.

Sort subroutine:

Aside from its demonstration purposes, you can use sorts in your own programs. Program 3 gives the listing of the modified version of program 2. The dumper won't do any intermediate swapping until the best number to be swapped is found. That will cut down the swapping to a maximum of 14 swap.

This subroutine assumes the numbers to be sorted are in an array N(NN), and that NN is the number of elements to be sorted.

As you can see from this program, 15 numbers can be sorted in about 30 seconds, including the time required to print the 15 numbers twice.

Special Note

You may wonder what mode the program is in; how can it have half the screen black, and what is the machanism behind the dumper...

The program is actually in text mode using only three colors, green, orange and black. When the dumper is in processing the program is actually building up 32 character line using STRING commands such as LEFT$, RIGHT$ and STRING$ on three types of string variables;

- S$ string of 22 blank black character (176)
- N$(i) string representation of the number to be sorted of 10 characters in length
- D$ string of 5 graphic characters for the dumper plus 17 blank black characters on the right.

So, the machanism used by the dumper to move a number out is by using LEFT$(S$,n) to fill the left part of the 32 characters line with blank, then add on the N$(?) and fill up the right part of the line by LEFT$(D$,m). This process has to be done ten times by increasing n from 1 to ten and decreasing m from 22 to 12. ie one character at a time to move a number out completely.

By the same token, to move a number inside a location, the program will change n and m in an opposite manner.

In program version 2, you can see the effect of the program PUSHing a number inside a location and PULLing out the existing number by applying the above machanisms on two N$(?) strings.

BUBBLE SORT VERSION 1

```
  10 'BUBBLE SORT VERSION 1
  20 CLEAR1000,32767
  30 GOTO9000
1000 'SORT
1010 FORI=(NN-1)TO1STEP-1
1020 FORJ=1TOI
1030 L=J+1
1040 IFN(J)<=N(L)THEN1240
1050 IFM=L THEN1080
1060 SOUND(200+M),1:IFL>M THENST=1ELSEST=-1
1070 FOR X=(M+ST)TOL STEPST:PRINT @(X-ST-1)*32+10,S$;
     :PRINT @(X-1)*32+10,D$;:NEXTX
1080 'MOVEOUT
1090 FORX=1TO10
1100 PRINT @(L-1)*32,LEFT$(S$,X)+N$(L)+
     LEFT$(D$,(22-X));
1110 NEXTX
1120 'SWAP DOWN
1130 PRINT @(J-1)*32,LEFT$(S$,10);
1140 PRINT @(L-1)*32,N$(J);
1150 'MOVEUP
1160 PRINT @(L-1)*32+10,S$;
1170 'MOVEIN
1180 FORX=10TO0STEP-1
1190 PRINT @(J-1)*32,LEFT$(S$,X)+N$(L)+
     LEFT$(D$,(22-X));
1200 NEXTX
1210 M=J:SOUND(200+M),1
1220 V=N(L):N(L)=N(J):N(J)=V
1230 V$=N$(L):N$(L)=N$(J):N$(J)=V$
1240 NEXTJ,I
1250 PRINT @(M-1)*32+10,CHR$(243)+CHR$(247)+CHR$(249)+
     CHR$(249)+CHR$(250);:RETURN
2000 'INPUT
2010 DIMN(15):DIMN$(15)'NUMBER ARRAY
2020 D$=CHR$(163)+CHR$(167)+CHR$(169)+CHR$(169)+
     CHR$(170)+STRING$(17,176)
2030 S$=STRING$(22,176)
2040 CLS:PRINT @0,
     "DO YOU WANT TO CHOOSE YOUR OWN  NUMBERS
     (Y OR N)?"
2050 LETB$=INKEY$:IFB$=""THEN2050
2060 IFB$="N"THEN2130
2070 PRINT"HOW MANY NUMBERS TO SORTED?      (MAX 15)"
2080 INPUTNN:IF(NN<0ORNN>15)THEN2080
2090 CLS:PRINT"PLEASE INPUT YOUR NUMBERS"
2100 FORI=1TONN
2110 INPUT N(I):V$=LEFT$(STR$(N(I)),9):
     N$(I)=V$+STRING$(10-LEN(V$),143)
2120 NEXTI:GOTO2160
2130 NN=15:FORI=1TONN
2140 N(I)=15*RND(0)+1:V$=LEFT$(STR$(N(I)),9):
     N$(I)=V$+STRING$(10-LEN(V$),143)
```

```
2150 NEXTI
2160 CLS(0)
2170 FORI=1TONN
2180 PRINT @(I-1)*32,N$(I)+S$;
2190 NEXTI
2200 M=NN
2210 RETURN
9000 'MAIN
9010 GOSUB2000'INPUT
9020 GOSUB1000'SORT
9030 IFPEEK(338)<>191THEN9030
9040 CLS:PRINT
     "DO YOU WANT TO SORT AGAIN?         (Y OR N)"
9050 V$=INKEY$:IFV$=""THEN9050
9060 IFV$="Y"THENRUN
9070 IFV$<>"N"THEN9050ELSESTOP
```

BUBBLE SORT   VERSION 2

```
  10 'BUBBLE SORT VERSION 2
  20 CLEAR1000,32767
  30 GOTO9000
1000 'SORT
1010 FORJ=1TO(NN-1)
1020 FORI=(J+1)TONN
1030 L=NN+J-I+1
1040 IFN(J)<=N(L)THEN1290
1050 IFM=L THEN1080
1060 IFL>M THENST=1ELSEST=-1
1070 FOR X=(M+ST)TOL STEPST:PRINT @(X-ST-1)*32+10,S$;
       :PRINT @(X-1)*32+10,D$;:NEXTX
1080 'MOVEOUT
1090 FORX=1TO10
1100 PRINT @(L-1)*32,LEFT$(S$,X)+N$(L)+
       LEFT$(D$,(22-X));
1110 NEXTX
1120 'TRAVEL
1130 FORX=(L-1)TOJ STEP-1:PRINT @X*32+10,S$;:
       PRINT @(X-1)*32+10,N$(L)+LEFT$(D$,12);:NEXTX
1140 'MOVEIN
1150 FORX=10TO0STEP-1
1160 PRINT @(J-1)*32,LEFT$(N$(J),X)+N$(L)+
       LEFT$(D$,(22-X));
1170 NEXTX
1180 'MOVEOUT
1190 FORX=1TO10:PRINT @(J-1)*32,LEFT$(N$(L),X)+N$(J)+
       LEFT$(D$,(22-X));
1200 NEXTX
1210 'TRAVEL
1220 FORX=(J+1)TOL:PRINT @(X-2)*32+10,S$;:
       PRINT @(X-1)*32+10,N$(J)+LEFT$(D$,12);
1230 NEXTX
1240 'MOVEIN
1250 FORX=10TO0STEP-1:PRINT @(L-1)*32,LEFT$(S$,X)+
       N$(J)+LEFT$(D$,(22-X));
1260 NEXTX
1270 M=L:V=N(L):N(L)=N(J):N(J)=V
1280 V$=N$(L):N$(L)=N$(J):N$(J)=V$
1290 NEXTI,J
1300 PRINT @(M-1)*32+10,CHR$(243)+CHR$(247)+
       CHR$(249)+CHR$(249)+CHR$(250);:RETURN
2000 'SORT
2010 DIMN(15):DIMN$(15)'NUMBER ARRAY
2020 D$=CHR$(163)+CHR$(167)+CHR$(169)+
       CHR$(169)+CHR$(170)+STRING$(17,176)
2030 S$=STRING$(22,176)
2040 CLS:PRINT @0,
       "DO YOU WANT TO CHOOSE YOUR OWN  NUMBERS
       (Y OR N)?"
2050 LETB$=INKEY$:IFB$=""THEN2050
2060 IFB$="N"THEN2130
2070 PRINT"HOW MANY NUMBERS TO SORTED?     (MAX 15)"
```

```
2080 INPUTNN:IF(NN<0ORNN>15)THEN2080
2090 CLS:PRINT"PLEASE INPUT YOUR NUMBERS"
2100 FORI=1TONN
2110 INPUT N(I):V$=LEFT$(STR$(N(I)),9):
        N$(I)=V$+STRING$(10-LEN(V$),143)
2120 NEXTI:GOTO2160
2130 NN=15:FORI=1TONN
2140 N(I)=15*RND(0)+1:V$=LEFT$(STR$(N(I)),9):
        N$(I)=V$+STRING$(10-LEN(V$),143)
2150 NEXTI
2160 CLS(0)
2170 FORI=1TONN
2180 PRINT @(I-1)*32,N$(I)+S$;
2190 NEXTI
2200 M=NN
2210 RETURN
9000 'MAIN
9010 GOSUB2000'INPUT
9020 GOSUB1000'SORT
9030 IFPEEK(338)<>191THEN9030
9040 CLS:PRINT
        "DO YOU WANT TO SORT AGAIN?       (Y OR N)"
9050 V$=INKEY$:IFV$=""THEN9050
9060 IFV$="Y"THENRUN
9070 IFV$<>"N"THEN9050ELSESTOP
```

BUBBLE SORT   VERSION 3

```
  10 'BUBBLE SORT VERSION 3
  20 CLEAR1000,32767
  30 GOTO9000
1000 'SORT
1010 FORJ=1TO(NN-1)
1020 MI=J
1030 FORI=(J+1)TONN
1040 L=NN+J-I+1
1050 IFN(J)<=N(L)THEN1070
1060 IFN(L)<N(MI) THENMI=L
1070 NEXTI
1080 IFJ<>MI THENL=MI ELSE1330
1090 IFM=L THEN1120
1100 IFL>M THENST=1ELSEST=-1
1110 FOR X=(M+ST)TOL STEPST:PRINT @(X-ST-1)*32+10,S$;
        :PRINT @(X-1)*32+10,D$;:NEXTX
1120 'MOVEOUT
1130 FORX=1TO10
1140 PRINT @(L-1)*32,LEFT$(S$,X)+N$(L)+
        LEFT$(D$,(22-X));
1150 NEXTX
1160 'TRAVEL
1170 FORX=(L-1)TOJ STEP-1:PRINT @X*32+10,S$;:
        PRINT @(X-1)*32+10,N$(L)+LEFT$(D$,12);:NEXTX
1180 'MOVEIN
1190 FORX=10TO0STEP-1
1200 PRINT @(J-1)*32,LEFT$(N$(J),X)+N$(L)+
        LEFT$(D$,(22-X));
1210 NEXTX
1220 'MOVEOUT
1230 FORX=1TO10:PRINT @(J-1)*32,LEFT$(N$(L),X)+N$(J)+
        LEFT$(D$,(22-X));
1240 NEXTX
1250 'TRAVEL
1260 FORX=(J+1)TOL:PRINT @(X-2)*32+10,S$;:
        PRINT @(X-1)*32+10,N$(J)+LEFT$(D$,12);
1270 NEXTX
1280 'MOVEIN
1290 FORX=10TO0STEP-1:PRINT @(L-1)*32,LEFT$(S$,X)+
        N$(J)+LEFT$(D$,(22-X));
1300 NEXTX
1310 M=L:V=N(L):N(L)=N(J):N(J)=V
1320 V$=N$(L):N$(L)=N$(J):N$(J)=V$
1330 NEXTJ
1340 PRINT @(M-1)*32+10,CHR$(243)+CHR$(247)+
        CHR$(249)+CHR$(249)+CHR$(250);:RETURN
2000 'INPUT
2010 DIMN(15):DIMN$(15)'NUMBER ARRAY
2020 D$=CHR$(163)+CHR$(167)+CHR$(169)+
        CHR$(169)+CHR$(170)+STRING$(17,176)
2030 S$=STRING$(22,176)
2040 CLS:PRINT @0,
        "DO YOU WANT TO CHOOSE YOUR OWN  NUMBERS
```

```
         (Y OR N)?"
2050 LETB$=INKEY$:IFB$=""THEN2050
2060 IFB$="N"THEN2130
2070 PRINT"HOW MANY NUMBERS TO SORTED?      (MAX 15)"
2080 INPUTNN:IF(NN<0ORNN>15)THEN2080
2090 CLS:PRINT"PLEASE INPUT YOUR NUMBERS"
2100 FORI=1TONN
2110 INPUT N(I):V$=LEFT$(STR$(N(I)),9):
         N$(I)=V$+STRING$(10-LEN(V$),143)
2120 NEXTI:GOTO2160
2130 NN=15:FORI=1TONN
2140 N(I)=15*RND(0)+1:V$=LEFT$(STR$(N(I)),9):
         N$(I)=V$+STRING$(10-LEN(V$),143)
2150 NEXTI
2160 CLS(0)
2170 FORI=1TONN
2180 PRINT @(I-1)*32,N$(I)+S$;
2190 NEXTI
2200 M=NN
2210 RETURN
9000 'MAIN
9010 GOSUB2000'INPUT
9020 GOSUB1000'SORT
9030 IFPEEK(338)<>191THEN9030
9040 CLS:PRINT
         "DO YOU WANT TO SORT AGAIN?       (Y OR N)"
9050 V$=INKEY$:IFV$=""THEN9050
9060 IFV$="Y"THENRUN
9070 IFV$<>"N"THEN9050ELSESTOP
```

Simultaneous Equations

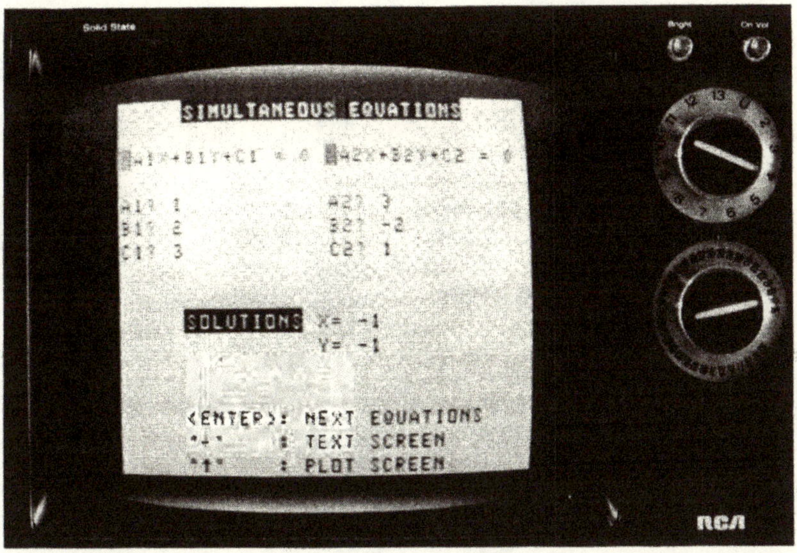

This program solves two simultaneous equations of the type
$$ax + by + c = 0$$

This equation is the general form of equation for a straight line,. and the 'solution' of two such lines is the mathematical term for the point where the two lines cross.

You will be asked by the program to enter the values of a, b and c for each of the two equations, and the program will find out for what values of x and y the lines meet.

If there is no solution - in other words the two lines are parallel and do not meet - the program will tell you so.

The program will then draw for you each of the two lines and show you where they cross on a relative scale.

Program consideration:

The actual calculation part of the program is fairly small - most of the program consist of getting the correct information from you, and then displaying the results to you (including the graph).

Line 3020 calculates the determinant D. If D is zero, no solution exists.

The block from 4020 - 4090 determines in which quadrant the intersection of the two lines occurs, and in which direction the graphs should be plotted.

Program Structure

```
10 - 70       Initialise screen and array

1000 - 1030   Input first equation

2000 - 2030   Input second equation

3000 - 3170   Calculate solution
                   if determinant = 0
                        then flash "NO SOLUTION" until (ENTER)
                               pressed
                   else
                        display solution screen

4000 - 5190   Plot graph screen
                   plot axises depend on solution (x,y)
                   plot lines based on adjusted scale to
                        show intersection of lines

9000 - 9040   Display solution or graph screen
                   "left arrow" for solution text screen
                   "up arrow" for graph plot screen
                   "(ENTER)" for next equations solving
```

Special Note

Because of the special architecture of the Dragon computer, it is extremely hard to display ASCII text information in the graphic mode unless, you design your own characters. That is one of the reason that you have to swap between two modes, the text and graphic mode for this application.

In line 5005, RX and RY are the scaling factor to ensure that the intersection of the two line equation is shown as near to the centre of the graphic screen as possible.

Try and see if you can understand how the change of axises depending on the X, Y solution is achieved from line 4030 to 4060.

SIMULTANEOUS EQUATIONS

```
10 'EQUATIONS
20 'TEXTMODE
30 PCLEAR4:CLS:SCREEN0,0
40 PRINT @5,"SIMULTANEOUS";CHR$(128);"EQUATIONS"
50 PRINT @64,CHR$(175);"A1X+B1Y+C1 = 0
        ";CHR$(191);"A2X+B2Y+C2 = 0"
60 DIMC(6)'COEFFICIENT ARRAY
70 DIMS$(7):DIMX$(7):DIMY$(7)
1000 'INPUT FIRST EQUATION
1010 PRINT @128,"";:INPUT"A1";C(1)
1020 PRINT @160,"";:INPUT"B1";C(2)
1030 PRINT @192,"";:INPUT"C1";C(3)
1040 'INPUT SECOND EQUATION
1050 PRINT @144,"";:INPUT"A2";C(4)
1060 PRINT @176,"";:INPUT"B2";C(5)
1070 PRINT @208,"";:INPUT"C2";C(6)
1080 'CALCULATE SOLUTION
1090 PRINT @293,"";
1100 D=C(2)*C(4)-C(1)*C(5)
1110 IFD<>0THEN1180
1120 PRINT"DEGENERATE:  "
1130 PRINT @305,"NO SOLUTION"
1140 FORI=1TO150:NEXTI
1150 PRINT @305,"
1160 FORI=1TO150:NEXTI
1170 IFPEEK(338)<>191THEN1130ELSERUN
1180 A=(C(3)*C(5)-C(2)*C(6))/D
1190 X$=STR$(A)
1200 B=(C(1)*C(6)-C(3)*C(4))/D
1210 Y$=STR$(B)
1220 PRINT"SOLUTIONS X= ";X$:PRINT @335,"Y= ";Y$
1230 PRINT @421,"<ENTER>: NEXT EQUATIONS"
1240 PRINT @453,CHR$(34);CHR$(95);CHR$(34);
        "     : TEXT SCREEN"
1250 PRINT @485,CHR$(34);CHR$(94);CHR$(34);
        "     : PLOT SCREEN";
2000 'GRAPHIC MODE
2010 PMODE3,1:COLOR1,2:PCLS
2020 'PLOTAXIS
2030 LINE(10,94)-(240,94),PSET
2040 LINE(125,8)-(125,180),PSET
2050 'CALCULATE SCALE
2060 IFA=0ANDB=0THENSC=1:GOTO3000
2070 IFABS(A)>ABS(B)THENSC=(115/(2*ABS(A)))
        ELSESC=(86/(2*ABS(B)))
3000 IFC(1)=0THENY1=94+C(3)/C(2)*SC:Y2=Y1:
        X1=10:X2=240:GOTO3080
3010 IFC(2)=0THENX1=125-C(3)/C(1)*SC:
        X2=X1:Y1=8:Y2=180:GOTO3080
3020 X1=240:Y1=94+(C(1)*115/SC+C(3))/C(2)*SC
3030 IFY1>180THENY1=180:
        X1=125-(C(3)-86/SC*C(2))/C(1)*SC
3040 IFY1<8THENY1=8:
```

```
        X1=125-(C(3)+86/SC*C(2))/C(1)*SC
3050 X2=10:Y2=94+(C(3)-115/SC*C(1))/C(2)*SC
3060 IFY2>180THENY2=180:
        X2=125-(C(3)-86/SC*C(2))/C(1)*SC
3070 IFY2<8THENY2=8:
        X2=125-(C(3)+86/SC*C(2))/C(1)*SC
3080 'DRAW FIRST LINE
3090 COLOR3,2:LINE(X1,Y1)-(X2,Y2),PSET
4000 'BUILD SECOND LINE
4010 IFC(4)=0THENY3=94+C(6)/C(5)*SC:
        Y4=Y3:X3=10:X4=240:GOTO4090
4020 IFC(5)=0THENX3=125-C(6)/C(4)*SC:
        X4=X3:Y3=8:Y4=180:GOTO4090
4030 X3=240:Y3=94+(C(4)*115/SC+C(6))/C(5)*SC
4040 IFY3>180THENY3=180:
        X3=125-(C(6)-86/SC*C(5))/C(4)*SC
4050 IFY3<8THENY3=8:
        X3=125-(C(6)+86/SC*C(5))/C(4)*SC
4060 X4=10:Y4=94+(C(6)-115/SC*C(4))/C(5)*SC
4070 IFY4>180THENY4=180:
        X4=125-(C(6)-86/SC*C(5))/C(4)*SC
4080 IF Y4<8THENY4=8:
        X4=125-(C(6)+86/SC*C(5))/C(4)*SC
4090 'DRAW SECOND LINE
4100 COLOR4,2:LINE(X3,Y3)-(X4,Y4),PSET
5000 SCREEN0,0:IFPEEK(338)=191THENRUN
5010 IFPEEK(341)<>223THEN5000
5020 SCREEN1,0:IFPEEK(338)=191THENRUN
5030 IFPEEK(343)<>223THEN5020
5040 GOTO5000
```

Lunar Lander

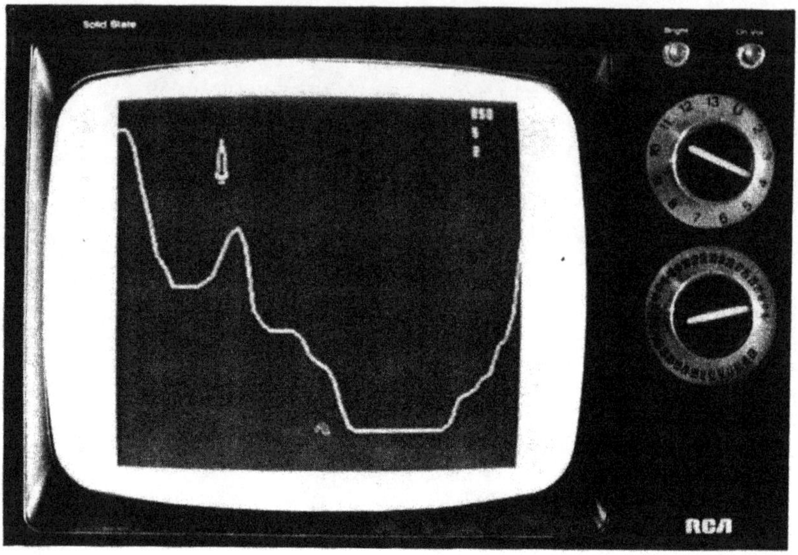

Can you land the rocket on the moons surface without running out of fuel or crashing? This is a real time game that requires you to think ahead and plan your course carefully.

You control the rocket by means of a main thruster that fires in the opposite direction to the ship and side thrusters that rotate the ship. The main thruster is fired by pressing the up arrow key while the side thrusters are controlled with the left and right arrow keys (the left key rotates the ship anticlockwise, the right key rotates the ship clockwise).

You must land with no horizontal velocity and as small a vertical velocity as possible or else you will crash. To make things even harder you only have a limited amount of fuel so don't take too long landing.

In the top right hand corner of the screen you will see three numbers. The top one is the amount of fuel remaining, the second is your horizontal velocity and the bottom one is your vertical velocity.

After each game you can play again by pressing the 'S' key.

Program structure

20 - 160	Initialization
500 - 540	Main loop 1 move rocket draw new rocket check keys and fire thrusters goto 1
1000 - 1200	Sets the graphics page to draw on and puts the rocket shape on it
1500 - 1640	Check the keyboard and fire the thrusters if a key was pressed
2000 - 2020	Update the position of the ship
2030 - 2290	End of game
2300	Check for 'S' key to restart
2310 - 2630	initialize shapes and strings for the rocket drawings
3000 - 3140	display fuel remaining
3150 - 3180	display horizontal velocity
3190 - 3220	display vertical velocity

Variables

LY()	Altitude of ground for each position on the screen
R1$-R8$	Rocket shapes
X,Y	Rocket position
VX,VY	Velocity components
AX,AY	Acceleration from firing the thrusters
G	Acceleration due to gravity
RO	Rotation aspect of the rocket
DO	Defines direction of rotation
FU	Fuel remaining

LUNAR LANDER

```
  20 PCLEAR 8: PMODE4,1: PCLS: PMODE4,5: PCLS
  30 PG=1
  40 DIM LY(50)
  50 GOSUB 2350
  60 R1$="BM+0,-9;NU3G1D2G1D9G1D2R6U2H1U9H1U2H1"
  70 R2$="BM+6,-6;NE2L1G1L1G6L1G2F3E2U1E6U1E1U1"
  80 R3$="BM+9,+0;NR3H1L2H1L9H1L2D6R2E1R9E1R2E1"
  90 R4$="BM+6,+6;NF2L1H1L1H6L1H2E3F2D1F6D1F1D1"
 100 R5$="BM+0,+9;ND3H1U2H1U9H1U2R6D2G1D9G1D2G1"
 110 R6$="BM-6,+6;NG3U1E1U1E6U1E2F3G2L1G6L1G1L1"
 120 R7$="BM-9,+0;NL3E1R2E1R9E1R2D6L2H1L9H1L2H1"
 130 R8$="BM-6,-6;NH2R1F1R1F6R1F2G3H2U1H6U1H1U1"
 140 X=10:Y=10:VX=5:VY=0:AX=0:AY=0:G=0.5:RO=1:
        DO=0:FU=1000:PG=5
 150 GOSUB 2500
 160 X=10:Y=10:VX=5:VY=0:AX=0:AY=0:G=0.5:RO=1:
        DO=0:FU=1000:PG=5
 500 '
 510 GOSUB 2000:' ALTER X,Y,VX,VY,RO
 520 GOSUB 1000
 530 GOSUB 1500
 540 GOTO 500
1000 IF PG=1 THEN PG=5 ELSE PG=1
1010 PMODE 4,PG:PCLS
1020 GOSUB2310
1030 IF ABS(X-128)>118 GOTO2270 ELSE IF Y<10 GOTO2270
1040 ID=INT(X*0.2+0.5)
1050 IF Y>LY(ID)-8 GOTO 2030
1060 D$="BM"+STR$(INT(X))+","+STR$(INT(Y))+";"
1070 DRAW D$
1080 ON RO GOTO 1090,1100,1110,1120,1130,1140,
        1150,1160
1090 DRAW R1$:GOTO1170
1100 DRAW R2$:GOTO1170
1110 DRAW R3$:GOTO1170
1120 DRAW R4$:GOTO1170
1130 DRAW R5$:GOTO1170
1140 DRAW R6$:GOTO1170
1150 DRAW R7$:GOTO1170
1160 DRAW R8$
1170 SCREEN 1,0:GOSUB 3000
1180 GOSUB 3150
1190 GOSUB 3190
1200 RETURN
1500 AX=0:AY=0
1510 IF FU<=0 THEN RETURN
1520 IF PEEK(341)<>223 GOTO 1570
1530 SOUND 10,1
1540 FU=FU-50:AX=XA(RO):AY=YA(RO)
1550 PSET(X+J1(RO),Y+K1(RO),1):
        PSET(X+J2(RO),Y+K2(RO),1):
        PSET(X+J3(RO),Y+K3(RO),1):
        PSET(X+J4(RO),Y+K4(RO),1)
```

```
1560 RETURN
1570 IF PEEK(343)=223 THEN P1=1 ELSE P1=0
1580 IF PEEK(344)=223 THEN P2=1 ELSE P2=0
1590 IF ABS(P1)+ABS(P2)=0 THEN RETURN
1600 SOUND 220,1
1610 FU=FU-10
1620 DO=SGN(DO-P1+P2)
1630 PSET(E1(RO),F1(RO),1):
        PSET(E2(RO),F2(RO),1):
        PSET(E3(RO),F3(RO),1):
        PSET(E4(RO),F4(RO),1)
1640 RETURN
2000 RO=RO+DO:IF RO>8 THEN RO=RO-8 :
        ELSE IF RO<1 THEN RO=RO+8
2010 X=X+VX+0.5*AX:Y=Y+VY+0.5*(AY+G):VX=VX+AX:
        VY=VY+AY+G
2020 RETURN
2030 IF RO=1 GOTO 2110
2040 CLS:PRINT @64,"ALL PERSONNEL KILLED.";
2050 PRINT @96,"PILOTS MUST LAND CRAFT UPRIGHT."
2060 PRINT @458,"TYPE 'S' TO RESTART.";
2070 FOR I=1 TO 1500:NEXTI
2080 IF PG=1 THEN PMODE 4,5 ELSE PMODE 4,1
2090 SCREEN1,0
2100 GOTO2300
2110 IF VY<3 GOTO 2160
2120 CLS
2130 PRINT @32,"RATE OF DESCENT TOO HIGH;";
2140 IF VY<7 THEN PRINT @96,"SEVERE INJURIES."; :
        ELSE PRINT @96,"ALL PERSONNEL KILLED."
2150 GOTO 2060
2160 IF ABS(VX)<3 GOTO 2240
2170 X0=INT(X+8*SGN(VX)):Y0=INT(Y+5):
        IF PG=1 THEN PG=5 ELSE PG=1
2180 PMODE 4,PG:PCLS
2190 GOSUB 2310:SCREEN 1,0
2200 DRAW"BM"+STR$(X0)+","+STR$(Y0)+";":
        IF VX>0 THEN DRAW R3$ ELSE DRAW R7$
2210 FOR I=1 TO 1500:NEXTI
2220 CLS:PRINT @64,"HORIZONTAL VELOCITY TOO GREAT
        - ALL KILLED."
2230 GOTO 2070
2240 CLS:PRINT @64,"PERFECT LANDING.";
2250 PRINT @128,"I'M A GOOD TEACHER.";
2260 GOTO 2070
2270 CLS:PRINT @128,"YOUR SHIP IS COMPLETLY";:
        PRINT @160,"OUT OF CONTROL.";:
        PRINT @196,"    ALL HOPE IS LOST !";
2280 PLAY"T30;O1;A;A;A;"
2290 PRINT @458,"TYPE 'S' TO RESTART.";
2300 I$=INKEY$:IF I$<>"S" GOTO 2300 ELSE GOTO 160
2310 ' DRAW SURFACE'
2320 LX=5:LINE(0,16)-(5,16),PSET
2330 FORI=1TO50:LX=LX+5:LINE-(LX,LY(I)),PSET:NEXTI
2340 RETURN
2350 FORI=1TO50:READ LY(I):NEXTI
```

```
2360 DATA 26,46,62,82,88,98,98,98,98,96
2370 DATA 92,82,72,68,78,110,116,120,120,120
2380 DATA 120,124,132,136,138,144,158,168,170,170
2390 DATA 170,170,170,170,170,170,170,170,170,170
2400 DATA 166,154,152,150,144,142,128,124,110,74
2410 RETURN
2500 FOR I=1TO8:READ XA(I),YA(I):NEXTI
2510 DATA 0,-1,0.707,-0.707,1,0,0.707,0.707,0,1,
     -0.707,0.707,-1,0,-0.707,-0.707
2520 FORI=1TO8
2530 READ J1(I),K1(I),J2(I),K2(I),J3(I),K3(I),
     J4(I),K4(I)
2540 NEXTI
2550 DATA -1,8,+1,8,-1,10,1,10
2560 DATA -5,6,-6,5,-6,7,-7,6
2570 DATA -8,-1,-8,1,-10,-1,-10,1
2580 DATA -5,-6,-6,-5,-6,-7,-7,-6
2590 DATA -1,-8,1,-8,-1,-10,1,-10
2600 DATA 5,-6,6,-5,6,-7,7,-6
2610 DATA 8,-1,8,1,10,-1,10,1
2620 DATA 5,6,6,5,6,7,7,6
2630 RETURN
3000 F$=STR$(FU):L=LEN(F$)
3010 I=2:DRAW"BM225,5;"
3020 NT=VAL(MID$(F$,I,1))+1
3030 ON NT GOTO 3040,3050,3060,3070,3080,3090,3100,
     3110,3120,3130
3040 DRAW"D4R2U4L2;BM+5,+0;":GOTO3140
3050 DRAW"BM+2,+0;D4;BM+3,-4;":GOTO3140
3060 DRAW"R2D2L2D2R2;BM+3,-4;":GOTO3140
3070 DRAW"R2D2NL2D2L2;BM+5,-4;":GOTO3140
3080 DRAW"D2R2NU2D2;BM+3,-4;":GOTO3140
3090 DRAW"NR2D2R2D2L2;BM+5,-4;":GOTO3140
3100 DRAW"NR2D4R2U2L2;BM+5,-2;":GOTO3140
3110 DRAW"R2D4;BM+3,-4;":GOTO3140
3120 DRAW"D4R2U2NL2U2L2;BM+5,+0;":GOTO3140
3130 DRAW"ND2R2D2NL2D2L2;BM+5,-4;"
3140 I=I+1:IF I>L THEN RETURN ELSE GOTO 3020
3150 F$=STR$(INT(VX)):L=LEN(F$)
3160 I=2:DRAW"BM225,15;"
3170 GOSUB 3020
3180 RETURN
3190 F$=STR$(INT(VY)):L=LEN(F$)
3200 I=2:DRAW"BM225,25;"
3210 GOSUB 3020
3220 RETURN
```

Space "Pursuit"

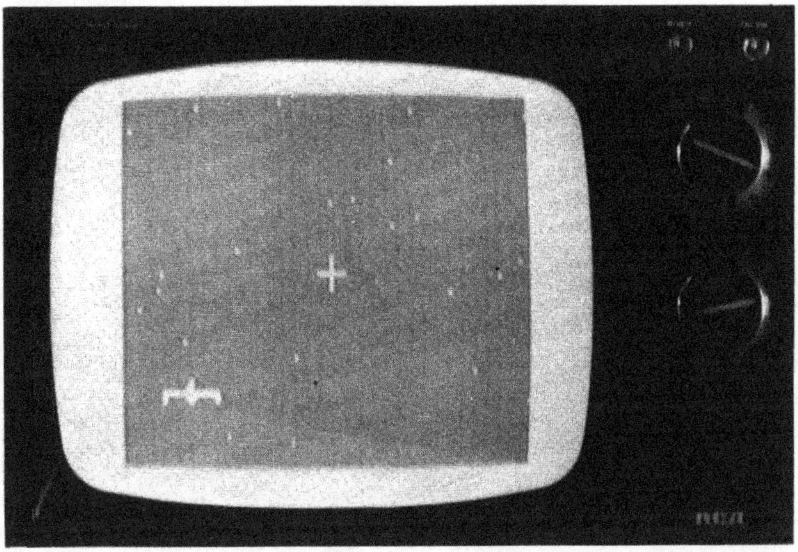

Copyright (c) Colin Carter

You are chasing the remaining ten enemy ships: how many can you destroy before they get home? You must line up your sights on each ship as it comes into range and hopefully blow it out of the universe. But don't take too long or it will get away.

You move your sight (shown as a cross on the screen) with the arrow keys, and you fire your explosive charges with the SPACE key.

Good luck and good hunting'

Program structure

10 - 230	Initialization
500 - 620	main loop
1000 - 1090	check for players input
1500 - 1620	draw everything
2000 - 2070	move sight
2500 - 2690	fire charges
3000 - 3070	end/restart game

Variables

S1(),S2(),S3()	Arrays for drawing the enemy ships
ST()	Array for drawing the sight
E1(),E2()	Explosion arrays
XC,YC	Position of sight
XS,YS	Position of enemy ship
F	Fire status
XF,YF	Position of explosion
HT	Count of number of hits

SPACE PURSUIT

```
  20 PCLEAR 6
  30 DIM S1(13, 8),S2(25,12),S3(38,20),ST(20,20)
        ,E1(11,11),E2(11,11)
  40 CLS(6):PRINT @264,"PLEASE WAIT.";
  50 PMODE 1,5:COLOR 2,3:PCLS
  60 FOR I=1 TO 25:X=RND(255):Y=RND(192):PSET(X,Y,5):
        NEXT I
  70 PMODE 1,1:COLOR 2,3:PCLS
  80 PMODE 1,3:COLOR 2,3:PCLS
  90 SCREEN 1,0
 100 A$="BM-4,+0;L12ND4R13E3NU3R1F3R12ND4L11G4L1H2"
 110 DRAW "BM 6,3;S2;C4;"+A$
 120 GET(1,1)-(14,9),S1,G
 130 PCLS:DRAW"BM12,6;S3;XA$;S4"
 140 PSET(12,6,2)
 150 GET(1,1)-(26,13),S2,G
 160 PCLS:DRAW"BM18,9;S4;XA$;S4"
 170 PSET(18,10,2):PSET(20,10,2)
 180 GET(1,1)-(39,21),S3,G
 190 A$="BM10,10;C2;NL8NR8NU8ND8"
 200 PCLS:DRAW A$
 210 GET(1,1)-(21,21),ST,G
 220 A$="L2U3G2F2E2H1"
 230 B$="R4H4L2G4D2F4R2E4U2"
 240 PCLS:DRAW "BM100,100;C8;XA$;C6;XB$;S4"
 250 GET(95,95)-(105,105),E1,G
 260 PCLS:DRAW"BM100,100;C6;XA$;C8;XB$;S4"
 270 GET(95,95)-(105,105),E2,G:PCLS
 280 PCOPY 5 TO 3:PCOPY 6 TO 4
 290 DC=20
 300 C=0:XC=128:YC=92:NS=0:DI=+1:HT=0:PP=0
 310 I=1:DX=0:DY=0:F=-1:S=-1
 320 CLS(6):PRINT @264,"BYE";:PRINT @384," ";
 500 SCREEN 1,0
 510 PMODE 1,1:PCLS
 520 PCOPY 5 TO 1:PCOPY 6 TO 2
 530 GOSUB 1000
 540 SCREEN 1,0
 550 PMODE 1,3:PCLS
 560 PCOPY 5 TO 3:PCOPY 6 TO 4
 570 GOSUB 1000
 580 IF NS>=10 GOTO 3000
 590 IF S>0 THEN I=I+DI:PP=PP+1
 600 IF I>19 THEN DI=-1
 610 IF I<1 THEN DI=+1:NS=NS+1:GOTO 500
 620 GOTO 500
1000 ' CHECK CONTROLS
1010 ME=341
1020 IF PEEK(ME)<>223 THEN ME=ME+1:
        IF ME<346 THEN GOTO 1020 ELSE GOTO1500
1030 ON ME-340 GOTO 1060,1050,1080,1070,1090
1040 GOTO 1500
1050 YC=YC+DC:GOTO1500
```

```
1060 YC=YC-DC:GOTO1500
1070 XC=XC+DC:GOTO1500
1080 XC=XC-DC:GOTO1500
1090 IF F<0 THEN F=0' FIRE !
1500 ' DRAW THINGS
1510 IF S>0 GOTO 1540
1520 IF RND(30)>2 GOTO 2000
1530 SX=0:SY=0:XS=RND(220)+20:YS=20+RND(152):S=+1:
     NS=NS+1
1540 SX=SX+RND(9)-5:SY=SY+RND(9)-5:XS=XS+SX:YS=YS+SY
1550 IF XS<38 THEN XS=38:SX=4
1560 IF XS>218 THEN XS=218:SX=-4
1570 IF YS<10 THEN YS=10:SY=4
1580 IF YS>180 THEN YS=180:SY=-4
1590 J=INT(I/5)+1:ON J GOTO 1620,1610,1600
1600 PUT(XS-18,YS-9)-(XS+20,YS+11),S3,PSET:GOTO2000
1610 PUT(XS-12,YS-5)-(XS+13,YS+7),S2,PSET:GOTO2000
1620 PUT(XS- 6,YS-3)-(XS+ 7,YS+5),S1,PSET
2000 ' MOVE SIGHT
2010 IF XC<10 THEN XC=10:CX=0
2020 IF XC>245 THEN XC=245:CX=0
2030 IF YC<10 THEN YC=10:CY=0
2040 IF YC>182 THEN YC=182:CY=0
2050 PUT(XC-10,YC-10)-(XC+10,YC+10),ST,AND
2060 IF F<0 GOTO 2690
2070 IF F>0 GOTO2520
2500 SOUND 240,2:XF=XC-CX:YF=YC-CY' ACTUAL FIRING
2510 PUT(XF-5,YF-5)-(XF+6,YF+6),E2,PSET
2520 F=F+1:IF F>3 THEN F=-1
2530 IF ABS(XF-XS)>10 GOTO 2690
2540 IF ABS(YF-YS)>10 GOTO 2690
2550 SOUND 253,1:SOUND 255,1
2560 SCREEN 1,0
2570 LINE(XF,YF)-(XS,YS),PSET
2580 LINE(XF,YF)-(XS,YS),PRESET
2590 PUT(XF-5,YF-5)-(XF+6,YF+6),E1,PSET
2600 LINE(XF,YF)-(XS,YS),PSET
2610 SOUND 254,1:SOUND 253,1
2620 PUT(XF-5,YF-5)-(XF+6,YF+6),E2,PSET
2630 FOR W=1 TO 5
2640 SOUND 255,1:SOUND 254,1
2650 LINE(XS,YS)-(RND(255),RND(192)),PSET
2660 NEXT W
2670 XS=500:PLAY"T7;L4;O3;A;O2;L2;C;L4;D;L2.;F;L4G;O3;
     AA;L2;A;L1;A"
2680 HT=HT+1:S=-1:I=1:DI=+1:GOTO1500
2690 RETURN
3000 FOR I=1 TO 10
3010 SOUND 180+I,1
3020 NEXT I
3030 PRINT @264,"YOU DESTROYED ";HT;
     " SHIPS OUT OF ";NS;
3040 IF HT>6 THEN PRINT @390,"YOU ARE A HERO.";
3050 PRINT @457,"PENALTY POINTS:";PP;
3060 I$=INKEY$:IF I$="" GOTO 3060
3070 IF I$="S" THEN GOTO300 ELSE GOTO 3060
5000 END
```

Bomber

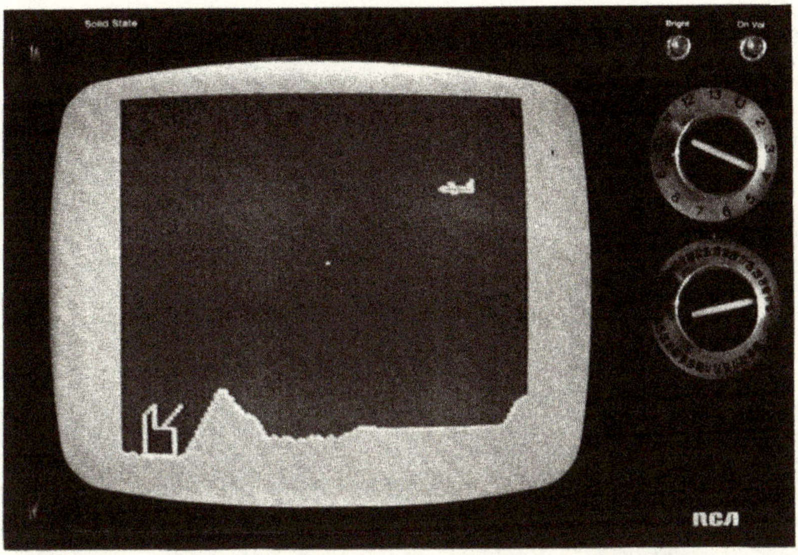

Your task is to blow the enemy bombers out of the sky with your anti-aircraft gun before they blow you to pieces. You control the elevation of your gun with the left and right arrow keys (left raises the gun and right lowers it). The gun is fired with the space bar.

You must plan your shots carefully because the enemy bombers may only be damaged and can still drop bombs on you or even worse they may crash into your gun as they fall.

Program structure

10 - 1150	initialize pictures
1160 - 1990	set up variables
2000 - 2920	main loop
2000 - 2070	monitor input
2100	extended delay for flak
2110 - 2160	send a new plane
2170 - 2310	move plane
2320 - 2370	drop a bomb
2380 - 2460	move bomb
2500 - 2920	move missile
3000 - 3110	elevate gun
4000 - 4140	end/restart game

Variables

P1(),P2()	Drawings of plane
B1()	Blank drawing
S(),C()	Co-ordinates for gun barrel
E$,E3$	Explosions
NP	Number of planes
A	Angle of elevation for gun barrel
TL	Delay for flak
TB	Time for falling bomb
TP	Time for falling plane
TN,TM	Time of missile flight
XN,YN,XM,YM	Missile co-ordinates
XB,YB	Bomb co-ordinates
XP,YP	Plane co-ordinates
VP	Planes velocity
KP,KM	Scaling constants

BOMBER

```
  20 PCLEAR 4:PMODE 3,1:COLOR 2,3
  30 DIM S(13),C(13),P1(22,8),B1(22,8),P2(22,8)
  40 CLS:PRINT @5,"PLEASE WAIT"
  50 FOR A=0 TO 13:READ S(A):READ C(A):NEXT A:
       'GUN POSITIONS
  60 DATA 0,16,2,16,4,16,6,15,7,14,9,13,10,12,11,
        11,12,10,13,8,14,6,15,4,15,2,15,0
  70 COLOR 2,3:PCLS(3):SCREEN 1,0
  80 'DRAW GROUND
  90 Y=186:EN=-1
 100 LINE(34,186)-(14,186),PSET
 110 FOR X=12 TO 0 STEP -2
 120 Y=Y+RND(3)-2:IF Y>194 THEN Y=194
 130 LINE-(X,Y),PSET
 140 NEXT X
 150 Y=186-RND(3)+1
 160 LINE(35,186)-(36,186),PSET
 170 FOR X=37 TO 41 STEP 2
 180 Y=Y-RND(3)+1
 190 LINE-(X,Y),PSET
 200 NEXT X
 210 FOR X=42 TO 61 STEP 2
 220 Y=Y-RND(3)-1
 230 LINE-(X,Y),PSET
 240 NEXT X
 250 FOR X=62 TO 90 STEP 1
 260 Y=Y+RND(3)-1:IF Y>194 THEN Y=194
 270 LINE-(X,Y),PSET
 280 NEXT X
 290 FOR X=92 TO 160 STEP 2:
       Y=Y+RND(3)-2:LINE-(X,Y),PSET:NEXT X
 300 Y2=Y
 310 LINE(160,Y)-(240,Y),PSET
 320 FOR X=242 TO 255 STEP 1:
       Y=Y-RND(3)+1:LINE-(X,Y),PSET:NEXT X
 330 PAINT(30,190),1,2
 340 'DRAW GUN SITE
 350 A$="BM14,185;C2;R9U7L6U6G3D10"
 360 DRAW "S8;"+ A$:PAINT(30,180),4,2
 370 LINE(26,170)-(37,159),PSET
 380 GET(0,1)-(22,9),B1,G
 390 'DRAW 'PLANE
 400 A$="BM2,5;C2;R8NU1R1U2D3L9U1BM6,3;R1D1;BM0,6;R1"
 410 DRAW A$
 420 GET(0,1)-(22,9),P1,G
 430 PUT(0,1)-(22,9),B1,PSET
 440 'EXPLOSION
 450 E3$="NU5NG5NR5NH5ND5NE5NL5NF5"
 460 GOTO 1980
1000 E$="BM"+STR$(XE)+","+STR$(YE)+";"
1010 IF XE=0THEN RETURN
1020 FOR I=1 TO 3
1030 DRAW E$+"C2;"+E3$
```

```
1040 SOUND 1,1
1050 DRAW E$+"C4;"+E3$
1060 SOUND 3,2:SOUND 2,1
1070 NEXT I
1080 DRAW E$+"C3;"+E3$
1090 IF P<0 GOTO 1140
1100 IF ABS(XP+11-XE)>12 GOTO1140
1110 IF ABS(YP+4-YE)>9 GOTO1140
1120 TP=1:NP=NP+1
1130 IF YE<150 THEN RETURN
1140 IF ABS(XE-26)>12 THEN RETURN
1150 EN=+1:RETURN
1160 'START ACTION & MONITORING
1980 A=7:TL=10:TB=0:TP=0:NP=0:TN=0:TM=0:P=-1:
     B=0:XN=0:XM=0:PP=0:VM=2:VP=3
1990 KP=3:KB=3:KM=2
2000 I$=INKEY$:IF I$="" GOTO 2110
2010 I=ASC(I$)
2020 IF I=32 GOTO3080
2030 IF I=94 THEN TL=TL+1:GOTO 2100
2040 IF I=10 THEN TL=TL-1: GOTO 2110
2050 IF I=8  GOTO 3010
2060 IF I=9 GOTO 3010
2070 GOTO 2110
2100 IF I=94 THEN TL=TL+1 ELSE TL=TL-1
2110 IF P>0 GOTO 2170
2120 IF RND(50)<49 GOTO 2320
2130 PP=PP+1:IF PP>20 GOTO 4090
2140 P=1:TP=0:XP=224:YP=30+RND(40):B=-1:TB=0
2150 PUT(XP,YP)-(XP+22,YP+8),P1,PSET
2160 PSET(XP+8,YP+7,2):PSET(XP+10,YP+7,2)
2170 GET(XP,YP-6)-(XP+28,YP+8),P2,G
2190 XP=XP-VP:YP=YP+KP*TP
2200 IF XP>1 GOTO 2300
2210 PUT(XP+VP,YP-KP*TP)-(XP+22+VP,YP+8-KP*TP),B1,PSET
2220 P=-1:IF B<0 THEN B=0
2230 GOTO 2500
2300 PUT(XP,YP-6)-(XP+28,YP+8),P2,PSET
2310 IF PPOINT(XP+26,YP+6)<>3 OR PPOINT(XP-2,YP+6)<>3
      THEN XE=XP:YE=YP:GOSUB 1000:
      IF EN>0 THEN GOTO 4000 ELSE GOTO2220
2320 IF B=0 GOTO 2500
2330 IF B>0 GOTO 2380
2340 IF RND(100)<98 GOTO 2500
2350 B=+1:XB=XP+10:YB=YP+8:TB=0
2360 PSET(XP+8,YP+7,3):PSET(XP+10,YP+7,3)
2370 GET(XP,YP-4)-(XP+28,YP+8),P2,G
2380 TB=TB+1
2390 PSET(XB,YB,3):PSET(XB+2,YB,3)
2400 XB=XB-VP:YB=YB+KB*TB
2410 IF XB<6 THEN B=0:GOTO 2500
2420 IF YB>190 THEN B=0:XE=XB:YE=190:GOSUB1000:
      IF EN>0 THEN GOTO 4000 ELSE GOTO2500
2430 IF PPOINT(XB,YB)=3 THEN
      PSET(XB,YB,2):PSET(XB+2,YB,2):GOTO2500
2440 XE=XB:YE=YB:B=0
```

```
2450 GOSUB 1000
2460 IF EN>0 GOTO4000
2500 IF XM=0 GOTO2700
2510 IF YM<10 GOTO2530
2520 PSET(XM,YM,3)
2530 TM=TM+1:XM=XM+VC:YM=YM-VS+KM*TM
2540 IF YM>195 THEN XM=0:GOTO2700
2550 IF XM>245 THEN XM=0:GOTO 2700
2560 IF TM>=TL GOTO 2620
2570 IF YM<10 GOTO2700
2580 IF PPOINT(XM,YM)<>3 GOTO 2620
2590 IF P<0 GOTO 2660
2600 IF ABS(XP+11-XM)>12 GOTO2660
2610 IF ABS(YP+4-YM)>9 GOTO 2660
2620 XE=XM:YE=YM:XM=0
2630 IF YM<10 GOTO2700
2640 GOSUB 1000:IF EN>0 THEN GOTO 4000
2650 GOTO 2700
2660 IF YM<10 GOTO2700
2670 PSET(XM,YM,2)
2700 IF XN=0 GOTO 2880
2710 IF YN<10 GOTO2730
2720 PSET(XN,YN,3)
2730 TN=TN+1:XN=XN+UC:YN=YN-US+KM*TN
2740 IF YN>195 THEN XN=0:GOTO2880
2750 IF XN>245 THEN XN=0:GOTO 2880
2760 IF TN>=TL GOTO 2620
2770 IF YN<10 GOTO2880
2780 IF PPOINT(XN,YN)<>3 GOTO 2620
2790 IF P<0 GOTO 2860
2800 IF ABS(XP+11-XN)>12 GOTO 2860
2810 IF ABS(YP+4-YN)>4 GOTO 2860
2820 XE=XN:YE=YN:XN=0
2830 IF YN<10 GOTO 2880
2840 GOSUB 1000:IF EN>0 GOTO4000
2850 GOTO 2880
2860 IF YN<10 GOTO 2880
2870 PSET(XN,YN,2)
2880 IF P<0 GOTO 2000
2890 IF PPOINT(XP+3,YP+8)<>3 GOTO 2910
2900 IF PPOINT(XP+15,YP+8)=3 GOTO 2000
2910 XE=XP+11:YE=YP+6:P=-1:GOSUB 1000:
        IF EN>0 GOTO 4000
2920 GOTO 2000
3000 'ELEVATE GUN
3010 LINE(26+C(A),170-S(A))-(26,170),PRESET
3020 DRAW"C2;"
3030 IF I=8 THEN A=A+1 ELSE A=A-1
3040 IF A<0 THEN A=0
3050 IF A>13 THEN A=13
3060 LINE-(26+C(A),170-S(A)),PSET
3070 GOTO 2110
3080 IF XM<>0 GOTO 3100
3090 CM=C(A):SM=S(A):XM=30+CM:YM=166-SM:TM=0:
        VC=CM*VM:VS=SM*VM:PSET(XM,YM,2):GOTO2110
3100 IF XN<>0 GOTO 2110
```

```
3110 CN=C(A):SN=S(A):XN=30+CN:YN=166-SN:TN=0:
        UC=CN*VM:US=SN*VM:PSET(XN,YN,2):GOTO 2110
4000 SOUND 50,3:SOUND 40,3:SOUND 30,3:SOUND 20,3:
        SOUND 10,8
4010 CLS:PRINT @5,"KILLED IN ACTION"
4020 PRINT @69,"SCORE: ";NP;" HITS"
4030 IF NP<10 GOTO4120
4040 IF NP>15 GOTO 4070
4050 PRINT @133,"POSTED A MEDAL"
4060 GOTO 4120
4070 PRINT @133,"NATIONAL HERO"
4080 GOTO 4120
4090 CLS
4100 PRINT @5,"RETURNING SOLDIER"
4110 GOTO 4020
4120 I$=INKEY$:IF I$="S" GOTO 70 ELSE GOTO 4120
4130 IF I$="S" GOTO 70
4140 GOTO 4120
4150 GOTO4150
5000 END
```

Dragon Invaders

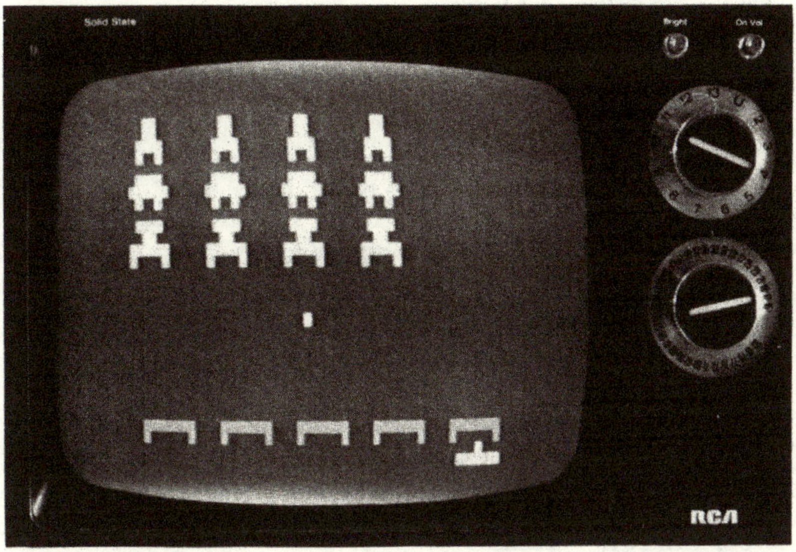

Watch out three squadrons of invaders are attacking your city and it is up to you to destroy them. You have three missile launchers to get them with (only one is used at a time though). Can you get them before they get you.

You move your launcher by moving your joystick to the left or right, and fire using the fire button.

Program structure

10 - 450	initialization
510 - 560	main loop
1000 - 1110	draw enemy invaders
1500 - 2100	if the player has fired a missile display it and check if it has hit anything
2500 - 2640	check for players input
3000 - 3090	pick a bomb and start it dropping
3500 - 3700	move all the dropping bombs
4000 - 4050	end/restart game

Variables

PI	Position of enemy fleet
PS	Position of players launcher
M1,M2	Co-ordinates of missile
G1-G4,H1-H4	Positions of enemy bombs
EX()	Existence(1) or not(-1) of an enmey ship in the enemy fleet
SC	Score

For those without joysticks

Delete lines 2530,2600 and 4050 and replace the following lines

```
2510 IF PEEK(344)=255 THEN 2520
2515 PS=PS+5: IF PS)25 THEN PS=25
2520 IF PEEK(343)=255 THEN 2540
2525 PS=PS-5: IF PS(0 THEN PS=0

2590 IF PEEK(345)()255 THEN 2610 ELSE RETURN

4040 IF PEEK(345)()255 THEN 50 ELSE 4040
```

This program is an attempt to write an arcade-style game using the block graphics available in text mode.

The invaders are displayed on the screen using a PRINT statement, and if you wanted to rewrite the program to use high resolution graphics, the entire program would need to be redesigned.

An example of an invader-style arcade game in high resolution is given elsewhere in this book - see ALIEN BLITZ on page 107.

You may like to see the effect on this program of speeding up the Dragon. Enter the program in the usual manner and save it to cassette. Then RUN the program to see its normal speed.

Hit the BREAK key to stop, and enter the command:

```
POKE 65495,Ø
```

then RUN the program.

You will be able to see it running faster, and you will hear all the sounds at a higher frequency. Note that you will need to hit the BREAK key to stop the program and that you will not be able to use the cassette recorder, etc., until you put the Dragon back into slow speed by entering the command:

```
POKE 65494,Ø
```

DRAGON INVADERS

```
 20 CLEAR 1500
 30 BS=0
 40 DIM EX(12)
 50 NM=3:SC=0
 60 CLS(0)
 70 X$=CHR$(128):X3$=X$+X$+X$:X6$=X3$+X3$
 80 XL$=X6$+X6$+X6$+X6$+X6$+X$
 90 XJ$=STRING$(8,X$)
100 ' FIRST SET'
110 Q1$=X$+CHR$(223)+X$
120 Q2$=CHR$(214)+CHR$(220)+CHR$(217)
130 R2$=CHR$(213)+CHR$(220)+CHR$(218)
140 ' SECOND SET'
150 Q3$=CHR$(225)+CHR$(227)+CHR$(226)
160 Q4$=CHR$(236)+CHR$(239)+CHR$(236)
170 R4$=CHR$(237)+CHR$(236)+CHR$(238)
180 ' THIRD SET'
190 Q5$=CHR$(241)+CHR$(243)+CHR$(242)
200 Q6$=CHR$(251)+CHR$(255)+CHR$(247)
210 R6$=CHR$(243)+CHR$(255)+CHR$(243)
220 Q7$=X3$
230 R7$=CHR$(248)+CHR$(128)+CHR$(244)
240 Q7$=X3$
250 R6$=CHR$(243)+CHR$(255)+CHR$(243)
260 G1$="":G2$="":FOR I=1TO4:G1$=G1$+Q1$+X3$:
      G2$=G2$+Q1$+X3$:NEXTI
270 G1$=G1$+XJ$:G2$=G2$+XJ$:FOR I=1TO4:
      G1$=G1$+Q2$+X3$:G2$=G2$+R2$+X3$:NEXTI
280 G1$=G1$+XJ$:G2$=G2$+XJ$:FOR I=1TO4:
      G1$=G1$+Q3$+X3$:G2$=G2$+Q3$+X3$:NEXTI
290 G1$=G1$+XJ$:G2$=G2$+XJ$:FOR I=1TO4:
      G1$=G1$+Q4$+X3$:G2$=G2$+R4$+X3$:NEXTI
300 G1$=G1$+XJ$:G2$=G2$+XJ$:FOR I=1TO4:
      G1$=G1$+Q5$+X3$:G2$=G2$+Q5$+X3$:NEXTI
310 G1$=G1$+XJ$:G2$=G2$+XJ$:FOR I=1TO4:
      G1$=G1$+Q6$+X3$:G2$=G2$+R6$+X3$:NEXTI
320 G1$=G1$+XJ$:G2$=G2$+XJ$:FOR I=1TO4:
      G1$=G1$+Q7$+X3$:G2$=G2$+R7$+X3$:NEXTI
330 LW=216:G1$=LEFT$(G1$,216):G2$=LEFT$(G2$,216)
340 BA$=CHR$(174)+CHR$(172)+CHR$(172)+CHR$(173)
350 T$=X$+X$+BA$
360 BA$=T$+T$+T$+T$+T$
370 SH$=X$+CHR$(129)+CHR$(131)+CHR$(139)+CHR$(131)+X$
380 PI=0:PK=65
390 PS=13:PU=13
400 M1=-1:M2=-1
410 H1=32:H2=32:H3=32:H4=32
420 FOR IE=1TO12:EX(IE)=+1:NEXTIE:FOR I=1TO4:LV(I)=3
      :NEXTI
430 DI=+1:LI=9
440 ' DRAW BARRIERS & SHIP'
450 PRINT @448,BA$;:PRINT @480+PS,SH$;
500 '
```

```
510 GOSUB 1000:'DRAW INVADAS'
520 GOSUB 3000:'DROP BOMB'
530 GOSUB 1500:'TRACK MISSILE'
540 GOSUB 3510:'MOVE BOMBS'
550 GOSUB 2500:'SEE JOY'
560 GOTO 510
570 '
1000 'PRINT INVADAS'
1010 PI=PI+DI
1020 PK=PK+2
1030 IF PK<63 THEN RESET(PK-3,0):RESET(PK-2,0):
     SET(PK,0,4):SET(PK-1,0,4):GOTO1060
1040 IF PK=63 THEN RESET(PK-2,0):RESET(PK-3,0):
     GOTO1060
1050 IF PK>128 THEN PK=1
1060 IF PI>=LI THEN DI=-1:GOTO 1110
1070 IF PI<=0 THEN DI=+1
1080 PRINT @32+PI,G1$;
1090 FOR I=1TO10:NEXTI
1100 PRINT @32+PI,G2$;
1110 RETURN
1500 'TRACK MISSILE'
1510 IF M2<0 THEN RETURN
1520 RESET(M1,M2)
1530 M2=M2-2:IF M2<0 THEN RETURN
1540 P=POINT(M1,M2)+1
1550 ON P GOTO 1630,4060,1560,1610,2100,1630,
     1640,1640,1640
1560 SOUND 50,1
1570 IF H1=Y THEN H1=32:GOTO1610
1580 IF H2=Y THEN H2=32:GOTO1610
1590 IF H3=Y THEN H3=32:GOTO1610
1600 H4=32
1610 RESET(M1,M2)
1620 M2=-1:RETURN
1630 SET(M1,M2,5):GOTO1520
1640 'GOT ONE'
1650 SOUND 100,1
1660 I=INT((M1-2*PI)/12)+1:J=P-6
1670 EX(J*4-4+I)=-1
1680 FOR II=1TO4
1690 LV(II)=0
1700 FOR JJ=3 TO 1 STEP -1
1710 IF EX(4*JJ+II-4)>0 GOTO 1740
1720 NEXT JJ
1730 GOTO 1750
1740 LV(II)=JJ
1750 NEXT II
1760 SC=SC+(4-J)*50
1770 PRINT @32,STRING$(224,X$);
1780 SOUND 100,1:PRINT @170,"SCORE: ";SC;
1790 L1=I*6+(J*J+J)*16-6
1800 L2=L1-32:L3=L2-32
1810 R1=LW-L1-6:R2=R1+32:R3=R2+32
1820 I6=I*6
1830 G1$=LEFT$(G1$,L2)+X6$+RIGHT$(G1$,R2):
```

```
     G1$=LEFT$(G1$,L1)+X6$+RIGHT$(G1$,R1)
1840 G2$=LEFT$(G2$,L2)+X6$+RIGHT$(G2$,R2):
     G2$=LEFT$(G2$,L1)+X6$+RIGHT$(G2$,R1)
1850 IF J<3 GOTO 1870
1860 G1$=LEFT$(G1$,L3)+X6$+RIGHT$(G1$,R3):
     G2$=LEFT$(G2$,L3)+X6$+RIGHT$(G2$,R3)
1870 FOR IE=12 TO 1 STEP -1
1880 IF EX(IE)>0 GOTO 1910
1890 NEXT IE
1900 CLS(0):GOTO260
1910 J=FIX((IE-1)/4)+1:I=IE-(J-1)*4
1920 LW=I*6+(J*J+J)*16
1930 G1$=LEFT$(G1$,LW):G2$=LEFT$(G2$,LW)
1940 FOR I=4 TO 1 STEP -1
1950 FOR J=1TO3
1960 IF EX(J*4-4+I)>0 GOTO 1990
1970 NEXT J
1980 NEXT I
1990 LI=35-6*I
2000 FOR J=1 TO 3
2010 IF EX(J*4-3)>0 GOTO 2080
2020 NEXT J
2030 FOR IE=1 TO 11:EX(IE)=EX(IE+1):NEXT IE:EX(12)=-1
2040 LW=LEN(G1$):G1$=RIGHT$(G1$,LW-6):
     G2$=RIGHT$(G2$,LW-6)
2050 LW=LW-6
2060 LI=LI+6
2070 GOTO2000
2080 FORIE=1TO 460-LW:NEXT IE
2090 DI=2*RND(2)-3:PI=RND(LI):
     PRINT @170,STRING$(15,X$);:GOTO1610
2100 RESET(PK,0):SOUND 230,1:PRINT @PK/2,CHR$(153);:
     SOUND 230,1:PRINT @PK/2,CHR$(150);:
     SOUND 230,1:PRINT @PK/2,CHR$(153);:
     PRINT @PK/2,X$;:PK=64:SC=SC+500:RETURN
2500 'MOVE ? FIRE ?'
2510 PS=INT(JOYSTK(0)/2)
2520 IF PS<0 THEN PS=0
2530 IF PS>25 THEN PS=25
2540 DS=SGN(PS-PU)
2550 PU=PU+DS
2560 PRINT @480+PU,SH$;
2570 IF PU<>PS THEN GOTO 2550
2580 PRINT @480+PS,SH$;
2590 IF PEEK(65280)=125 GOTO 2610
2600 IF PEEK(65280)<>253 THEN RETURN
2610 IF M2>0 THEN RETURN
2620 SOUND 180,1:M1=2*PS+6:M2=28
2630 IF POINT(M1,28)>0 THEN PRINT @448+M1/2,X$;:M2=-1:
     RETURN
2640 SET(M1,M2,5):GOSUB1510:RETURN
3000 'DROP BOMB'
3010 I=RND(4):IF LV(I)=0 THEN RETURN
3015 K=I: FOR J=1 TO I: IF LV(J)=0 THEN K=K-1: NEXT J
3020 H=LV(I)*4+3
3030 G=(6*K+PI-4)*2-1
```

```
3040 IF H1>31 THEN H1=H:G1=G:GOTO3090
3050 IF H2>31 THEN H2=H:G2=G:GOTO3090
3060 IF H3>31 THEN H3=H:G3=G:GOTO3090
3070 IF H4>31 THEN H4=H:G4=G:GOTO3090
3080 RETURN
3090 SET(G,H,2):RETURN
3500 'MOVE BOMBS'
3510 H1=H1+4:H2=H2+4:H3=H3+4:H4=H4+4:K=0
3520 IF H1<36 THEN H=H1:G=G1:GOTO3570
3530 IF H2<36 THEN H=H2:G=G2:GOTO 3570
3540 IF H3<36 THEN H=H3:G=G3:GOTO 3570
3550 IF H4<36 THEN H=H4:G=G4:GOTO 3570
3560 RETURN
3570 RESET(G,H-4):IF H>31 THEN K=32:GOTO3630
3580 IF H<>27 GOTO3600
3590 IF POINT(G,28)=3 THEN RESET(G,28):K=32:SOUND 180,1:GOTO
3630
3600 P=POINT(G,H)+1
3610 ON P GOTO 3670,3690,3670,3620,3620,3680,
        3670,3670,3670
3620 SOUND 180,1:RESET(G,H):K=32
3630 IF ABS(G-G1)+ABS(H-H1)=0 THEN H1=H+K:K=0:GOTO3530
3640 IF ABS(H-H2)+ABS(G-G2)=0 THEN H2=H+K:K=0:GOTO3540
3650 IF ABS(H-H3)+ABS(G-G3)=0 THEN H3=H+K:K=0:GOTO3550
3660 H4=H4+K:K=0:RETURN
3670 SET(G,H,2):GOTO3630
3680 M2=-1:GOTO3620
3690 FOR I=1 TO 5:SOUND 10,2:SOUND 10,1:NEXT I
3700 K=32:NM=NM-1:IF NM<=0 THEN GOTO 4010 :
        ELSE GOTO3630
4000 'FINISHED GAME'
4010 CLS:PRINT @0,"SCORE : ";SC;
4020 IF SC>BS THEN BS=SC
4030 PRINT @64,"BEST SCORE : ";BS;
4040 IF PEEK(65280)=125 GOTO 50
4050 IF PEEK(65280)=253 THEN GOTO 50 ELSE GOTO 4040
5000 END
```

Race Driver

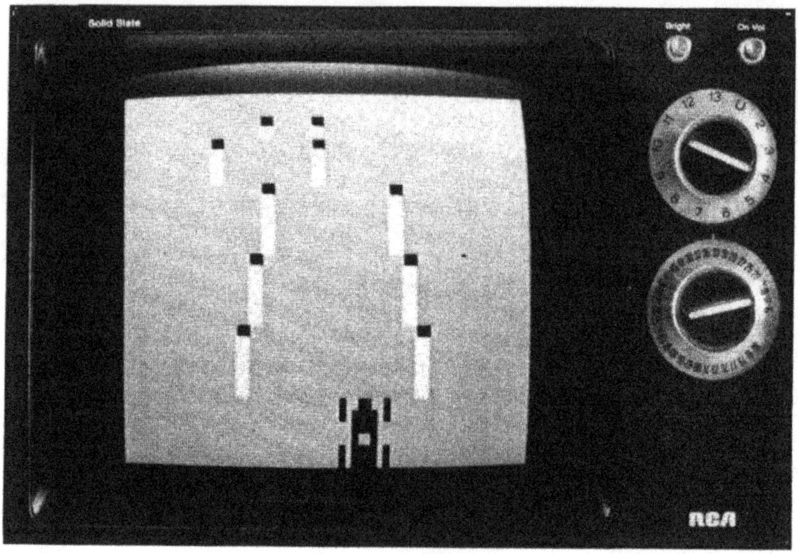

Can you maneouver your car between the posts on this treacherously narrow race course and reach the finish safely. The road has some very nasty bends and curves so take care and try to plan ahead. Your aim is to finish the course with as few penalty points as possible. You get penalties for hitting the posts at the side of the road or for running off the road itself.

Your car is steered with the left and right arrow keys. GOOD LUCK.

Program structure

10 - 350	Initialization
500 - 610	main loop
1000 - 1060	Check input
1070 - 1160	Update coordinates of the center of the road
1500 - 1510	Print top row of posts
1600 - 1630	Print center row of posts
1700	Print bottom row of posts
2000 - 2130	Check for a collision
3000 - 3100	Do last stages of the game
4000 - 4100	Print final message and restart

Variables

F1\$-F3\$	Car characters
K1\$-K9\$,KA\$-KC\$	Crash characters
P1\$,P2\$	Pole characters
CT	Count of poles passed
WA-WE	Half width at levels A to E
A2-E2	Position of centre of road at levels A to E
F	Position of car

RACE DRIVER

```
 20 CLEAR600
 30 F1$=CHR$(143)+CHR$(133)+CHR$(136)+CHR$(132)
      +CHR$(138)+CHR$(143)
 40 F2$=CHR$(143)+CHR$(143)+CHR$(129)+CHR$(130)
      +CHR$(143)+CHR$(143)
 50 F3$=CHR$(143)+CHR$(133)+CHR$(128)+CHR$(128)
      +CHR$(138)+CHR$(143)
 60 K4$=CHR$(133)+CHR$(143)+CHR$(142)+CHR$(128)
      +CHR$(141)+CHR$(143)
 70 K5$=CHR$(143)+CHR$(143)+CHR$(138)+CHR$(131)
      +CHR$(133)+CHR$(143)
 80 K6$=CHR$(143)+CHR$(133)+CHR$(131)+CHR$(131)
      +CHR$(130)+CHR$(143)
 90 K7$=STRING$(6,CHR$(143))
100 K8$=CHR$(143)+CHR$(143)+CHR$(129)+CHR$(130)
      +CHR$(143)+CHR$(143)
110 K9$=CHR$(143)+CHR$(133)+CHR$(131)+CHR$(131)
      +CHR$(143)
120 K$=STRING$(6,CHR$(143))
130 KA$=CHR$(143)+CHR$(131)+CHR$(143)+CHR$(143)
      +CHR$(142)+CHR$(143)
140 KB$=CHR$(143)+CHR$(135)+CHR$(141)+CHR$(138)
      +CHR$(143)+CHR$(135)
150 KC$=CHR$(143)+CHR$(140)+CHR$(140)+CHR$(143)
      +CHR$(139)+CHR$(143)
160 K1$=CHR$(143)+CHR$(132)+CHR$(128)+CHR$(141)
      +CHR$(143)+CHR$(138)
170 K2$=CHR$(143)+CHR$(138)+CHR$(131)+CHR$(133)
      +CHR$(143)+CHR$(143)
180 K3$=CHR$(143)+CHR$(129)+CHR$(131)+CHR$(131)
      +CHR$(138)+CHR$(143)
190 F$=F1$+STRING$(26,CHR$(143))+F2$
      +STRING$(26,CHR$(143))+F3$
200 C1$=STRING$(32,CHR$(143)):C2$=C1$+C1$:C3$=C2$+C1$
      :C4$=C2$+C2$
210 P1$=CHR$(195):P2$=CHR$(207)
300 CLS
310 PRINT @0,STRING$(32,CHR$(223));
320 T=0:S=0:R=0:A2=48:B2=80:C2=144:D2=240:E2=336
330 F=432:DX=0:FI=0:PP=0:OB=4
340 WA=2:WB=4:WC=5:WD=6:WE=7:UW=63-WE:LW=WE+32
350 CT=0
500 CT=CT+1:IF CT>50  GOTO4000
510 GOSUB 1000:' INKEY
520 GOSUB 1070:' UPDATE CENTRES
530 GOSUB 1000
540 GOSUB 1500:' PRINT A&B
550 GOSUB 1000
560 GOSUB 1600:' PRINT C&D
570 GOSUB 1000
580 GOSUB 1700:' PRINT E
590 GOSUB 1000
600 GOSUB 2000:' CRASH ?
```

```
 610 GOTO 500
1000 ' CHECK CONTROLS
1010 IF PEEK(343)=223 THEN F=F-1:GOTO 1030
1020 IF PEEK(344)=223 THEN F=F+1:GOTO 1030
1030 IF F<417 THEN F=417
1040 IF F>441 THEN F=441
1050 PRINT @F,F$;
1060 RETURN
1070 E2=D2+96:D2=C2+96:C2=B2+64:B2=A2+32
1080 IF FI=0 THEN A2=A2+RND(15)-8
1090 IF A2>UW THEN A2=UW:GOTO 1110
1100 IF A2<LW THEN A2=LW
1110 A1=A2-WA:A3=A2+WA
1120 B1=B2-WB:B3=B2+WB
1130 C1=C2-WC:C3=C2+WC
1140 D1=D2-WD:D3=D2+WD
1150 E1=E2-WE:E3=E2+WE
1160 RETURN
1500 PRINT @32,C1$;:PRINT @A1,P1$;:PRINT @A3,P1$;
1510 PRINT @64,C2$;:PRINT @B1,P1$;:PRINT @B3,P1$;:
       PRINT @B1+32,P2$;:PRINT @B3+32,P2$;:RETURN
1600 PRINT @128,C3$;:PRINT @C1,P1$;:PRINT @C3,P1$;:
       PRINT @C1+32,P2$;:PRINT @C3+32,P2$;:
       PRINT @C1+64,P2$;:PRINT @C3+64,P2$;
1610 PRINT @224,C3$;
1620 PRINT @D1,P1$;:PRINT @D3,P1$;:PRINT @D1+32,P2$;:
       PRINT @D3+32,P2$;:PRINT @D1+64,P2$;:
       PRINT @D3+64,P2$;
1630 RETURN
1700 PRINT @320,C3$;:PRINT @E1,P1$;:PRINT @E3,P1$;:
       PRINT @E1+32,P2$;:PRINT @E3+32,P2$;:
       PRINT @E1+64,P2$;:PRINT @E3+64,P2$;
2000 REM LEFT POLE?
2010 IF F>E1+96 GOTO 2050
2020 IF F<E1+93 GOTO 2080
2030 GOTO2070
2040 ' RIGHT POLE ?
2050 IF F<E3+92 THEN RETURN
2060 IF F>E3+96 GOTO 2080
2070 PP=PP+100:GOTO 2110
2080 FOR I=1 TO 4:SOUND 180,1:NEXT I
2090 PP=PP+50
2100 RETURN
2110 SOUND 3,2:PRINT @F,K1$;:PRINT @F+32,K2$;:
       PRINT @F+64,K3$;:SOUND 2,1:PRINT @F,K4$;:
       PRINT @F+32,K5$;:PRINT @F+64,K6$;:SOUND 3,2:
       PRINT @F,K7$;:PRINT @F+32,K8$;:
       PRINT @F+64,K9$;:SOUND 2,1
2120 PRINT @F,KA$;:PRINT @F+32,KB$;:PRINT @F+64,KC$;:
       SOUND 1,1:SOUND 1,1:PRINT @F,K$;:
       PRINT @F+32,K$;:PRINT @F+64,K$;:SOUND 1,1
2130 RETURN
3000 FI=FI+1:ON FI GOTO 3010,3020,3030,3040,3050
3010 PRINT @32,C1$;:PRINT @A1,CHR$(142)+CHR$(141);:
       RETURN
3020 PRINT @32,C1$;:PRINT @64,C2$;:
```

```
         PRINT @B1,CHR$(129)+CHR$(131)+CHR$(131)
         +CHR$(130);:PRINT @B1+32,CHR$(135);:
         PRINT @B1+35,CHR$(139);:RETURN
3030 PRINT @32,C4$;:PRINT @160,C2$;:
         PRINT @C1-96," F I N I S H";:
         FOR I=0 TO 160 STEP 32:
         PRINT @C1-96+I,CHR$(138);:
         PRINT @C1-84+I,CHR$(133);:NEXT I:RETURN
3040 PRINT @32,C4$;:PRINT @C1-96," F I N I S H";:
         FOR I=0 TO 192 STEP 32:
         PRINT @C1-96+I,CHR$(138);:
         PRINT @C1-84+I,CHR$(133);:NEXT I:RETURN
3050 CLS:PRINT @0,STRING$(32,CHR$(223));:
         PRINT @F,F1$;:PRINT @F+32,F2$;:
         PRINT @F+64,F3$;:
         PRINT @7,CHR$(138)+CHR$(128)+CHR$(135)
         +CHR$(138)+CHR$(143)+CHR$(129)+CHR$(136)
         +CHR$(143)+CHR$(133)+CHR$(143)+CHR$(140)
         +CHR$(128)+CHR$(120)+CHR$(130)+CHR$(133);
3060 FOR I=32 TO 448 STEP 32:PRINT @7+I,CHR$(138);:
         PRINT @21+I,CHR$(133);:NEXT I
3070 SOUND 140,3:SOUND140,3:SOUND140,3
3080 CLS:PRINT @0,STRING$(32,CHR$(223));
3090 PRINT @192,"THE NUMBER OF PENALITY POINTS";:
         PRINT @260,"SET AGAINST YOU WAS";:
         PRINT @338,PP;" POINTS";
3100 RETURN
4000 GOSUB 3000
4010 GOSUB 1000
4020 GOSUB 1070
4030 GOSUB 1000
4040 IF FI<3 THEN GOSUB 1600
4050 GOSUB 1000
4060 IF FI<4 THEN GOSUB 1700
4070 GOSUB 1000
4080 GOSUB 2000
4090 IF FI<5 GOTO 4000
4100 I$=INKEY$:IF I$<>"S" GOTO 4100 ELSE GOTO 300
5000 END
```

Chopper

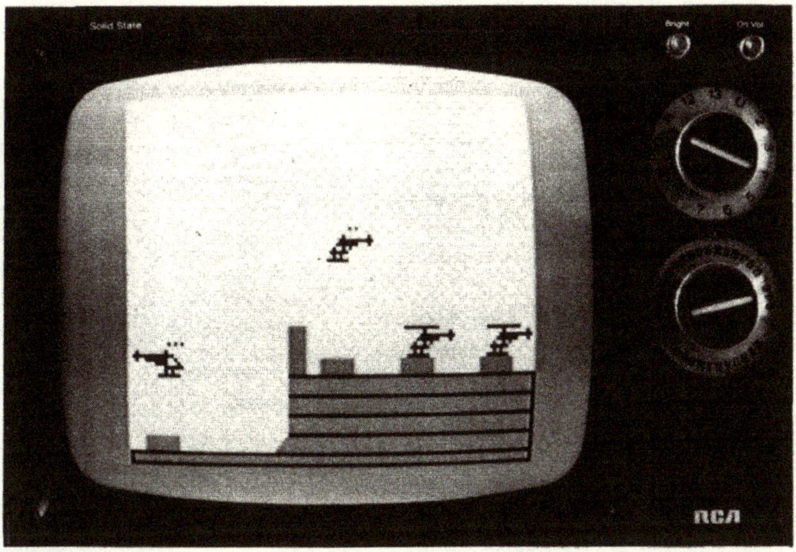

Copyright (c) Colin Carter

You are the sole survivor of a squadron of helicopters, and your task is to invade the city and destroy the last of the enemy choppers. There are three of the enemy left and they will come at you one at a time. Can you get all of them before they get you - be warned it is very hard to do.

The up and down arrow keys move your chopper up and down while the right arrow fires your gun. Use the 'S' key to restart at the end of the game.

Program structure

5 - 680	Initialization
1000 - 1500	main loop
1010 - 1040	Blade rotation
1050 - 1080	move enemy
1090 - 1140	move up
1150 - 1170	move down
1180 - 1290	enemy firing
1300 - 1430	player firing
1440 - 1450	end game
1460 - 1490	blade rotation

Variables

XO,YO	Position of helicopter
XE,YE	Position of enemy
OD,ED	Location of blades
FC	Firing limit count
F	Firing count for enemy

CHOPPER

```
 10 PCLEAR 4
 20 PMODE 1,1
 30 COLOR 1,3:PCLS(2)
 40 SCREEN1,0
 50 DIM C1(17),C2(17),C3(15),C4(15),BL(17)
 60 GET(1,1)-(41,31),BL,G
 70 P$="T255;O1;V31;L1;3;L255;3;P60;V15;L10;2;
      L255;2;P40;V2;L100;1;L255;1;"
 80 DRAW"C1"
 90 LINE(0,185)-(10,185),PSET
100 LINE-(10,175),PSET
110 LINE-(30,175),PSET
120 LINE-(30,185),PSET
130 LINE-(90,185),PSET
140 LINE-(100,175),PSET
150 LINE-(100,120),PSET
160 LINE-(110,120),PSET
170 LINE-(110,145),PSET
180 LINE-(120,145),PSET
190 LINE-(120,135),PSET
200 LINE-(140,135),PSET
210 LINE-(140,145),PSET
220 LINE-(170,145),PSET
230 LINE-(170,135),PSET
240 LINE-(190,135),PSET
250 LINE-(190,145),PSET
260 LINE-(220,145),PSET
270 LINE-(220,135),PSET
280 LINE-(240,135),PSET
290 LINE-(240,145),PSET
300 LINE-(255,145),PSET
310 PAINT(150,190),1,1
320 DRAW"C4"
330 LINE(255,145)-(255,196),PSET
340 LINE-(0,196),PSET
350 LINE-(0,185),PSET
360 LINE(100,155)-(255,155),PSET
370 LINE(100,165)-(255,165),PSET
380 LINE(100,175)-(255,175),PSET
390 LINE(0,185)-(255,185),PSET
400 LINE(100,145)-(255,145),PSET
410 ' PMODE1,3:COLOR 1,3:PCLS(2)
420 SCREEN1,0
430 DRAW"C3"
440 CIRCLE(4,158),3
450 A$="BM7,159;M26,159;F6L8;M7,159;BM18,168;
      R4NU2R4NU2R4;BM22,156;D8"
460 B$="M-19,+0;G6R8;M-2,-6;BM+3,+10;L4NU2L4NU2L4;
      BM+12,-4;E4R2L3ND1L5;BM+1,-4;D3R15NU2ND2"
470 DRAW A$
480 PAINT(18,160),3,3
490 GET(0,140)-(40,170),C1,G
500 DRAW"BM152,96;"+ B$
```

```
510 GET(120,80)-(152,107),C3,G
520 GET(120,88)-(152,115),C4,G
530 FOR Y=88 TO 108
540 PUT(120,Y)-(152,Y+27),C3,PSET:NEXTY
550 PUT(170,108)-(202,135),C3,PSET
560 PUT(220,108)-(252,135),C3,PSET
570 PUT(0,100)-(40,130),C1,PSET
580 GET(0,108)-(40,138),C2,G
590 FOR Y=104 TO 144 STEP4
600 PUT(0,Y)-(40,Y+28),C1,PSET
610 NEXT Y
620 LINE(172,120)-(192,120),PSET
630 LINE(224,120)-(244,120),PSET
640 XE=120:YE=108:ED=2
650 YO=144:OD=10
660 DE=-4:YE=108
670 FC=0
680 F=0
1000 ' MAIN LOOP
1010 PSET(XE+6,YE+ED,3):PSET(XE+10,YE+ED,3):
     PSET(XE+18,YE+ED,2):PSET(XE+22,YE+ED,2)
1020 FOR DX=0TO12 STEP 4
1030 PSET(8+DX,YO+OD,3):PSET(24+DX,YO+OD,2)
1040 NEXT DX
1050 IF YE=108 THEN PUT(XE,YE)-(XE+32,YE+27),C4,PSET
1060 YE=YE+DE:IF YE<=10 THEN DE=+4:ED=12:GOTO1060
1070 IF YE>110 THEN DE=-4:ED=2:GOTO1060
1080 IF DE<0 THEN PUT(XE,YE)-(XE+32,YE+27),C4,PSET :
     ELSE PUT(XE,YE)-(XE+32,YE+27),C3,PSET
1090 IF PEEK(341)<>223 GOTO 1150
1100 IF YO=144 THEN PUT(0,YO)-(40,YO+30),C2,PSET
1110 IF OD=12 THEN PUT(0,YO)-(40,YO+30),C2,PSET
1120 IF YO<=10 THEN GOTO1180 ELSEYO=YO-4:OD=4
1130 PUT(0,YO)-(40,YO+30),C2,PSET
1140 GOTO 1180
1150 IF PEEK(342)<>223 GOTO1180
1160 IF YO>=142 GOTO 1180 ELSE YO=YO+4:OD=12
1170 PUT(0,YO)-(40,YO+28),C1,PSET
1180 IF YE>90 THEN GOTO 1460 ELSE F=F+RND(3)
1190 IF F<10 GOTO 1300
1200 F=0
1210 SOUND250,1
1220 YS=YE+ED+10
1230 FOR XX=XE TO 30 STEP-8
1240 PSET(XX,YS,3):PSET(XX,YS,2)
1250 NEXT XX
1260 IF ABS(YO+OD+6-YS)-6>0 GOTO1300
1270 FOR I=1TO5:PSET(RND(35),YO+OD+RND(12),4):
     PLAY P$:PSET(RND(35),YO+OD+RND(12),1):NEXT I
1280 SOUND 100,2
1290 GOTO1450
1300 FC=FC+1:IF PEEK(344)<>223 GOTO 1460
1310 IF YO>100 THEN XL=100 ELSE XL=250
1320 SOUND 250,1
1330 YS=YO+OD+10
1340 IF FC<4 THENGOTO1460 ELSE FC=0
```

```
1350 FOR XX=40 TO XL STEP 8
1360 PSET(XX,YS,3):PSET(XX,YS,4):PSET(XX,YS,2):
     PSET(XX,YS,2)
1370 NEXT XX
1380 IF ABS(YE+ED+6-YS)-6>0GOTO1460
1390 FORI=1TO5:PSET(XE+RND(28),YE+ED+RND(9),4):
     PLAY P$:PSET(XE+RND(28),YE+ED+RND(9),1):NEXTI
1400 PUT(XE-5,YE)-(XE+35,YE+30),BL,PSET
1410 XE=XE+50
1420 YE=108
1430 IF XE<230 GOTO 1460
1440 FOR I=1 TO 7:SOUND 50+20*I,1:NEXT I
1450 I$=INKEY$:IF I$="S" THEN PCLS(2):GOTO80 :
     ELSE GOTO 1450
1460 PSET(XE+6,YE+ED,2):PSET(XE+10,YE+ED,2):
     PSET(XE+18,YE+ED,3):PSET(XE+22,YE+ED,3)
1470 FOR DX=0TO12STEP4
1480 PSET(8+DX,YO+OD,2):PSET(24+DX,YO+OD,3)
1490 NEXT DX
1500 GOTO1000
```

Pinball

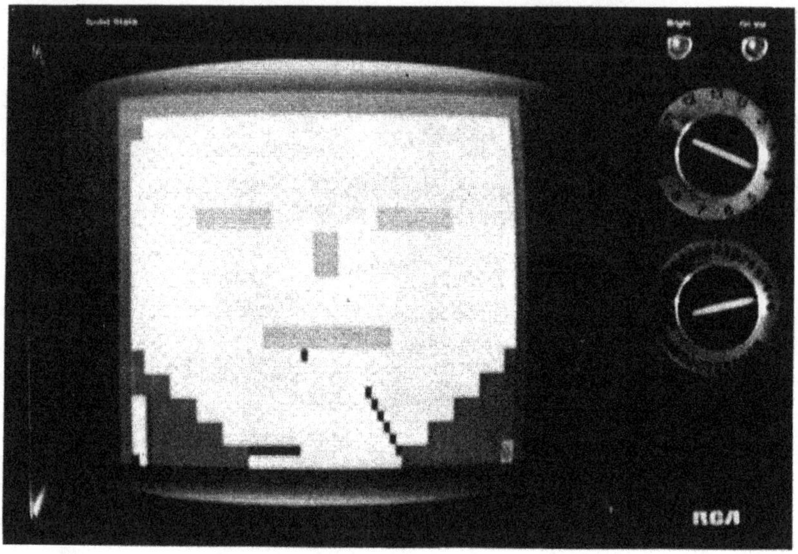

Now you can have a pinball parlour right on your own computer. You have three balls to play with so see how long you can last.

The balls are set into motion with the Up arrow key while your flippers are controlled by the 'Q' key (for the left flipper) and the '@' key (for the right flipper). And just like the real thing it takes a bit of practice to control the ball in play.

Program structure

100 - 260	Draw the pinball machine
500 - 530	initialization
540 - 730	Main loop for the 3 balls
550	Wait for 'S' key to restart game
560	release ball
690 - 730	Section for the ball in play
1000 - 1130	initialize data for a particular angle of travel
1500 - 1510	A bit of fun
2000 - 2380	Move the ball one step
3000 - 3660	Check keys for flipper movement
4000 - 4080	Display score

Variables

K	Angle of travel
NB	Number of balls left
PA, PB	Position of flippers
SC	Score

PINBALL

```
 100 ' DRAW TABLE'
 110 CLS(5)
 120 FOR I=0 TO 14:PRINT @I,CHR$(191);:
        PRINT @31-I,CHR$(191);:PRINT @I*32,CHR$(191);:
        PRINT @I*32+31,CHR$(191);:NEXT I
 130 PRINT @15,CHR$(191)+CHR$(191);:
        PRINT @480,CHR$(191);:POKE1535,191
 140 FOR J=1TO4
 150 J2=(16-J)*32:J3=J2+31
 160 FOR I=1 TO 2*(5-J)+1
 170 PRINT @J2+I,CHR$(175);:PRINT @J3-I,CHR$(175);
 180 NEXT I
 190 NEXT J
 200 PRINT @353,CHR$(175);:PRINT @382,CHR$(175);
 210 E$=STRING$(6,CHR$(143)):BL$=STRING$(6,CHR$(207))
 220 PRINT @166,E$;:PRINT@180,E$;:
        PRINT @207,CHR$(255);CHR$(255);:
        PRINT @239,CHR$(255);CHR$(255);
 230 FOR I=0TO9:PRINT @331+I,CHR$(239);:NEXTI
 240 FOR I=1 TO 4:PRINT @489+I,CHR$(195);:
        PRINT @502-I,CHR$(195);:NEXTI
 250 FOR I=0 TO 128 STEP 32:PRINT @353+I,CHR$(207);:
        NEXTI
 260 PRINT @33,CHR$(191);
 500 SC=0:NB=3:PRINT @504,STRING$(7,CHR$(175));
 510 W=1000:PB=1:PA=1
 520 GOSUB 4000:' PRINT SCORE
 530 RESET(2,31)
 540 PRINT @385,CHR$(207);:PRINT @353,CHR$(207);:
        IF NB>0 GOTO 560
 550 I$=INKEY$:IF I$="S" GOTO 500 ELSE GOTO 550
 560 IF PEEK(341)<>223 GOTO 560:' FIRE ?
 570 NB=NB-1
 580 E=-1
 590 SOUND 100,1
 600 PRINT @481,CHR$(203);
 610 FOR I=449 TO 65 STEP -32
 620 PRINT @I+32,CHR$(207);:PRINT @I,CHR$(205);:
        PRINT @I,CHR$(203);
 630 NEXT I
 640 PRINT @385,CHR$(175);:PRINT @353,CHR$(175);
 650 IF NB>0 THEN RESET(2,31)
 660 KJ=RND(8):GOSUB 1000
 670 X=3:Y=4
 680 SOUND 240,1
 690 GOSUB 2000:' MOVE IT
 700 IF E>0 GOTO540
 710 GOSUB 3000:' CHECK Q ?
 720 GOSUB 3500:' CHECK @ ?
 730 GOTO 690
1000 ON KJ GOTO
        1010,1020,1030,1040,1050,1060,1070,1080,
        1090,1100,1110,1120
```

```
1010 K=1:DX=-1:DY=+1:GOTO1130
1020 K=2:DX=-1:DY=+2:GOTO1130
1030 K=2:DX=+1:DY=+2:GOTO1130
1040 K=1:DX=+1:DY=+1:GOTO1130
1050 K=3:DX=+2:DY=+1:GOTO1130
1060 K=3:DX=+2:DY=-1:GOTO1130
1070 K=1:DX=+1:DY=-1:GOTO1130
1080 K=2:DX=+1:DY=+2:GOTO1130
1090 K=2:DX=-1:DY=-2:GOTO1130
1100 K=1:DX=-1:DY=-1:GOTO1130
1110 K=3:DX=-2:DY=-1:GOTO1130
1120 K=3:DX=-2:DY=+1
1130 RETURN
1500 PRINT @339,BL$;:PRINT @307,CHR$(239);CHR$(239);:
     PRINT @180,BL$;:FOR I=1 TO 100:NEXTI:
     PRINT @180,E$;:PRINT @307,CHR$(207)+CHR$(207)
     ;:PRINT @339,CHR$(239)+CHR$(239);
1510 RETURN
2000 ' MOVE IT'
2010 X2=X+DX:Y2=Y+DY
2020 IF Y2>31 THEN SOUND 5,2:E=+1:SET(X,Y,5):RETURN
2030 P=POINT(X2,Y2)+1
2040 ON P GOTO 2050,2110,2260,2150,2190,2260,2260,
     2310,2350
2050 SOUND 10,1
2060 IF X<32 GOTO 2090
2070 IF PA>2 THEN DX=-DX:SET(X,Y,5):X=X+DX:RESET(X,Y)
     ELSE DY=-DY:SET(X,Y,5):Y=Y+DY:RESET(X,Y)
2080 RETURN
2090 IF PB>2 THEN DX=-DX:SET(X,Y,5):X=X+DX:RESET(X,Y)
     ELSE DY=-DY:SET(X,Y,5):Y=Y+DY:RESET(X,Y)
2100 RETURN
2110 SOUND 160,1
2120 IF X=10 OR X=11 THEN DX=-DX ELSE DY=-DY
2130 SC=SC+100:GOSUB4000
2140 RETURN
2150 SOUND 240,1
2160 IF X>31 THEN KJ=7+RND(5) ELSE KJ=4+RND(5)
2170 GOSUB 1000
2180 RETURN
2190 SOUND 240,1
2200 IF POINT(X+DX,Y-DY)<>5 GOTO 2220
2210 DY=-DY:RETURN
2220 IF POINT(X-DX,Y+DY)<>5 GOTO 2240
2230 DX=-DX:RETURN
2240 KJ=RND(12):GOSUB1000
2250 RETURN
2260 IF POINT(X,Y+SGN(DY))=0 GOTO 2050
2270 IF POINT(X+SGN(DX),Y)=0 GOTO 2050
2280 IF POINT(X+SGN(DX),Y+SGN(DY))=0 GOTO 2050
2290 SET(X,Y,5):RESET(X2,Y2):X=X2:Y=Y2
2300 RETURN
2310 SOUND 150,1
2320 IF X=20 OR X=21 THEN DX=-DX ELSE DY=-DY
2330 SC=SC+50:GOSUB4000
2340 RETURN
```

```
2350 SOUND 170,1:SOUND 170,1
2360 IF X=11 OR X=16 THEN DY=-DY ELSE DX=-DX
2370 SC=SC+500:GOSUB 4000
2380 RETURN
3000 ON PB GOTO 3010,3050,3080,3110,3140
3010 IF PEEK(339)<>239 THEN RETURN
3020 FOR XB=27 TO 22 STEP -1:SET(XB,30,5):NEXT XB
3030 RESET(22,29):RESET(23,29):RESET(24,28):
       RESET(25,28):RESET(26,27)
3040 PB=2:RETURN
3050 SET(26,27,5):SET(25,28,5):SET(24,28,5):
       SET(23,29,5):SET(22,29,5):SET(21,30,5)
3060 FOR XB=21 TO 25:RESET(XB,50-XB):NEXT XB
3070 PB=3:RETURN
3080 FOR XB=25 TO 21 STEP -1:SET(XB,50-XB,5):NEXT XB
3090 RESET(20,29):RESET(21,28):RESET(21,27):
       RESET(22,26):RESET(22,25):RESET(23,24)
3100 PB=4:RETURN
3110 SET(23,24,5):SET(22,25,5):SET(22,26,5):
       SET(21,27,5):SET(21,28,5)
3120 FOR YB=29 TO 23 STEP -1:RESET(20,YB):NEXT YB
3130 PB=5:RETURN
3140 FOR YB=23 TO 29:SET(20,YB,5):NEXT YB
3150 FOR XB=21 TO 27:RESET(XB,30):NEXT XB
3160 PB=1:RETURN
3500 ON PA GOTO 3510,3550,3580,3610,3640
3510 IF PEEK(338)<>251 THEN RETURN
3520 FOR XB=36 TO 42:SET(XB,30,5):NEXT XB
3530 RESET(41,29):RESET(40,29):RESET(39,28):
       RESET(38,28):RESET(37,27)
3540 PA=2:RETURN
3550 SET(37,27,5):SET(38,28,5):SET(39,28,5):
       SET(40,29,5):SET(41,29,5):SET(42,30,5)
3560 FOR XB=42 TO 38 STEP -1: RESET(XB,XB-13):NEXT XB
3570 PA=3:RETURN
3580 FOR XB=38 TO 42:SET(XB,XB-13,5):NEXT XB
3590 RESET(43,29):RESET(42,28):RESET(42,27):
       RESET(41,26):RESET(41,25):RESET(40,24)
3600 PA=4:RETURN
3610 SET(40,24,5):SET(41,25,5):SET(41,26,5):
       SET(42,27,5):SET(42,28,5)
3620 FOR YB=29 TO 23 STEP -1:RESET(43,YB):NEXT YB
3630 PA=5:RETURN
3640 FOR YB=23 TO 29:SET(43,YB,5):NEXT YB
3650 FOR XB=42 TO 36 STEP-1:RESET(XB,30):NEXT XB
3660 PA=1:RETURN
4000 ' PRINT SCORE'
4010 S$=STR$(SC)
4020 L=LEN(S$)-1
4030 PRINT @511-L,RIGHT$(S$,L);
4040 IF SC<W THEN RETURN
4050 W=W+1000
4060 GOSUB 1500
4070 IF W>100000 THEN E=+1:FOR I=10 TO 100 STEP 10:
       SOUND 140+I,1:NEXT I
4080 RETURN
5000 END
```

Alien Blitz

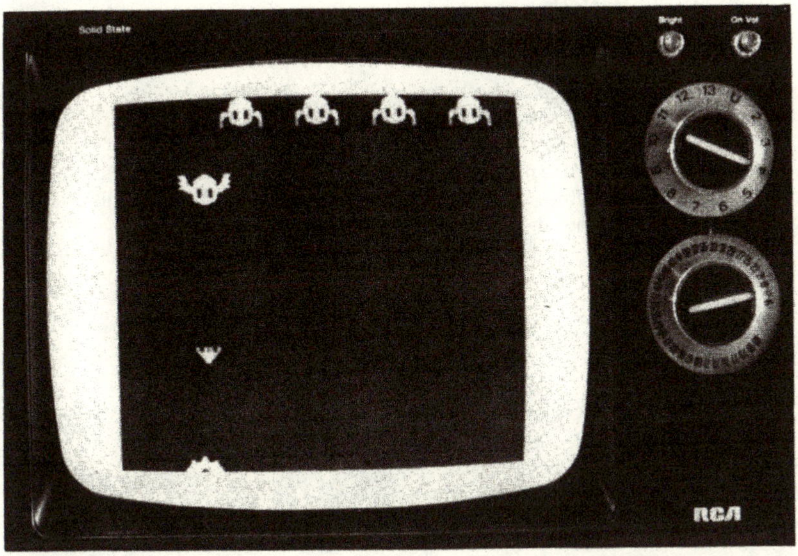

You are the sole defender of the space station. Suddenly overhead you see them - a convoy of enemy aliens. They must know of your power because they stay safely out of your tractor beam reach.

What's this? - slowly one of them separates itself from the rest of the fleet and swoops down on your position. Is it possible that it's flapping its wings, or is that a space illusion?

No time to worry about that - there are missiles falling. Got to get them, those guys are fast; quick; get out the tractor beam and pull him in. Got him. But wait - another alien is detaching himself from the convoy . . .

Programming considerations:

This program is an arcade game for the DRAGON loosely based on similar games to be found on video machines.

As such the main programming considerations are speed and visual effects. Sound is only used when necessary, as it would slow things down too much otherwise.

Therefore a minimum of work is to be done in each cycle, to keep speed at a maximum. Only 3 variables are to be updated each cycle:

- coordinates of swooping alien
- column position of player

The main loop is divided into two cycles, one for wings up shape and one for wings down shape. This allows the player and alien to move faster as no decision needs to be made within the main cycle as to the shape to be drawn.

Program Structure:

10 - 60	Define shapes, draw convoy
90 - 350	First part of cycle update all positions
360 - 530	Second part of cycle
1000 - 1440	Successful hits by player on alien come here to simulate the tractor sucking in the alien.
1400 - 1440	explodes the player when he is hit.
1500 - 1540	Destruction of enemy convoy
9000 - 9170	Builds the arrays that are to be put on the screen to draw the aliens, player and bombs.

ALIEN BLITZ

```
 10 PCLEAR 4: PMODE 4,1: SCREEN 1,0: PCLS: VR=1536
 20 GOSUB 9000
 25 PCLS
 30 V=184: S=0: G=40
 35 X=16+S: Y=0
 40 FOR Z=0 TO 192-S STEP 48
 50 PUT (X+Z,0)-(X+Z+31,15),AR,PSET
 60 NEXT Z
 90 PUT (G,V)-(G+23,V+7),EL,PSET
100 G=G+8*(PEEK(343)=223)-8*(PEEK(344)=223)
110 IF G<0 THEN G=0
120 IF G>232 THEN G=232
130 PUT (G,V)-(G+23,V+7),LB,PSET
190 PUT (X,Y)-(X+31,Y+15),EA,PSET
200 X=X+8*((Y<32)-(Y>24)-2*SGN(G-X)*(RND(0)>.5)):
        IF X>224 THEN X=0
205 IF X<0 THEN X=224
210 Y=Y+8
220 PUT (X,Y)-(X+31,Y+15),AU,PSET
230 IF Y=V-16 THEN 1400
240 IF RND(0)>.15 THEN 300
245 SOUND 100,2
250 FOR I=Y+16 TO V-8 STEP 8:
        PUT (X+8,I)-(X+23,I+7),BM,PSET:
        PUT (X+8,I)-(X+24,I+7),EB,PSET: NEXT I
260 IF G-X<=16 AND G-X>=-8 THEN 1420
300 IF PEEK(345)<>223 THEN 350
310 M=20: IF G=X OR G=X+8 THEN M=16+Y
320 LINE (11+G,183)-(11+G,M),PSET: SOUND 200,2:
        IF M>20 THEN 1000
330 LINE (11+G,183)-(11+G,M),PRESET
350 PUT (G,V)-(G+23,V+7),EL,PSET
360 G=G+8*(PEEK(343)=223)-8*(PEEK(344)=223)
370 IF G<0 THEN G=0
380 IF G>232 THEN G=232
390 PUT (G,V)-(G+23,V+7),LB,PSET
400 PUT (X,Y)-(X+31,Y+15),EA,PSET
410 X=X+8*((Y<32)-(Y>24)-2*SGN(G-X)*(RND(0)>.5)):
        IF X>224 THEN X=0
420 IF X<0 THEN X=224
430 Y=Y+8
440 PUT (X,Y)-(X+31,Y+15),AD,PSET
450 IF Y=V-16 THEN 1400
460 IF RND(0)>.15 THEN 490
465 SOUND 100,2
470 FOR I=Y+16 TO V-8 STEP 8: PUT
(X+8,I)-(X+23,I+7),BM,PSET:: PUT (X+8,I)-(X+24,I+7),EB,PSET:
NEXT I
480 IF G-X<=16 AND G-X>=-8 THEN 1420
490 IF PEEK(345)<>223 THEN 90
500 M=20: IF G=X OR G=X+8 THEN M=16+Y
510 LINE (11+G,183)-(11+G,M),PSET: SOUND 200,2:
        IF M>20 THEN 1000
```

```
 520 LINE (11+G,183)-(11+G,M),PRESET
 530 GOTO 90
1000 FOR Y=Y+8 TO V-16 STEP 8
1010 PUT (X,Y-8)-(X+31,Y+7),EA,PSET:
       PUT (X,Y)-(X+31,Y+15),AK,PSET
1015 NEXT Y
1020 PUT (X,V-16)-(X+31,V-1),EA,PSET
1200 S=S+48
1210 IF S<240 THEN 35
1220 GOTO 1500
1400 PUT(X,Y)-(X+31,Y+15),EA,PSET
1410 IF ABS(X-G)>8 THEN 35
1420 FOR I=1 TO 11: SCREEN 1,1: SOUND 80,2:
       SCREEN 1,0: SOUND 150,1: NEXT I
1430 FOR X=1 TO 1000: NEXT X
1440 GOTO 25
1500 CLS: PRINT @160,"   CONGRATULATIONS - YOU HAVE
       DESTROYED THE ENTIRE ENEMY FLEET"
1510 PLAY "C#CO-BO+ACO-BO+C#12"
1520 PRINT: PRINT "WATCH OUT - HERE THEY COME AGAIN"
1530 FOR I=1 TO 3: SOUND 197,17: SOUND 89,2: NEXT I
1535 SCREEN 1,0
1540 GOTO 25
9000 FOR I=1 TO 21
9010 READ N
9020 FOR X=VR+N TO VR+N+224 STEP 32
9030 READ A: POKE X,A: NEXT X
9040 NEXT I
9050 DIM AR(14),AU(14),AD(14),AK(14),LB(5),BM(4)
9051 DIM EA(14),EL(5),EB(4)
9052 GET (0,100)-(31,115),EA,G
9053 GET (0,100)-(23,107),EL,G
9054 GET (0,100)-(15,107),EB,G
9060 DIM Z(7): GET (40,8)-(55,23),Z,G
9070 PUT (88,8)-(103,23),Z,PSET
9071 PUT (136,8)-(151,23),Z,PSET
9072 PUT (184,8)-(199,23),Z,PSET
9080 GET (32,8)-(63,23),AR,G
9081 GET (80,8)-(111,23),AU,G
9082 GET (128,8)-(159,23),AD,G
9083 GET (176,8)-(207,23),AK,G
9084 GET (48,40)-(71,47),LB,G
9085 GET (112,40)-(127,47),BM,G
9090 RETURN
9100 DATA 516,14,31,28,24,16,16,16,16,519,112,
       248,56,24,8,8,8,8
9110 DATA 261,3,15,63,127,127,127,255,227,262,192,
       240,252,254,254,254,255,199
9120 DATA 517,227,227,99,99,127,63,7,0,518,199,199,
       198,198,254,252,224,0
9130 DATA 266,240,112,56,248,124,62,255,30,269,
       15,14,28,31,62,124,255,120,522,7,0,0,0,0,
       0,0,0,525,224,0,0,0,0,0,0,0
9140 DATA 272,0,0,0,0,0,0,0,7,275,0,0,0,0,0,0,
       224,528,30,255,62,124,248,56,112,240,531,
       120,255,124,62,31,28,14,15
```

```
9150 DATA 278,16,16,16,16,24,28,31,14,281,8,8,8,
       8,24,56,248,112
9160 DATA 1286,0,0,12,15,31,63,127,255,1287,24,60,
       60,255,255,255,231,129,1288,0,0,48,240,
       248,252,254,255
9170 DATA 1294,66,66,38,27,15,7,3,1,1295,66,66,
       100,216,240,224,192,128
```

Eliminator

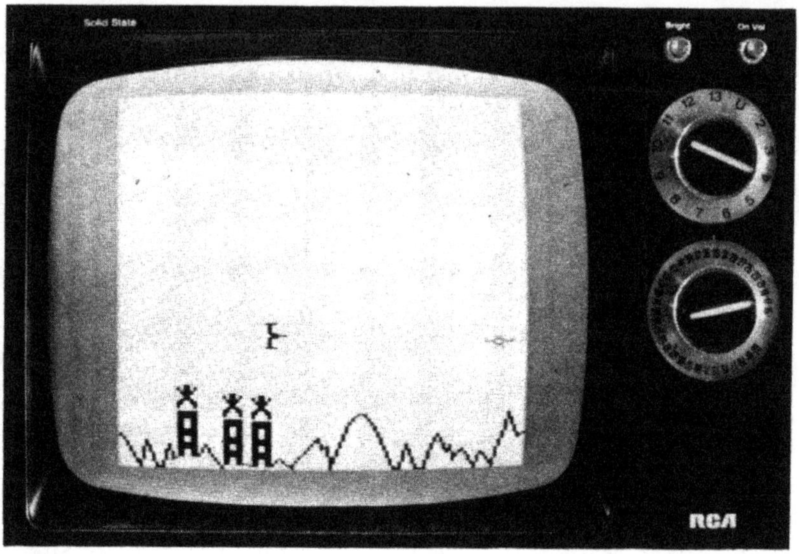

You are the protector and defender of the humanoids on the surface of the planetoid. Your task is to ELIMINATE the invader ALIEN.

You must prevent at all costs their attempts to kidnap the humanoids under your care. Their survival and the survival of their planetoid depends on you.

The planetoid you are guarding is only a small one, but it is impossible to fly too low above the ground. You can only travel in one direction up and down.

The enemy kidnappers have sufficient intelligence to evade your only weapon, the horizontal laser beam. You must not allow them to descend below your lowest possible flight path or else you will not be able to stop their invasion but by losing your humanoid.
When the invaders descend below your lowest fly path, they will change to a small detecting unit until a humanoid is captured.

Can you perform evasive action, shoot down the invaders and protect the humanoids?

Playing the game:

You are in control of the space craft in the centre of the screen. Your forward momentum does not allow you any flexibility in moving sideways.

Your only controls are therefore up and down, using the "up arrow" and the "down arrow".

You have at your disposal a laser blaster, controlled by pressing the "spacebar" key, which will destroy the kidnapping invaders, but it only brings temporary relief. As soon as you shoot one, the next one appears.

Your craft can sustain only one damage, after all humanoids are kidnapped, the game finish.

Programming considerations:

There are no available commands in BASIC in order to simulate the movement of the spacecraft against the surface of the planet.
Even if there were suitable commands, horizontal scrolling of the screen would be painfully slow in BASIC

The only solution available, and the one that is used here, is to have the horizontal scrolling routine written in 6809 machine language. You will find this routine, 67 bytes long, in the DATA statement at lines 7130 to 7190.
For those who are interested in machine language programming, there is a listing of the source code of the scrolling subroutine attached.

What this routine does is to take each line of the screen, and wrap it around. In mode 3 graphic each pixel can only have four possible colours represented by two bits of an eight bits byte. In this program, the scrolling is one horizontal byte at a time ie.four horizontal pixels at a time
(there are 128 identifiable horizontal pixels in pmode 3)
ie. the characters that were at (0,0), (2,0), (4,0), (8,0) will go to (30,0), (0,0), (2,0), (4,0).

Theoretically, we can scroll the whole screen (3072 bytes); but knowing that the land and humanoids are all located withinthe bottom 48 vertical pixels of the screen, we can scroll that 48 rows of bytes and save 75% of time. SO practically, that is what the machine language routine is doing, scrolling the bottom 48 rows.
This machine language routine is fully relocatable - in

other words, you don't need to know anything about machine language to use it. Simply use a program similar to that in lines 7040 to 7110. Because this routine is fully relocatable, you can specify any address that will not be overwritten as the address it should be POKEd into.

You may be interested in trying to adapt this routine for other programs. You can be sure that Melbourne House is always keen to see any exciting programs you may develop.

The rest of the program is mainly taken up with keeping track of the variables relating to the spaceship (XX,SY) and alien (AX,AY).

Structure of the program:

```
10 - 30        Reserve 500 bytes for string and set BASIC
               system upper limit to 32671
               Branch to lower part of program

1000 - 1180    Fighter routine
                   check fighter movement up/down
                   check resultant position
                   draw fighter
                   if fire laser blast
                       then fire laser
                            if alien hit by laser
                              then increase score
                                   blank alien
                            return
                   else
                       return

1190 - 2130    Alien routine
                   generate alien if not exist
                   if below lowest flight path
                       then blank big alien
                            draw seeking shape
                            return
                   else
                       avoid fighter laser gun head
                       if crash with fighter
                            flash screen, blank alien, return

3000 - 3170    Scroll routine
                   scroll land and humanoids
                   test searching alien down for humanoid
                   if yes then capture

4000 - 4600    Build land routine

5000 - 5210    draw shapes routine

6000 - 6150    Main loop
```

```
            Initialisation
            Draw shapes
            Buildland
        L1: Fighter routine
            Alien routine
            Scroll routine
            if game control <> 0 then goto L1
            Display score, wait for (ENTER) key to
                restart
7000 - 7250 Initialisation
            set string and numeric variables
            read in the machine language routine
```

ELIMINATOR

```
  10 'ELIMINATOR
  20 CLEAR500,32671
  30 GOTO6000'MAIN
1000 'FIGHTER
1010 DY=((PEEK(341)=223)-(PEEK(342)=223))*4
1020 IFDY=0THEN1060
1030 SY=SY+DY
1040 IFSY<0THENSY=0
1050 IFSY>123THENSY=123
1060 PUT(90,SY)-(105,SY+20),F,PSET
1070 IFPEEK(345)<>223THENRETURN
1080 COLOR4,2
1090 FY=SY+10
1100 PLAY"V20;O3;L32;12"
1110 LINE(106,FY)-(220,FY),PSET
1120 PLAY"V20;O1;L64;1"
1130 LINE(106,FY)-(220,FY),PRESET
1140 GP=SY+10
1150 IF((GP>AY+8)OR(GP<AY+2)OR(AX<105)OR(AX>220))THEN
        RETURN
1160 AE=0:SC=SC+100
1170 PUT(AX,AY)-(AX+21,AY+10),BK,PSET
1180 RETURN
1190 'ALIEN
2000 IFAE=0THENAE=1:AX=230:AY=RND(121)
2010 IFAY<=131THENGOTO2050
2020 IFAE=2THENRETURN
2030 IFAE=1THENGOSUB1170:AE=2:AY=139:
        PUT(AX+6,AY)-(AX+13,AY+4),B,PSET
2040 RETURN
2050 IF((AY<SY)AND(AX>90)) THENAY=AY-2ELSEAY=AY+2
2060 AX=AX-2
2070 IFAX<0THENAX=0
2080 IFAY<0THENAY=0
2090 IF(PPOINT(AX,AY+5)<>4ANDPPOINT(AX+19,AY+5)<>4)
        THEN GOTO2120
2100 FORI=1TO20:SCREEN1,1:FORJ=1TO10:NEXTJ:SCREEN1,0:
        FORJ=1TO10:NEXTJ:NEXTI
2110 AE=0:PUT(AX,AY)-(AX+21,AY+10),BK,PSET:RETURN
2120 PUT(AX,AY)-(AX+21,AY+10),A,PSET
2130 RETURN
3000 'SCROLL
3010 N=USR0(0)
3020 IFAE<>2THENRETURN
3030 PX=AX+8
3040 PLAY"V30;L128;O4;12"
3050 FORI=144TO159
3060 IFPPOINT(PX,I)=4THENGOTO3080
3070 NEXTI:PLAY"V30;L64;O2;1":RETURN
3080 PUT(AX,I-3)-(AX+21,I+11),BK,PSET
3090 GC=GC-1:AE=0:OX=AX+4:NX=AX+15
3100 FORI=139TO4STEP-3
3110 SOUND(255-I),1
```

```
3120 PUT(AX,I)-(AX+21,I+10),A,PSET
3130 PUT(OX,I+7)-(NX,I+19),M,PSET
3140 PUT(OX,I+20)-(NX,I+23),BK,PSET
3150 NEXTI
3160 I=I+3:PUT(AX,I)-(AX+25,I+19),BK,PSET
3170 RETURN
4000 'BUILDLAND
4010 SY=RND(130):AE=0:GC=3:SC=0
4020 PCLS2:SCREEN1,0
4030 TX=0:OX=0:OY=163+RND(36):FY=OY
4040 FORI=1TO3
4050 TX=TX+INT(RND(74)/2)*2+12:TY=179+RND(12)
4060 GOSUB4500'DRAWLAND
4070 PUT(TX,TY)-(TX+11,TY-23),T,PSET
4080 PUT(TX,TY-24)-(TX+11,TY-36),M,PSET
4090 OX=TX+12:OY=TY
4100 NEXTI
4110 TX=255:TY=FY:GOSUB4500
4120 RETURN
4500 'DRAWLAND
4510 COLOR3,2
4520 NX=OX+RND(7)+1
4530 N=RND(0):SG=(N>.5)-(N<=.5)
4540 NY=OY+SG*(RND(13)+1)
4550 IFNX>TX  THENNX=TX
4560 IFNX=TX  THENNY=TY
4570 IFNY>191THENNY=191
4580 IFNY<163THENNY=163
4590 LINE(OX,OY)-(NX,NY),PSET
4600 IFNX=TX  THENRETURNELSEOX=NX:OY=NY:GOTO4520
5000 'DRAWSHAPE
5010 PMODE3,1:PCLS2
5020 DIMF(15)
5030 DRAW"C4BM0,4R2NR4D5R2NR2D1NR8D1NR2L2D5L2R6"
5040 GET(0,0)-(15,20),F,G
5050 'DRAWALIEN
5060 DIMA(6)
5070 DRAW"C1BM125,3F1R3NE1F1L6D1L6NU1R6D1R6U1
        R6NU1L6D1G1NF1L3G1"
5080 GET(118,1)-(139,11),A,G
5090 'SMARTBOMB
5100 DIMB(1)
5110 DRAW"C1BM152,3R1F1D2NG1R3NF1U2E1"
5120 GET(152,3)-(159,7),B,G
5130 'DRAWTOWER
5140 DIMT(7)
5150 DRAW"C3BM4,191U23R2D23U4R2U3R2D3R2ND4R2N
        D4U19L2ND19L2D3L2U3R4D9L2D3L2U3"
5160 GET(4,191)-(15,168),T,G
5170 'DRAWMAN
5180 DIMM(3)
5190 DRAW"C4BM4,156F3R1U4R2D4R2NE3L2D3R2D2E1R1ND3
        L2U1L4NU3L2D2H1D3"
5200 GET(4,167)-(15,155),M,G
5210 RETURN
6000 'MAIN
```

```
6010 GOSUB6160'INIT
6020 GOSUB5000'DRWSHP
6030 GOSUB4000'BUILDLAND
6040 GOSUB1000'FIGHTER
6050 GOSUB1190'ALIEN
6060 GOSUB3000'SCROLL
6070 IFGC<>0THENGOTO6040
6080 SCREEN0,0:CLS
6090 PRINT @201,"YOUR SCORE "
6100 PRINT @213,SC:PRINT @487,"<ENTER> TO RESTART";
6110 FORI=1TO20:NEXTI
6120 PRINT @213,"            ":
        PRINT @487,"                    ";
6130 FORI=1TO20:NEXTI
6140 IFPEEK(338)<>191THEN GOTO6100
6150 GOTO6030
6160 'INIT
7000 DIMBK(17)
7010 CLS
7020 GET(0,0)-(33,15),BK,G
7030 E$="V25;L8;1;L16;1;1 ;5;L8;1;5;L16;5;5;8;5"
7040 RESTORE
7050 FORI=32672TO32754
7060 PRINT @201,"            "
7070 READN:POKEI,N
7080 PRINT @201,"INITIALISING"
7090 SOUND200,1
7100 NEXTI
7110 DEFUSR0=32672
7120 RETURN
7130 'DATA
7140 DATA  16,142,0,48,142,24,16,166,16,238,17,239,
        16,238,19,239
7150 DATA  18,238,21,239,20,238,23,239,22,238,25,239,
        24,238,27,239
7160 DATA  26,238,29,239,28,238,31,239,30,238,1,239,
        132,238,3,239
7170 DATA  2,238,5,239,4,238,7,239,6,238,9,
        239,8,238,11,239
7180 DATA  10,238,13,239,12,230,15,231,14,167,15,
        48,136,32,49,63
7190 DATA  38,181,57
7200 CLS
7210 FORI=338TO345
7220 PRINTI;" = ",PEEK(I)
7230 NEXTI
7240 IF INKEY$=""THEN7240
7250 GOTO7200
```

HORIZONTAL SCROLL ROUTINE FOR ELIMINATOR

```
0E00                          ORG $7F80
0600                   SCSTRT EQU $1800
7F80 108E0030                 LDY #48        NUMBER OF LINES
7F84 8E1810                   LDX #SCSTRT+16 MIDDLE OF FIRST
7F87 A610              B@     LDA -16,X      *** MOVE
7F89 EE11                     LDU -15,X      ** LINE
7F8B EF10                     STU -16,X      *  ACROSS
7F8D EE13                     LDU -13,X      *
7F8F EF12                     STU -14,X
7F91 EE15                     LDU -11,X
7F93 EF14                     STU -12,X
7F95 EE17                     LDU -9,X
7F97 EF16                     STU -10,X
7F99 EE19                     LDU -7,X
7F9B EF18                     STU -8,X
7F9D EE1B                     LDU -5,X
7F9F EF1A                     STU -6,X
7FA1 EE1D                     LDU -3,X
7FA3 EF1C                     STU -4,X
7FA5 EE1F                     LDU -1,X
7FA7 EF1E                     STU -2,X
7FA9 EE01                     LDU 1,X
7FAB EF84                     STU ,X
7FAD EE03                     LDU 3,X
7FAF EF02                     STU 2,X
7FB1 EE05                     LDU 5,X
7FB3 EF04                     STU 4,X
7FB5 EE07                     LDU 7,X
7FB7 EF06                     STU 6,X
7FB9 EE09                     LDU 9,X
7FBB EF08                     STU 8,X
7FBD EE0B                     LDU 11,X
7FBF EF0A                     STU 10,X
7FC1 EE0D                     LDU 13,X
7FC3 EF0C                     STU 12,X       *
7FC5 E60F                     LDB 15,X       *
7FC7 E70E                     STB 14,X       **
7FC9 A70F                     STA 15,X       ***
7FCB 308820                   LEAX 32,X      NEXT LINE
7FCE 313F                     LEAY -1,Y      DECREMENT COUNT
7FD0 26B5                     BNE B@         LOOP IF NOT FINISHED
7FD2 39                       RTS

7FD3                          END
```

Meteor Storm

METEOR STORM places you at the controls of a space craft hurtling through the asteroid belt. On your display you see the pleasant view of the solar system as seen from mid space.

In the distance, you can see Saturn with its rings.

Suddenly command control warns you of a METEOR STORM' Before your very eyes, you see a meteor growing in size and sound as it heads directly for your ship' To confirm the desparate situation, your on board radar shows the approach of the asteroid.

METEOR STORM is 3-Dimensional computer gaming at its most exciting.

Running the program:

After you press (RUN) (ENTER), there is a short period of INITIALISATION time for the program to generate shapes and initialise variables. Then you will see the familiar console display come to life.

A cross hair in the middle of the screen marks the direction your laser beams is aimed at. To manipulate the beam, use the following controls:

"four arrows" to control up/down/left/right movement
"spacebar" to fire

Note that as with most BASIC programs, only one key can be pressed at a time. You may have noticed by now that your DRAGON computer is quite slow in its keyboard scanning; so long as any key is pressed it will think that the first recognised key remains pressed until you actually release all keys and repress the desired one.

The cross hair control features full wrap-around - in other words, going too far to the right will bring you to the left of the screen, and so on.

You can fire at any time, but missing the asteroid results only in the dull sound of the laser hurtling into the void. A hit on any solid part of the asteroid however will explode the asteriod into a big blast.

As you penetrate deeper into the METEOR STORM, they start coming at you faster and faster. How many can you shoot with only three lives?

Programming considerations:

This program makes extensive use of the graphic building facilities of the Dragon, such as CIRCLE, LINE PSET, LINE PRESET, DRAW, PAINT.

At the beginning of the program, the meteor shapes are drawn using the DRAW and relative DRAW facilities whereas the explosion shapes are drawn by using the PRESET and PSET facilities based on a special format read in through the DATA statement.

These meteor and explosion shapes that were drawn are stored into individual shape arrays using the GET command and will be retrieved later by the PUT command. Using the GET & PUT will only require the shape to be drawn once before you GET it. Further reference of the shape is achieved by using the PUT command which is much faster than redrawing it.

LINE, CIRCLE, PAINT commands are used to draw the console as well as the radar shapes. This is the only time in the entire program they are drawn!

Structure of the program:

```
10 - 20        Direct the control to bottom part of the
               program so that the BASIC system can find each
               subroutine faster as they are located as near
               the start of the program as possible.

1000 - 1190    Meteor Routine
                   generate meteor if none exist
                   delay as the meteor approaches
                   draw meteor shapes depending on which stage
                   if crash console
                      call crash routine (9100 - 9600)
                      blank meteor and radar

2000 - 2160    Test hitting target meteor
                 If spacebar not pressed
                   then return
                 else
                   if centre of cross not meteor
                       then return
                   else
                       flash between big and small explosion
                       blank explosion and return

               Useful variables are:
                 C1, C2  top position of crosshair
                 C3, C4  bottom position of crosshair
                 NS      number of lives
                 MC      meteor stage (range 0 - 7)
                 MX, MY  position of meteor

3000 - 3150    Spaceship routine
                   if arrow key pressed
                       then blank old cross
                            calculate new position
                            wrap around
                   draw cross

6000 - 6160    Main loop
                   draw shape
                   initialisation
                   game initialisation
               L1: draw saturn
                   meteor routine
                   test hitting target meteor
                   ship routine
                   if more ship left
                       then goto L1
                   else
                       display score and wait for restart

7000 - 7590    Initialisation
                   initialise string, numeric variables
                   draw all shapes and store into shape arrays
```

8000 - 9090 Shape routine
draw meteor, explosion shapes

9010 - 9600 Crash console routine
blank ship left in radar control
crash screen, flash and blank

Special notes:

As the program is using mode 1 graphic, the extensive use of graphic shapes makes the program very expensive in memory. Since your Dragon has about 32,000 bytes of RAM (Random Access Memory) you shouldn't have any problem of running short of memory.

However, it is helpful to know that mode 1 graphic use up two pages of graphic screen ie 3072 bytes of memory.

As the meteor is approaching the console, the volume of the sound increases by using the V(1-30) parameter in the PLAY instruction. This together with the increasing size of the meteor will give you a real feeling the the meteor is crashing towards you.

METEOR STORM

```
  10 'METEOR STORM
  20 GOTO6000'MAIN
1000 'METEOR
1010 IFMC<>0THEN1050
1020 IFRND(0)<.3THENRETURN
1030 MX=INT(RND(196)/2)*2+2:MY=INT(RND(100)/2)*2+2:
       MC=7
1040 RX=120:RY=174:DM=3
1050 IFDM<>0THENDM=DM-1:RETURNELSEDM=3
1060 ONMC GOTO1070,1080,1090,1100,1110,1120,1130
1070 PUT(MX,MY)-(MX+55,MY+57),BK,PSET:GOTO1140
1080 PUT(MX,MY)-(MX+55,MY+57),M5,PSET:GOTO1140
1090 PUT(MX+12,MY+12)-(MX+43,MY+43),M4,PSET:GOTO1140
1100 PUT(MX+16,MY+18)-(MX+39,MY+39),M3,PSET:GOTO1140
1110 PUT(MX+22,MY+22)-(MX+35,MY+35),M2,PSET:GOTO1140
1120 PUT(MX+24,MY+24)-(MX+31,MY+31),M1,PSET:GOTO1140
1130 PUT(MX+26,MY+26)-(MX+29,MY+29),M0,PSET
1140 IF(MC<>6ANDMC<>1)THEN
       PUT(RX,RY)-(RX+7,RY+7),BK,PSET:RX=RX-16
1150 MC=MC-1:IFMC>0THENPLAY"V"+STR$((7-MC)*5)+";
       L64;O"+STR$(RND(5))+";1"
1160 RO$="C4BM"+STR$(RX)+R$
1170 DRAWRO$
1180 IFMC<>0THENRETURN
1190 GOSUB9100'CRASH
1200 PUT(MX,MY)-(MX+55,MY+57),BK,PSET
1210 PUT(RX,RY)-(RX+7,RY+7),BK,PSET
1220 RETURN
2000 'CRASHTEST
2010 IFPEEK(345)<>K THENRETURN
2020 IFPPOINT(C1+2,C2+2)<>4THENRETURN
2030 EC=6:SC=SC+(8-MC)*20
2040 ES=2
2050 ONES GOTO2060,2070
2060 PUT(MX,MY)-(MX+57,MY+55),BE,PSET:GOTO2080
2070 PUT(MX,MY)-(MX+57,MY+55),SE,PSET
2080 ES=ES-1
2090 E1$="V30;O"+STR$(RND(3))+";L255"+";"+
       STR$(RND(12))
2100 PLAYE1$
2110 IFES<>0THEN2050
2120 EC=EC-1
2130 IFEC<>0THEN2040
2140 PUT(MX,MY)-(MX+57,MY+57),BK,PSET
2150 MC=0:PUT(RX,RY)-(RX+7,RY+7),BK,PSET
2160 RETURN
3000 'GUN
3010 DX=0:DY=0
3020 IFPEEK(341)=K THENDY=-8
3030 IFPEEK(342)=K THENDY=8
3040 IFPEEK(343)=K THENDX=-8
3050 IFPEEK(344)=K THENDX=8
3060 IF(DX=0ANDDY=0)THEN3140
```

```
3070 PUT(C1,C2)-(C3,C4),BK,PSET
3080 C1=C1+DX:C2=C2+DY
3090 IFC1<8THENC1=242
3100 IFC1>242THENC1=8
3110 IFC2<4THENC2=158
3120 IFC2>158THENC2=4
3130 C3=C1+5:C4=C2+5
3140 PUT(C1,C2)-(C3,C4),CR,PSET
3150 RETURN
6000 'MAIN
6010 GOSUB8000'DRAWSHAPE
6020 GOSUB7000'INIT
6030 GOSUB7500'GAMEINIT
6040 PUT(66,22)-(81,35),ST,PSET
6050 GOSUB1000'METEOR
6060 GOSUB2000'CRASH
6070 GOSUB3000'GUN
6080 IFNS<>0THEN6040
6090 CLS:SCREEN0,0:PRINT @201,"YOUR";CHR$(128);
     "SCORE ":PRINT @495,"TO";CHR$(128);"RESTART";
6100 PRINT @213,SC:PRINT @487,"<ENTER>";
6110 FORI=1TO100:NEXTI
6120 PRINT @213,"       ":PRINT @487,"        ";
6130 FORI=1TO100:NEXTI
6140 IFPEEK(338)<>191THEN6100
6150 PUT(C1,C2)-(C3,C4),BK,PSET
6160 PMODE1,1:SCREEN1,0:GOTO6030
7000 'INIT
7010 DIMCR(1):DIMST(2)
7020 S$="D2G2D4L2D4E2F2U2R2F2U4L2U4L2"
7030 R$=",174R2G2R6U2D4L4G2R4"
7040 K=223'KEY
7050 CLS:PMODE1,1:COLOR3,2:PCLS:SCREEN1,0
7060 DRAW"C1BM128,96R2H2G2F2"
7070 GET(126,94)-(131,99),CR,G
7080 'CORNERS
7090 COLOR3,2
7100 CIRCLE(10,10),10,,1,.5,.75
7110 CIRCLE(244,10),10,,1,.75,1
7120 CIRCLE(244,156),10,,1,0,.25
7130 CIRCLE(10,156),10,,1,.25,.5
7140 CIRCLE(10,178),8,,1,.25,.75
7150 CIRCLE(154,178),8,,1,.25,.75
7160 CIRCLE(130,178),8,,1,.75,.25
7170 CIRCLE(244,178),8,,1,.75,.25
7180 'FILL LINES
7190 LINE(10,164)-(242,164),PSET
7200 LINE(10,0)-(242,0),PSET
7210 LINE(0,10)-(0,154),PSET
7220 LINE(254,10)-(254,154),PSET
7230 LINE(10,168)-(128,168),PSET
7240 LINE(10,186)-(128,186),PSET
7250 LINE(154,186)-(242,186),PSET
7260 LINE(154,168)-(242,168),PSET
7270 'FILL EDGE
7280 PAINT(254,190),3,3
```

```
7290 PAINT(0,0),3,3
7300 PAINT(254,0),3,3
7310 'DRAW SATURN
7320 DRAW"C3BM70,22R6F2L10G2R8G2L6
     BM+12,0R2G2L2F2L10F2R6"
7330 GET(66,22)-(81,35),ST,G
7340 'CANNON
7350 DRAW"C1BM18,174L8F2R10D2R8BM-12,0L4F2R10
     BM-4,2L8G2R8"
7360 'GUN
7370 DRAW"C1BM128,96R2H2G2F2"
7380 GET(126,94)-(131,99),CR,G
7390 RETURN
7500 'GAMEINIT
7510 'SHIPLEFT
7520 COLOR4,2
7530 DRAW"BM230,172"+S$
7540 DRAW"BM208,172"+S$
7550 DRAW"BM186,172"+S$
7560 DRAW"BM164,172"+S$
7570 NS=4:MC=0:SC=0
7580 C1=126:C2=94:C3=131:C4=99
7590 RETURN
8000 'SHAPES
8010 'METEORSHAPES
8020 CLS:PRINT @201,"INITIALISING"
8030 PMODE1,1:COLOR4,2:PCLS
8040 DIMBK(45):DIMM0(1):DIMM1(1):DIMM2(2):
     DIMM3(6):DIMM4(12):DIMM5(40)
8050 T1$="L128;O2;12"
8060 GET(0,0)-(57,57),BK,G
8070 DRAW"BM2,40R3D2L3"
8080 PLAY T1$
8090 'SHAPE1
8100 PLAYT1$
8110 DRAW"BM2,22;R2F2L6F2R4D2"
8120 'SHAPE2
8130 PLAYT1$
8140 DRAW "BM6,0;R2F2L6G2R4E2F2F2L6H2G2L2F2
     R10D2G2L2U2L4"
8150 'SHAPE3
8160 DRAW"BM50,0;F2L4G8F10R6E4U10L6E2L4H2G8F8R6
     E2U2H6G2D4L6U4E2R2F2D4F2R2F2E4U2H2G2NL2E2R4U2"
8170 'SHAPE4
8180 PLAYT1$
8190 DRAW"BM92,0NR2G2NR8D2L4F2L6G2R6G2L4D2R8U2
     R4NU2F2L2H2G2D2L6D2R6F2L8F2R6D2L6D2R2D2R8N
     U4D4L2R6U2L10R14U2L4U6F2U2E2R8G6R2U18F2
     D14U4E2L6U2R6H4L2U4L6E2D8L2D4NL2U4E2U6L6"
8200 'SHAPE5
8210 PLAYT1$
8220 DRAW"BM164,0;R1;BM-1,2;R3;BM-3,2;R7;BM-7,2;R9;
     BM-11,2;R13;BM-13,2;R21;BM-23,2;R5;BM+3,0;
     R27;BM-37,2;R5;BM+17,0;R13;BM-49,2;R1;
     BM+11,0;R5;BM+9,0;R5;BM+7,0;R11"
8230 DRAW"BM-49,2;R3;BM+7,0;R5;BM+5,0;R1;BM+9,0;
```

```
        R1;BM+9,0;R11;BM-53,2;R15;BM+17,0;R5;BM+7,0
        ;R11;BM-55,2;R13;BM+9,0;R5;BM+19,0;R7;
        BM-53,2;R11;BM+9,0;R5;BM+11,0;R1;BM+9,0;R5"
8240 DRAW"BM-51,2;R11;BM+9,0;R3;BM+13,0;R1;BM+7,0;
        R7;BM-49,2;R9;BM+9,0;R1;BM+9,0;R1;BM+5,0;R1;
        BM+3,0;R9;BM-45,2;R7;BM+7,0;R3;BM+9,0;R1;
        BM+9,0;R11"
8250 DRAW"BM-47,2;R9;BM+5,0;R1;BM+9,0;R3;BM+9,0;
        R11;BM-45,2;R7;BM+13,0;R5;BM+9,0;R9;BM-43,2;
        R9;BM+11,0;R7;BM+7,0;R7;BM-39,2;R11;BM+19,0;
        R9;BM-39,2;R15;BM+15,0;R7;BM-35,2;R15;
        BM+11,0;R9"
8260 DRAW"BM-35,2;R33;BM-35,2;R35;BM-37,2;R9;
        BM+7,0;R19;BM-9,2;R7;BM-7,2;R5;BM-7,2;R5"
8270 'GETSHAPE
8280 PLAYT1$
8290 GET(2,40)-(5,43),M0,G
8300 GET(0,22)-(7,29),M1,G
8310 GET(0,0)-(13,13),M2,G
8320 GET(40,0)-(63,21),M3,G
8330 GET(80,0)-(111,31),M4,G
8340 GET(142,0)-(197,57),M5,G
8350 'EXPLODESHAPES
8360 PCLS:RESTORE
8370 DIMSE(40):DIMBE(40)
8380 PLAYT1$
8390 L=16:PX=88:PY=92
8400 GOSUB8470
8410 L=28:PX=140:PY=80
8420 GOSUB8470
8430 GET(74,80)-(131,135),SE,G
8440 GET(142,80)-(199,135),BE,G
8450 PLAY"L16;O4;1"
8460 RETURN
8470 'DRAW EXPLODE
8480 FOR I=1TOL
8490 M=1'ONMODE
8500 Y=PY
8510 X=PX
8520 READD'READ DATA
8530 M=-M
8540 IF D=-1 THENGOTO8620
8550 IF D=0 THENGOTO8520
8560 FORJ=1TOD
8570 IFM=-1 THENPRESET(X,Y)ELSEPSET(X,Y)
8580 X=X+2
8590 PLAYT1$
8600 NEXTJ
8610 GOTO8520
8620 PY=PY+2
8630 NEXTI
8640 RETURN
8650 DATA-1
8660 DATA4,5,-1
8670 DATA4,1,3,1,-1
8680 DATA1,3,2,1,3,3,-1
```

```
8690 DATA0,2,4,1,6,1,-1
8700 DATA4,1,2,2,2,1,2,1,-1
8710 DATA0,2,2,1,1,1,1,2,1,1,2,1,-1
8720 DATA0,1,3,8,2,2,-1
8730 DATA0,1,2,1,2,6,4,1,-1
8740 DATA0,1,2,1,1,8,3,1,-1
8750 DATA1,1,1,2,1,2,2,1,2,1,2,1,-1
8760 DATA1,1,5,3,3,1,1,2,-1
8770 DATA2,4,5,3,1,1,-1
8780 DATA7,2,6,1,-1
8790 DATA8,2,3,3,-1
8800 DATA9,5,-1
8810 'BIGEXPLODE
8820 DATA13,3,-1
8830 DATA1,2,8,2,3,2,-1
8840 DATA3,1,6,1,7,2,7,1,-1
8850 DATA3,5,14,3,1,1,-1
8860 DATA 2,2,4,1,5,4,6,2,-1
8870 DATA2,1,10,1,4,1,6,2,-1
8880 DATA2,1,4,3,16,1,-1
8890 DATA6,1,2,2,3,1,11,3,-1
8900 DATA5,1,7,2,1,6,6,2,-1
8910 DATA5,1,6,1,8,2,-1
8920 DATA2,1,6,1,1,1,11,1,5,1,-1
8930 DATA1,1,6,1,5,1,9,1,3,1,-1
8940 DATA1,1,6,1,4,1,4,1,8,1,-1
8950 DATA1,1,6,1,4,1,5,1,7,1,-1
8960 DATA1,2,6,1,3,1,5,1,5,1,-1
8970 DATA2,2,1,1,3,1,9,1,5,1,-1
8980 DATA3,1,1,1,5,1,6,1,5,2,-1
8990 DATA5,1,5,2,10,2,-1
9000 DATA5,1,6,2,6,1,5,1,-1
9010 DATA5,2,6,2,6,1,5,1,-1
9020 DATA6,3,11,1,6,2,-1
9030 DATA17,3,6,1,3,1,-1
9040 DATA25,1,3,1,-1
9050 DATA5,1,5,1,4,1,7,2,-1
9060 DATA5,1,6,4,6,2,2,1,-1
9070 DATA6,1,11,1,7,1,-1
9080 DATA6,2,5,1,3,1,7,1,-1
9090 DATA8,2,4,3,7,1,-1
9100 'CRASH
9110 COLOR4,2
9120 ONNS GOTO 9130,9140,9150,9160
9130 PUT(160,172)-(169,185),BK,PSET:GOTO9170
9140 PUT(182,172)-(191,185),BK,PSET:GOTO9170
9150 PUT(204,172)-(213,185),BK,PSET:GOTO9170
9160 PUT(226,172)-(235,185),BK,PSET
9170 NS=NS-1
9180 LINE(128,96)-(100,88),PSET
9190 LINE-(80,64),PSET
9200 LINE-(44,44),PSET
9210 LINE-(26,24),PSET
9220 LINE-(4,12),PSET
9230 LINE(136,96)-(160,94),PSET
9240 LINE-(178,114),PSET
```

```
9250 LINE-(208,118),PSET
9260 LINE-(228,128),PSET
9270 LINE-(246,152),PSET
9280 LINE(128,102)-(140,118),PSET
9290 LINE-(138,140),PSET
9300 LINE-(134,160),PSET
9310 LINE(128,96)-(78,116),PSET
9320 LINE-(56,140),PSET
9330 LINE-(28,150),PSET
9340 LINE-(10,152),PSET
9350 LINE(126,90)-(124,74),PSET
9360 LINE-(130,54),PSET
9370 LINE-(126,30),PSET
9380 LINE-(134,6),PSET
9390 LINE(136,86)-(162,64),PSET
9400 LINE-(190,54),PSET
9410 LINE-(208,34),PSET
9420 LINE-(240,10),PSET
9430 HI$="V30;O1;L"+STR$(16*RND(3))+";"+STR$(RND(12))
9440 CC=10
9450 SCREEN1,1:PLAYHI$
9460 SCREEN1,0:PLAYHI$
9470 CC=CC-1:IFCC<>0THEN9450
9480 LINE(128,96)-(100,88),PRESET
9490 LINE-(80,64),PRESET:LINE-(44,44),PRESET:
       LINE-(26,24),PRESET:LINE-(4,12),PRESET
9500 LINE(136,96)-(160,94),PRESET
9510 LINE-(178,114),PRESET:LINE-(208,118),PRESET:
       LINE-(228,128),PRESET:LINE-(246,152),PRESET
9520 LINE(128,102)-(140,118),PRESET
9530 LINE-(138,140),PRESET:LINE-(134,160),PRESET
9540 LINE(128,96)-(78,116),PRESET
9550 LINE-(56,140),PRESET:LINE-(28,150),PRESET:
       LINE-(10,152),PRESET
9560 LINE(126,90)-(124,74),PRESET
9570 LINE-(130,54),PRESET:LINE-(126,30),PRESET:
       LINE-(134,6),PRESET
9580 LINE(136,86)-(162,64),PRESET
9590 LINE-(190,54),PRESET:LINE-(208,34),PRESET:
       LINE-(240,10),PRESET
9600 RETURN
```

Car Race

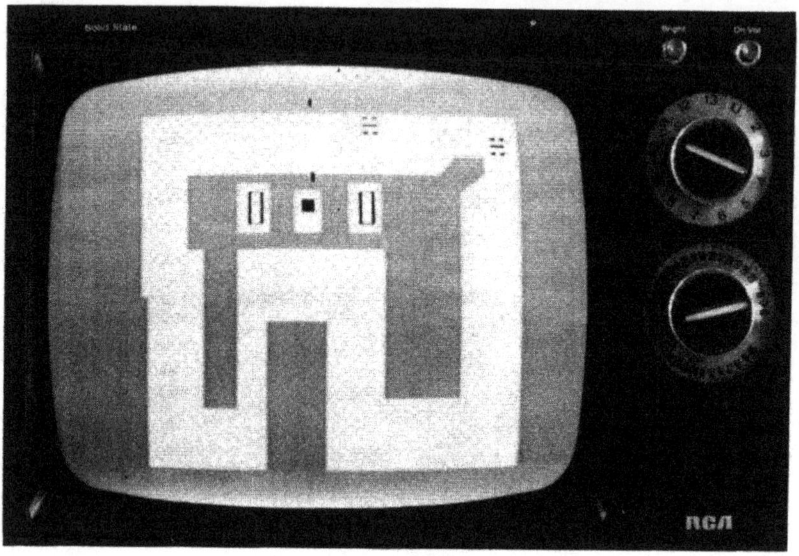

Race your cars around the track trying to be the first to complete ten laps. This game is for two people each having control of one of the cars. The game is best played using two joysticks but can be run from the keyboard if desired.

You must wait for the green light before you start moving your car or you will be penalised. The cars cannot crash but you will lose valuable time running into walls or the other persons car. In fact it is a good idea to try and stay in front of the other car to make it harder for it to turn without crashing. Finally you must traverse the track in an anti-clockwise direction or your laps will not be counted.

The cars are controlled by moving the joystick in the direction that you want the car to travel.

CAR RACE

```
  10 DIM A1(6),A2(6),A4(6),A5(6),B1(6),B2(6),B4(6),
       B5(6),RL(9),GL(9)
  20 DIM X(13),Y(13)
  30 PMODE 3,1:SCREEN 1,0:COLOR 2,1:PCLS(2)
  40 A$="R2D1L2"
  50 A$="BM10,10;"+A$+"BM10,18;"+A$+"BM16,10;"+A$
       +"BM16,18;"+A$+"BM10,14;R9D1L9"
  60 DRAW "C3;"+A$:GET(10,10)-(30,20),A2,G:
       GET(0,10)-(20,20),A4,G
  70 PCLS(2):DRAW"C4;"+A$:GET(10,10)-(30,20),B2,G:
       GET(0,10)-(20,20),B4,G
  80 A$="BM10,10;D4;BM10,16;D4;BM18,16;D4;BM18,10;D4;
       BM14,10;D10"
  90 PCLS(2):DRAW"C3;"+A$:GET(10,0)-(20,20),A5,G:
       GET(10,10)-(20,30),A1,G
 100 DRAW"C4;"+A$:GET(10,0)-(20,20),B5,G:
       GET(10,10)-(20,30),B1,G
 110 PCLS(2):DRAW"C4;BM124,54;D6R6U6L6":
       PAINT(128,56),4,4:GET(120,50)-(136,70),RL,G
 120 PCLS(2):DRAW"C1;BM124,60;D6R6U6L6":
       PAINT(128,64),1,1:GET(120,50)-(136,70),GL,G
 130 FOR I=1 TO 9:READ X(I),Y(I):NEXT I
 140 DATA 18,103,18,190,90,190,90,115,130,115,130,
       190,250,190,250,9,14,9
 150 PCLS(1):DRAW"C2":LINE(14,9)-(14,103),PSET
 160 FOR I=1 TO 9:LINE-(X(I),Y(I)),PSET:NEXT I
 170 FOR I=1 TO 13:READ X(I),Y(I):NEXT I
 180 DATA 50,80,50,160,75,160,75,80,165,80,165,155,
       215,155,215,50,230,40,230,30,210,30,200,40,40,40
 190 LINE(40,40)-(40,80),PSET
 200 FOR I=1 TO 13:LINE-(X(I),Y(I)),PSET:NEXT I
 210 PAINT(30,50),2,2
 220 L1=0:L2=0:S1=0:S2=0
 230 GOSUB 1000:' LAP COUNTER
 240 GOSUB 1500:' STARTER
 250 RH=JOYSTK(0):RV=JOYSTK(1):
       LH=JOYSTK(2):LV=JOYSTK(3)
 260 GOSUB2000
 270 GOTO 250
1000 DRAW"C2;":LINE(145,46)-(163,70),PSET,BF:
       LINE(75,46)-(93,70),PSET,BF
1010 IL=0:NN=L1:DRAW"BM80,50;C3"
1020 IF NN<0 THEN NN=0
1030 ON NN+1 GOTO 1040,1050,1060,1070,1080,1090,1100,1110,
       1120,1130
1040 DRAW"D16R8U16L8":GOTO1140
1050 DRAW"BM+8,+0;D16":GOTO1140
1060 DRAW"R8D8L8D8R8":GOTO1140
1070 DRAW"R8D8NL8D8L8":GOTO1140
1080 DRAW"D8R4NU4NR4D8":GOTO1140
1090 DRAW"NR8D8R8D8L8":GOTO1140
1100 DRAW"NR8D16R8U8L8":GOTO1140
1110 DRAW"R8D16":GOTO1140
```

```
1120 DRAW"D16R8U8NL8U8L8":GOTO1140
1130 DRAW"ND8R8D8NL8D8L8"
1140 IL=IL+1:IF IL=2 GOTO1160
1150 DRAW"BM150,50;C4;":NN=L2:GOTO1020
1160 IF L1=9 GOTO 1180
1170 IF L2<9 THEN RETURN
1180 FOR JS=1 TO 4:SOUND 50,1:SOUND 150,2:NEXT JS
1190 I$=INKEY$:IF I$="S" THEN GOTO 220 ELSE GOTO 1190
1200 RETURN
1500 PUT(110,50)-(126,70),RL,PSET
1510 DRAW"BM120,1;C4;D3;BM120,40;D4"
1520 X1=155:X2=155
1530 ON RND(2) GOTO 1540,1550
1540 Y1=10:Y2=20:GOTO1560
1550 Y2=10:Y1=20
1560 PUT(X1,Y1)-(X1+20,Y1+10),A2,PSET:
          PUT(X2,Y2)-(X2+20,Y2+10),B2,PSET
1570 RD=RND(50)
1580 FOR I=1 TO 50+RD
1590 RH=JOYSTK(0):RV=JOYSTK(1):
          LH=JOYSTK(2):LV=JOYSTK(3)
1600 GOSUB 2000
1610 NEXT I
1620 IF X1<120 THEN S1=0 ELSE S1=1:L1=-1
1630 IF X2<120 THEN S2=0 ELSE S2=1:L2=-1
1640 PUT(110,50)-(126,70),GL,PSET
1650 RETURN
2000 ' MOVE CARS'
2010 ' CAR ONE'
2020 IF LH<LV THEN GOTO2050
2030 IF LH+LV<63 THEN D=1 ELSE D=4
2040 GOTO2060
2050 IF LH+LV<63 THEN D=2 ELSE D=5
2060 IF S1>0 GOTO 2100
2070 IF D<>2 GOTO 2100
2080 IF X1<120 GOTO 2290
2090 S1=1:L1=-1:GOTO2290
2100 ON D GOTO 2140,2120,2290,2130,2110
2110 P=X1+1:Q=Y1+20:R=X1+9:S=Y1+20:PQ=X1+4:
          RS=Y1+15:GOTO2150
2120 P=X1-10:Q=Y1+1:R=X1-10:S=Y1+9:PQ=X1-10:
          RS=Y1+1:GOTO2150
2130 P=X1+20:Q=Y1+1:R=X1+20:S=Y1+9:PQ=X1+15:
          RS=Y1+5:GOTO2150
2140 P=X1+1:Q=Y1-10:R=X1+9:S=Y1-10:PQ=X1+4:RS=Y1-5
2150 ' CHECK POINT AHEAD'
2160 IF QA<0 THEN QA=1:GOTO 2290
2170 IF PPOINT(P,Q)<>2 GOTO 2260ELSE
          IF PPOINT(R,S)<>2 GOTO 2260ELSE
          IF PPOINT(PQ,RS)<>2GOTO2260
2180 ON D GOTO 2190,2200,2290,2210,2220
2190 Y1=Y1-10:PUT(X1,Y1)-(X1+10,Y1+20),A1,PSET:
          GOTO2230
2200 X1=X1-10:PUT(X1,Y1)-(X1+20,Y1+10),A2,PSET:
          GOTO2230
2210 X1=X1+10:PUT(X1-10,Y1)-(X1+10,Y1+10),A4,PSET:
```

```
        GOTO2230
2220 Y1=Y1+10:PUT(X1,Y1-10)-(X1+10,Y1+10),A5,PSET
2230 IF Y1>35 GOTO 2290
2240 IF ABS(X1-105)>3 GOTO 2290
2250 IF D=2 THEN SOUND 160,2:L1=L1+1:GOSUB 1000
2260 PLAY"T255;A#;A;A-;A#;A;A-"
2270 QA=-1
2280 ' CAR TWO'
2290 IF RH<RV THEN IF RH+RV<63 THEN D=2:GOTO2310 :
        ELSE D=5:GOTO2310
2300 IF RH+RV<63 THEN D=1 ELSE D=4
2310 IF S2>0 GOTO 2350
2320 IF D<>2 GOTO 2350
2330 IF X2<120 THEN RETURN
2340 S2=1:L2=-1:RETURN
2350 ON D GOTO 2360,2370,2530,2380,2390
2360 P=X2+1:Q=Y2-10:R=X2+9:S=Y2-10:PQ=X2+4:RS=Y2-5:
        GOTO2400
2370 P=X2-10:Q=Y2+1:R=X2-10:S=Y2+9:PQ=X2-5:RS=Y2+5:
        GOTO2400
2380 P=X2+20:Q=Y2+1:R=X2+20:S=Y2+9:PQ=X2+15:RS=Y2+5:
        GOTO 2400
2390 P=X2+1:Q=Y2+20:R=X2+9:S=Y2+20:PQ=X2+4:RS=Y2+15
2400 ' PT AHEAD'
2410 IF QB<0 THEN QB=1:GOTO2530
2420 IF PPOINT(P,Q)<>2 THEN GOTO 2510 ELSE
        IF PPOINT(R,S)<>2 THEN GOTO 2510ELSE
        IF PPOINT(PQ,RS)<>2GOTO2510
2430 ON D GOTO 2440,2450,2530,2460,2470
2440 Y2=Y2-10:PUT(X2,Y2)-(X2+10,Y2+20),B1,PSET:
        GOTO2480
2450 X2=X2-10:PUT(X2,Y2)-(X2+20,Y2+10),B2,PSET:
        GOTO2480
2460 X2=X2+10:PUT(X2-10,Y2)-(X2+10,Y2+10),B4,PSET:
        GOTO2480
2470 Y2=Y2+10:PUT(X2,Y2-10)-(X2+10,Y2+10),B5,PSET
2480 IF Y2>35 GOTO2530
2490 IF ABS(X2-105)>3 GOTO 2530
2500 IF D=2 THEN SOUND 160,2:L2=L2+1:GOSUB1000
2510 PLAY"T255;A#;A;A-;A#;A;A-"
2520 QB=-1
2530 RETURN
2540 GOTO 2540
```

Ten Pin Bowling

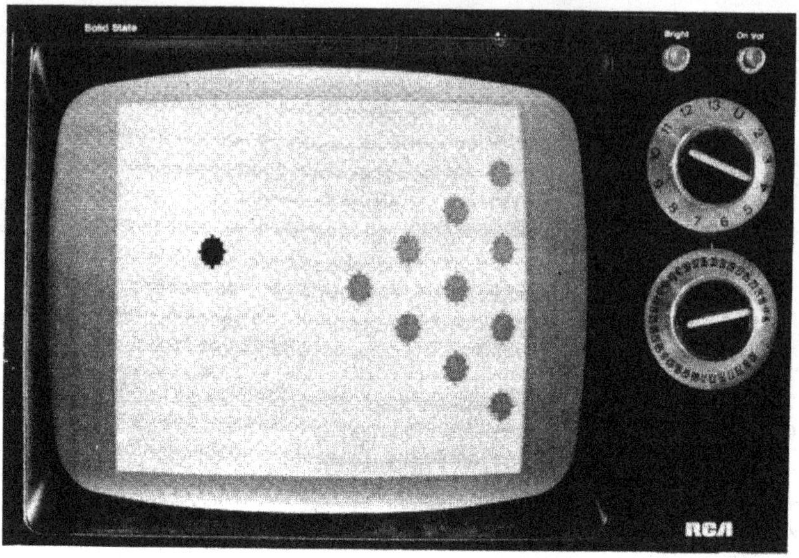

Copyright (c) Colin Carter

How well can you do at ten pin bowls on your DRAGON. The game can be played by one or two people at a time with the computer keeping track of the scores. The scoring is done in the proper ten bin bowling fashion, and it even gives you an 11th frame if you are good enough to deserve one.

When the game is run you will see the pins set up on the right of the screen. Your ball will appear on the left and move up and down the screen until you hit the SPACE key, when it will bowl down the alley at the pins. Just like in the real game, a direct hit on the front pin will not give you a strike, so you will have to practice to get your technique just right.

Program structure

5 - 260		Initialization
270 - 910		main loop
	290 - 320	all pins exist except pin 4
	340 - 370	set up the pins
	400	no pin hit yet
	410 - 480	move players ball up and down and wait for space key
	490 - 550	move ball forward to the pins
	560 - 600	move the ball through the pins
	610 - 770	score
	780 - 910	prepare for next turn
1000 - 1070		move ball
2000 - 2540		track "ball - pin" hits
3000 - 3040		move ball
4000 - 4310		compute score and display data
4320 - 4340		end/restart game
4500 - 4630		draw digits for numbers
4700 - 4730		draw frame indicator
5000 - 5450		track "pin - pin" hits

Variables

EX()	Defines the status of all the pins
W()	Data for angle of impact and rebound
F	Frame counter
S	Ball one / Ball two indicator
T()	Frame scores
PO()	Positions of pins
HT()	Pin hit or not indicators
B()	Ball drawing
BL()	Blank drawing
X,Y	Co-ordinates of the ball

TEN PIN BOWLING

```
 10 PCLEAR 4
 20 DIM BL(19,19),B(19,19),PI(19,19),PO(2,11),
      HT(11),EX(11),W(16)
 30 PMODE 1,1:PCLS(2):COLOR 4,2
 40 GET(1,1)-(20,20),B,G
 50 CIRCLE(10,10),9,4
 60 PAINT(10,10),4,4
 70 GET(1,1)-(20,20),BL,G
 80 PCLS(2)
 90 CIRCLE(10,10),9,1
100 PAINT(10,10),1,1
110 GET(1,1)-(20,20),PI,G
120 FOR P=-5 TO 5
130 Q=P+6
140 READ PO(1,Q):READ PO(2,Q)
150 NEXT P
160 DATA 240,155,240,115,210,135,100,100,180,115,
      150,95,180,75,210,95,210,55,240,75,240,35
170 FOR I=1 TO 16:READ W(I):NEXT I
180 DATA -2,-2,0,0,0,0,2,2,-2,-2,0,0,0,0,2,2
190 CLS:PRINT @200,"HOW MANY PLAYERS ?";
200 I$=INKEY$:IF I$="" GOTO 200
210 I=VAL(I$):IF I=0 GOTO 200
220 IF I>2 GOTO 200
230 T(1)=0:T(2)=0:CLS
240 NP=I
250 N=1:F=1:S=1:GOSUB4000
260 F=1:N=1:EN=-1:TN=1
270 REM: BEGIN A BOWL
280 S=0
290 FOR I=1 TO 11
300 EX(I)=+1
310 NEXT I
320 EX(4)=-1
330 PMODE 1,1:PCLS(2):SCREEN 1,0
340 FOR I=1 TO 11
350 IF I=4 GOTO 370
360 PUT(PO(1,I)-9,PO(2,I)-9)-
      (PO(1,I)+10,PO(2,I)+10),PI,PSET
370 NEXT I
380 S=S+1
390 X0=15:X1=X0-9:X2=X0+10:Y0=12:DY=+5
400 FOR I=1 TO 11:HT(I)=10:NEXT I
410 Y1=Y0-9:Y2=Y0+10
420 PUT(X1,Y1)-(X2,Y2),BL,PSET
430 I$=INKEY$:IF I$<>"" GOTO 490
440 Y0=Y0+DY
450 IF Y0>180 THEN DY=-DY:GOTO440
460 IF Y0<15 THEN DY=-DY:GOTO440
470 PUT(X1,Y1)-(X2,Y2),B,PSET
480 GOTO 410
490 FOR X=X0-2 TO 135 STEP 5
500 PUT(X1,Y1)-(X2,Y2),B,PSET
```

```
510 X1=X-9:X2=X+10
520 PUT(X1,Y1)-(X2,Y2),BL,PSET
530 NEXT X
540 ZN=INT(ABS(95-Y0)*0.2)+1
550 IF Y0>95 THEN ZN=-ZN
560 FOR PS=1 TO 12
570 GOSUB 5000
580 GOSUB 2000
590 GOSUB 1000
600 NEXT PS
610 I=1:SC=0
620 IF EX(I)<0 THEN SC=SC+1
630 I=I+1:IF I=4 GOTO 630
640 IF I<12 GOTO 620
650 IF S=2 GOTO 740
660 B1=SC
670 IF F<11 THEN T(N)=T(N)+B1
680 IF ST(N)>0 THEN T(N)=T(N)+B1:ST(N)=ST(N)-1:
     IF ST(N)>1 GOTO 680
690 IF B1<10 GOTO 720
700 IF F<11 THEN ST(N)=ST(N)+2:FOR I=0 TO 14:
     SOUND 180+I,1:NEXT I:FOR I=1 TO 7:
     SOUND 196,2:NEXT I
710 GOTO 780
720 IF F<11 GOTO 380
730 IF ST(N)>0 GOTO 380 ELSE GOTO 780
740 B2=SC-B1
750 IF F<11 THEN T(N)=T(N)+B2
760 IF ST(N)>0 THEN T(N)=T(N)+B2:ST(N)=ST(N)-1
770 IF B1+B2=10 THEN IF F<11 THEN ST(N)=ST(N)+1:
     FOR I=1 TO 3:SOUND120,2:SOUND160,1:NEXT I
780 'WHO'S TURN ?
790 IF F>9 GOTO 820
800 IF N<NP THEN N=NP:GOTO900
810 F=F+1:N=1:GOTO900
820 IF F>10 GOTO 840
830 IF N<NP THEN N=NP:GOTO900
840 IF N<NP THEN N=NP:IF ST(N)>0 GOTO 900 :
     ELSE GOTO 850
850 N=1:F=F+1
860 IF ST(N)>0 GOTO 900
870 N=NP
880 IF ST(N)>0 GOTO 900
890 EN=+1
900 GOSUB 4000
910 GOTO 270
1000 IF X2>254 THEN RETURN
1010 FOR I=1 TO 3
1020 PUT(X1,Y1)-(X2,Y2),B,PSET
1030 X1=X1+10:X2=X2+10
1040 IF X2>254 THEN RETURN
1050 PUT(X1,Y1)-(X2,Y2),BL,PSET
1060 NEXT I
1070 RETURN
2000 IF PS>3 GOTO 2480
2010 ON PS GOTO 2020,2080,2250
```

```
2020 IF ABS(HT(6))>1 THEN RETURN
2030 IF HT(6)=1 THEN HT(5)=1:ET=5:GOTO2060
2040 IF HT(6)=0 THEN HT(8)=0:ET=8:GOTO2060
2050 IF HT(6)=-1 THEN HT(7)=-1:ET=7:GOTO2060
2060 GOSUB 3000
2070 RETURN
2080 IF HT(5)>1 GOTO 2160
2090 ON (HT(5)+3) GOTO 2100,2110,2120,2130
2100 ET=7:GOTO2140
2110 ET=8:GOTO2140
2120 ET=2:GOTO2140
2130 ET=3
2140 HT(ET)=HT(5)
2150 GOSUB 3000
2160 IF HT(7)>2 THEN RETURN
2170 ON (HT(7)+3) GOTO 2240,2180,2190,2200,2210
2180 ET=9:GOTO2220
2190 ET=10:GOTO2220
2200 ET=8:GOTO2220
2210 ET=5
2220 HT(ET)=HT(7)
2230 GOSUB 3000
2240 RETURN
2250 IF HT(9)>2 GOTO 2320
2260 ON (HT(9)+3) GOTO 2320,2270,2320,2280,2290
2270 ET=11:GOTO2300
2280 ET=10:GOTO2300
2290 ET=8
2300 HT(ET)=HT(9)
2310 GOSUB 3000
2320 IF HT(8)>2 GOTO 2400
2330 ON (HT(8)+3) GOTO 2340,2350,2400,2360,2370
2340 ET=9:GOTO2380
2350 ET=10:GOTO2380
2360 ET=2:GOTO2380
2370 ET=3
2380 HT(ET)=HT(8)
2390 GOSUB 3000
2400 IF HT(3)>1 THEN RETURN
2410 ON (HT(3)+3) GOTO 2420,2430,2470,2440
2420 ET=8:GOTO2450
2430 ET=2:GOTO2450
2440 ET=1
2450 HT(ET)=HT(3)
2460 GOSUB 3000
2470 RETURN
2480 IF HT(1)=-2 THEN HT(2)=-2:ET=2:GOSUB 3000
2490 IF HT(2)=2 THEN HT(1)=2:ET=1:GOSUB 3000
2500 IF HT(2)=-2 THEN HT(10)=-2:ET=10:GOSUB3000
2510 IF HT(10)=2 THEN HT(2)=2:ET=2:GOSUB 3000
2520 IF HT(10)=-2 THEN HT(11)=-2:ET=11:GOSUB3000
2530 IF HT(11)=2 THEN HT(10)=2:ET=10:GOSUB3000
2540 RETURN
3000 IF EX(ET)<0 THEN RETURN
3010 EX(ET)=-1
3020 PUT(PO(1,ET)-9,PO(2,ET)-9)-
```

```
        (PO(1,ET)+10,PO(2,ET)+10),B,PSET
3030 SOUND 235,1
3040 RETURN
4000 PMODE 1,3:PCLS
4010 SCREEN 1,0
4020 FOR QS=1 TO NP
4030 IC=INT(T(QS)*0.01+0.01)
4040 YD=30
4050 IF IC=0 GOTO 4080
4060 XD=54+(QS-1)*100
4070 GOSUB 4500
4080 IC=INT(T(QS)*0.1+0.01)-10*IC
4090 XD=74+(QS-1)*100
4100 GOSUB 4500
4110 IC=T(QS)-10*IC
4120 IF IC>99 THEN IC=IC-INT(T(QS)/100+0.01)*100
4130 XD=94+(QS-1)*100
4140 GOSUB 4500
4150 NEXT QS
4160 YD=100:F2=F
4170 IF NP=1 THEN XD=54:GOTO4200
4180 IF N=1 THEN XD=54:F2=F:GOTO 4200
4190 XD=154
4200 IF EN>0 GOTO 4320
4210 GOSUB 4700
4220 XD=XD+20
4230 IC=INT(F2*0.1+.01)
4240 GOSUB 4500
4250 XD=XD+20
4260 IC=F2-IC*10
4270 GOSUB 4500
4280 SCREEN 1,0
4290 FOR I=1 TO 2000:NEXT I
4300 SOUND 150,2
4310 RETURN
4320 SOUND 150,2:SOUND 180,1
4330 EN=-1
4340 I$=INKEY$:IF I$<>"S" GOTO 4340 ELSE GOTO 190
4500 DRAW"BM"+STR$(XD)+","+STR$(YD)+";"
4510 ON (IC+1) GOTO 4520,4530,4540,4550,4560,4570,
        4580,4590,4600,4610
4520 A$="L8D16R8U16":GOTO 4620
4530 A$="D16":GOTO 4620
4540 A$="NL8D8L8D8R8":GOTO4620
4550 A$="NL8D8NL8D8L8":GOTO4620
4560 A$="D8ND8L8U8":GOTO4620
4570 A$="L8D8R8D8L8":GOTO 4620
4580 A$="L8D16R8U8L8":GOTO4620
4590 A$="NL8D16":GOTO 4620
4600 A$="L8D16R8U8NL8U8":GOTO4620
4610 A$="ND16L8D8R8"
4620 DRAW A$
4630 RETURN
4700 DRAW"BM"+STR$(XD)+","+STR$(YD)+";"+"L8D8NR6D8"
4710 IF ST(1)>0 THEN DRAW"BM110,38;C4;NU8NL8ND8NR8" :
        ELSE DRAW"BM110,38;C1;NU8ND8NL8NR8"
```

```
4720 IF ST(2)>0 THEN DRAW"BM210,38;C4;NU8ND8NR8NL8" :
        ELSE DRAW"BM210,38;C1;NL8NU8NR8ND8;C4"
4730 RETURN
5000 IF PS>4 THEN RETURN
5010 ON PS GOTO 5020,5090,5190,5330
5020 IF ABS(ZN)>4 THEN RETURN
5030 IF EX(6)<0 THEN RETURN
5040 OT=6
5050 IF ABS(ZN)=4 THEN H=2:GOTO5080
5060 IF ABS(ZN)=3 THEN H=1:GOTO5080
5070 H=ABS(ZN)-1
5080 HT(6)=H*SGN(ZN):GOTO5420
5090 IF ABS(ZN)>8 THEN RETURN
5100 IF ZN>0 THEN OT=7 ELSE OT=5
5110 IF EX(OT)<0 THEN RETURN
5120 A=ABS(ZN)
5130 IF A=8 THEN H=2:GOTO5180
5140 IF A>5 THEN H=1:GOTO5180
5150 IF A<3 THEN H=-2:GOTO5180
5160 IF A=3 THEN H=-1:GOTO 5180
5170 H=0
5180 HT(OT)=H*SGN(ZN):GOTO5420
5190 IF ABS(ZN)>12 THEN RETURN
5200 IF ABS(ZN)=1 THEN RETURN
5210 IF ABS(ZN)<5 THEN OT=8:GOTO5240
5220 IF ZN>0 THEN OT=9:GOTO5240
5230 OT=3
5240 A=ABS(ZN)
5250 IF EX(OT)<0 THEN RETURN
5260 ON (A-1) GOTO 5280,5280,5290,5310,5300,5280,5270,
        5270,5280,5280,5290
5270 H=0:GOTO5320
5280 H=1:GOTO5320
5290 H=2: GOTO 5320
5300 H=-1:GOTO 5320
5310 H=-2
5320 HT(OT)=H*SGN(ZN):GOTO5420
5330 IF ABS(ZN)>16 THEN RETURN
5340 A=ABS(ZN)
5350 IF ZN<0 GOTO 5380
5360 IF ZN>8 THEN OT=11:GOTO5400
5370 OT=10:GOTO5400
5380 IF A>8 THEN OT=1:GOTO5400
5390 OT=2
5400 IF EX(OT)<0 THEN RETURN
5410 HT(OT)=W(A)*SGN(ZN)
5420 EX(OT)=-1
5430 PUT(PO(1,OT)-9,PO(2,OT)-9)-
        (PO(1,OT)+10,PO(2,OT)+10),B,PSET
5440 SOUND 225,1
5450 RETURN
5460 END
```

Flight Simulator

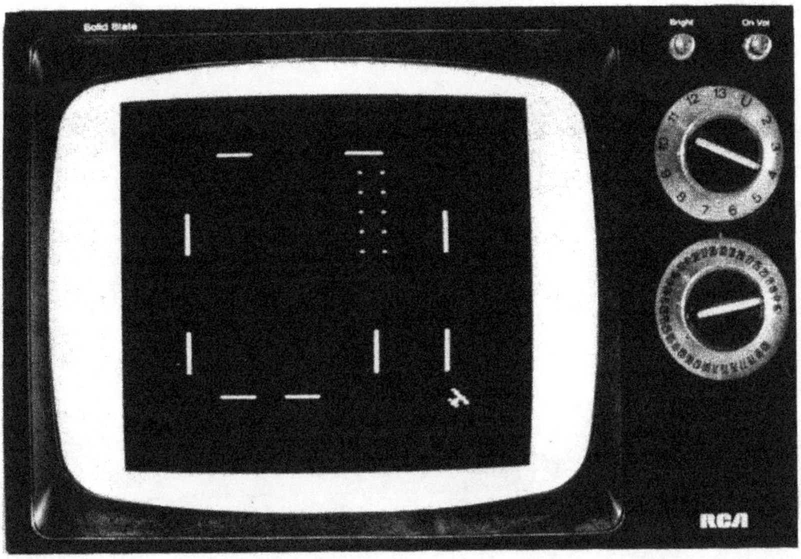

Now you can use your DRAGON computer to put you in command of a small light aircraft. You must safely navigate around the field and land on the airstrip. Because of the treacherous area that the landing field is situated in you must follow the marked course carefully or will crash and spin into the ground.

The game is played in two sections, firstly you see an aerial view from above the plane showing the landing area and the airstrip. The 'safe' approach is shown as a dashed line. Should you manage this section and get close to the strip you will move into the second stage where you will have a 3-D view out of the windscreen of your plane. In this section you can see the horizon, the landing strip (if it is within your field of view) and your altimeter on the instrument panel. Your altimeter is a dial type (with only one dial), you start at about 1000 feet and the dial will move clockwise as you climb and anti-clockwise as you descend.

The plane is controlled using the joystick in the same manner as a real plane. Pushing the joystick to the right/left banks your plane to the right/left while pushing it forward will put you into a dive and pulling it back will make your plane climb.

This game is best played with a joystick becouse it simulates the controls of a plane better. However for those without joysticks some changes can be made to allow the keyboard to be used to control the plane. Because most planes don't have keyboards the game does not react like a real plane if the keyboard is used. You may be interested in trying the game with the keyboard since it plays quite differently.

Program structure

Stage 1

10 - 150	initialization
210 - 240	main loop
Subroutines	
500 - 1100	initial drawings
2000 - 2400	draw areodrome and plane
2500 - 2560	monitor joystick
5500 - 5690	crash / restart game

Variables

X,Y	Position of plane
A()-E2()	Drawings of plane
K	Index to drawings
DK	Increment for K
J-	Joystick variables

Stage 2

310 - 340	initialization
410 - 450	main loop
Subroutines	
3000 - 3040	monitor joystick
4000 - 4240	compute position and data for view
4500 - 4790	draw view
5000 - 5110	crash or land sequence

Variables

D	Distance to far end of runway
L	Length of runway
DD	Decrement for D
H	Height
AT	Climb/descent attitude
W	Width of runway
F	Scaling factor
YH	Y coordinate of horizon
YT	Y coordinate of far end of runway
YF	Y coordinate of near end of runway
X1-X6,Y1-Y6	Screen coordinates of runway images
XC	X coordinate of center of runway
TG	Scaling factor for deviation from horizontal

Using a keyboard for control

Delete line 2510 and lines 3010 to 3030 then insert the following lines

```
205 JH=32: JV=32

2510 IF PEEK(343)=247 THEN JH=JH-16: IF JH(0 THEN JH=0
2511 IF PEEK(344)=247 THEN JH=JH+16: IF JH)64 THEN JH=64
2512 IF PEEK(341)=247 THEN JV=JV-16: IF JV(0 THEN JV=0
2513 IF PEEK(342)=247 THEN JV=JV+16: IF JV)64 THEN JV=64

3010 IF PEEK(343)=247 THEN J2=J2-8 ELSE IF PEEK(344)=247
     THEN J2=J2+8 ELSE J2=31
3020 IF J2(0 THEN J2=0 ELSE IF J2)64 THEN J2=64
3030 IF PEEK(343)=247 THEN J5=J5-8 ELSE IF PEEK(344)=247
     THEN J5=J5+8 ELSE J5=31
3035 IF J5(0 THEN J5=0 ELSE IF J5)64 THEN J5=64
```

FLIGHT SIMULATOR

```
 20 PCLEAR 6
 30 DIM PK(11)
 40 CLS(0):PMODE2,1:PCLS(0):PMODE2,3:PCLS(0):
       PMODE2,5:PCLS(0)
 50 FORI=1TO11:READ PK(I):NEXTI
 60 DATA 16,12,5,1,19,5,128,23,1,9,20
 70 FOR I=1TO11:POKE 1255+I,PK(I):NEXTI
 80 DIM DX(33),DY(33),R1(16),R2(16),XS(7),YS(7)
 90 DIM A(6),A2(6),B(6),B2(6),B3(6),B4(6),C(6),
       C2(6),C3(6),C4(6),D(6),D2(6),D3(6),D4(6),
       E(6),E2(6)
100 PMODE 2,1
110 PCLS(0)
120 FA=+1:FB=-1
130 GOSUB 500
140 X=200:Y=185:K=2:DK=0:PG=1
150 FG=-1
200 '
210 GOSUB2000
220 SCREEN 1,1
230 GOSUB 2500
240 GOTO 210
300 '
310 Q=-1:F2=200:P=1/500:T=1/128:S=1:L=1000:W=20:
       DD=500:G=1
320 F=1E+3:AT=0
330 DV=0:D=10000:H=500:RC=0:J1=31:J2=31:J4=31:J5=31
340 GOTO420
400 '
410 GOSUB3000:'ASK JOY'
420 GOSUB4000:'COMPUTE POSITIONS
430 GOSUB4500:'DRAW
440 SCREEN 1,1
450 GOTO410
490 '
500 F$="NU6NL2NR4D1ND5NL2R6NU3D2"
510 DRAW"BM4,8;"+F$
520 GET(0,0)-(20,20),E,G
530 F$="NU6NR2NL4D1ND5NR2L6NU3D2"
540 PCLS(0):DRAW"BM16,8;"+F$
550 GET(0,0)-(20,20),E2,G
560 F$="NL6NR6NU2D1NL6NR6D7NL2NR2D1NL2NR2"
570 PCLS(0):DRAW"BM8,4;"+F$
580 GET(0,0)-(20,20),A,G
590 F$="NL6NR6ND2U1NL6NR6U7NL2NR2U1NL2NR2"
600 PCLS(0):DRAW"BM8,16;"+F$
610 GET(0,0)-(20,20),A2,G
620 F$="R1NE3NG4D1NH1F3NE2NG1"
630 PCLS(0):DRAW"BM6,6;"+F$
640 GET(0,0)-(20,20),C,G
650 F$="NH3NF4D1NE1G3NH2NF1"
660 PCLS(0):DRAW"BM14,6;"+F$
670 GET(0,0)-(20,20),C2,G
```

```
680 F$="NG3NE4U1NF1H3G1R1L1NE2G1"
690 PCLS(0):DRAW"BM14,14;"+F$
700 GET(0,0)-(20,20),C3,G
710 F$="R1NF3NH4U1NG1E3F1R1L1H1NH1"
720 PCLS(0):DRAW"BM6,14;"+F$
730 GET(0,0)-(20,20),C4,G
740 F$="NU3R1E4NU1BM-4,+2;D1G4BM+3,-2;D5G1D1E4U1"
750 PCLS(0):DRAW"BM6,6;"+F$
760 GET(0,0)-(20,20),B,G
770 F$="L1NU3L1H4NU1BM+4,+2;D1F4BM-3,-2;D5F1D1H4U1"
780 PCLS(0):DRAW"BM14,6;"+F$
790 GET(0,0)-(20,20),B2,G
800 F$="ND3R1F4BM-4,-2;U1H5BM+4,+2;ND1U5H1U1F4"
810 PCLS(0):DRAW"BM6,14;"+F$
820 GET(0,0)-(20,20),B4,G
830 F$="L1ND3L1G4BM+4,-2;U1E5BM-4,+2;ND1U5E1U1G4"
840 PCLS(0):DRAW"BM14,14;"+F$
850 GET(0,0)-(20,20),B3,G
860 F$="R1E1NU2G1L2NU1R1ND4R1F1R1F1R2NU1D2"
870 PCLS(0):DRAW"BM6,6;"+F$
880 GET(0,0)-(20,20),D,G
890 F$="L1L1H1NU2F1R2NU1L1ND4L1G1L1G1L2NU1D2"
900 PCLS(0):DRAW"BM14,6;"+F$
910 GET(0,0)-(20,20),D2,G
920 F$="L1L1G1ND2E1R2ND1L1NU4L1H1L1H1L2ND1U2"
930 PCLS(0):DRAW"BM14,14;"+F$
940 GET(0,0)-(20,20),D3,G
950 F$="R1F1ND2H1L2ND1R1NU4R1E1R1E1R2ND1U2"
960 PCLS(0):DRAW"BM6,14;"+F$
970 GET(0,0)-(20,20),D4,G
980 PH$="BM200,140;U20;BM200,80;U20;BM160,30;L20;
     BM80,30;L20;BM40,60;D20;BM40,120;D20;
     BM60,152;R20;BM100,152;R20;BM156,140;U20"
990 FOR K=1 TO 33:READ DX(K),DY(K):NEXT K
1000 DATA 4,-14,0,-20,-4,-14,-8,-16,-12,-16,-14,-14,
     -16,-12,-16,-8,-14,-4,-20,0,-14,4,-16,8,
     -16,12,-14,14,-12,16,-8,16,-4,14,0,20
1010 DATA 4,14,8,16,12,16,14,14,16,12,16,8,14,4,20,
     0,14,-4,16,-8,16,-12,14,-14,12,-16,8,-16,4,-14
1020 PMODE 2,5:PCLS
1030 CIRCLE(128,255),100,5,0.4,0.50,1
1040 CIRCLE(128,170),18
1050 PMODE 2,3:PCLS
1060 FOR I=0 TO 16:READ R1(I),R2(I):NEXT I
1070 DATA 0,15,6,14,11,11,14,6,15,0,14,-6,11,-11,
     6,-14,0,-15,-6,-14,-11,-11,-14,-6,-15,
     0,-14,6,-11,11,-6,14,0,14
1080 FOR I=1 TO 7:READ  XS(I),YS(I):NEXTI
1090 DATA -10,15,-20,25,-34,32,-30,48,-12,44,24,
     55,45,44
1100 RETURN
1110 '
2000 'DRAW DROME & PLANE'
2010 IF FB>0 GOTO 310
2020 IF PG=1 THEN PG=3 ELSE PG=1
2030 PMODE 2,PG:PCLS
```

```
2040 FOR YD=30 TO 80 STEP 10:
        PSET(148,YD,5):PSET(162,YD,5):NEXT YD
2050 X=X+INT(FA*DX(K+SGN(DK))):
        Y=Y+INT(FA*DY(K+SGN(DK))):K=K+DK
2060 DRAW PH$
2070 IF K=0 THEN K=32
2080 IF K=34 THEN K=2
2090 IF X<10 THEN X=15:GOTO 5500
2100 IF X>245 THEN X=240: GOTO 5500
2110 IF Y<10 THEN Y=15: GOTO 5500
2120 IF Y>186 THEN Y=186: GOTO 5500
2130 IF X<80 THEN FG=+1
2140 IF ABS(X-110)>30 GOTO2160
2150 IF ABS(Y-92)<20 GOTO5500
2160 IF FG<0 THEN GOTO 2180 ELSE
        IF ABS(X-155)>15 GOTO2180
2170 IF K=2 OR K=34 THEN FB=+1
2180 X1=X-10:Y1=Y-10:X2=X+10:Y2=Y+10
2190 IF K>16 GOTO 2300
2200 K2=K/2
2210 ON K2 GOTO 2220,2230,2240,2250,2260,2270,
        2280,2290
2220 PUT(X1,Y1)-(X2,Y2),A,OR:RETURN
2230 PUT(X1,Y1)-(X2,Y2),B,OR:RETURN
2240 PUT(X1,Y1)-(X2,Y2),C,OR:RETURN
2250 PUT(X1,Y1)-(X2,Y2),D,OR:RETURN
2260 PUT(X1,Y1)-(X2,Y2),E,OR:RETURN
2270 PUT(X1,Y1)-(X2,Y2),D4,OR:RETURN
2280 PUT(X1,Y1)-(X2,Y2),C4,OR:RETURN
2290 PUT(X1,Y1)-(X2,Y2),B4,OR:RETURN
2300 K2=K/2-8
2310 ON K2 GOTO 2320,2330,2340,2350,2360,2370,
        2380,2390,2400
2320 PUT(X1,Y1)-(X2,Y2),A2,OR:RETURN
2330 PUT(X1,Y1)-(X2,Y2),B3,OR:RETURN
2340 PUT(X1,Y1)-(X2,Y2),C3,OR:RETURN
2350 PUT(X1,Y1)-(X2,Y2),D3,OR:RETURN
2360 PUT(X1,Y1)-(X2,Y2),E2,OR:RETURN
2370 PUT(X1,Y1)-(X2,Y2),D2,OR:RETURN
2380 PUT(X1,Y1)-(X2,Y2),C2,OR:RETURN
2390 PUT(X1,Y1)-(X2,Y2),B2,OR:RETURN
2400 PUT(X1,Y1)-(X2,Y2),A,OR:RETURN
2410 '
2500 'CONTROL'
2510 JH=JOYSTK(0):JV=JOYSTK(1)
2520 IF JH>47 THEN DK=-2:GOTO 2550
2530 IF JH<17 THEN DK=2:GOTO2550
2540 DK=0
2550 FA=0.2:IF ABS(JH-32)>20 THEN FA=0.25
2560 RETURN
2570 '
3000 'JOY STICK
3010 J2=JOYSTK(0)
3020 'J2=31
3030 J5=JOYSTK(1)
3040 RETURN
```

```
3050 '
4000 'COMPUTE'
4010 DD=D/10
4020 AT=AT+P*(J5-31):H=H+DD*AT:D=D-DD:DL=D-L
4030 IF D<L AND H<50 GOTO5070
4040 IF ABS(AT)>0.2 THEN AT=0.2*SGN(AT)
4050 IF DL<=0 THEN DL=1E-4
4060 IF D<300 GOTO 5040
4070 IF H<=0 GOTO 5000
4080 RC=(J2-31)*S+RC:XC=128-RC:DV=Q*RC+DV
4090 X5=W*F/(DL+H):X1=-X5
4100 X6=W*F/(D+H):X2=-X6
4110 X4=(X2+X6)*.5
4120 X3=(X1+X5)*.5
4130 TG=(31-J2)*0.01
4140 YH=70+250*AT:YL=YH-XC*TG:YR=(256-XC)*TG+YH
4150 YF=H*F2*RD+YH:YT=H*F2/DL+YH
4160 IF D<F THEN YF=200:GOTO4190
4170 YF=YF+10000/(D-900)
4180 IF YF-YT<10 THEN YF=YT+10
4190 IF YT>YH+50 THEN YT=YH+50
4200 Y1=YF+X1*TG:Y5=YF+X5*TG:Y3=(Y1+Y5)*.5
4210 Y2=YT+X2*TG:Y6=YT+X6*TG:Y4=(Y2+Y6)*.5
4220 X1=XC+X1:X2=XC+X2:X3=XC+X3:X4=XC+X4:
     X5=XC+X5:X6=XC+X6
4230 IF D>L THEN RETURN ELSE IF H>50 THEN RETURN ELSE
     IF ABS(AT)<.11 GOTO 5070
4240 RETURN
4250 '
4500 'DRAW'
4510 'PRINT #-2,D,H,YT,YF,X1,Y1,X2,Y2,X3,Y3,X4,Y4,
     X5,Y5,X6,Y6
4520 IF PG=1 THEN PG=3 ELSE PG=1
4530 PMODE2,PG:PCOPY 5 TO PG:PCOPY 6 TO PG+1
4540 FOR I=1TO7:'DRAW STARS'
4550 X9=XC-XS(I):IF ABS(X9-128)>126 GOTO 4580
4560 Y9=YH-YS(I):IF Y9*(YH-Y9)<0 GOTO 4580
4570 PSET(X9,Y9,5)
4580 NEXT I
4590 XL=0:XR=255
4600 IF YL<0 THEN XL=256*YL/(YL-YR):YL=0:GOTO4620
4610 IF YL>196 THEN XL=256*(YL-196)/(YL-YR):YL=196
4620 IF YR<0 THEN XR=256*YL/(YL-YR):YR=0:GOTO4640
4630 IFYR>196 THEN XR=256*(YL-196)/(YL-YR):YR=196
4640 LINE(XL,YL)-(XR,YR),PSET
4650 XA=X1:XB=X2:YA=Y1:YB=Y2:GOSUB4730
4660 XA=X3:XB=X4:YA=Y3:YB=Y4:GOSUB4730
4670 XA=X5:XB=X6:YA=Y5:YB=Y6:GOSUB4730
4680 AL=H:I=150
4690 IF AL>500 THEN AL=AL-500:I=I+5:PSET(I,170,5):
     GOTO4690
4700 AL=INT(AL*0.032+.5)
4710 LINE(128,170)-(128+R1(AL),170-R2(AL)),PSET
4720 RETURN
4730 M=(XB-XA)/(YB-YA):XQ=XA:YQ=YA
4740 DQ=(YB-YA)*.1
```

```
4750 IF ABS(XQ-128)>126 GOTO 4780
4760 IF ABS(YQ-80)>76 GOTO 4780
4770 PSET(XQ,YQ,5)
4780 YQ=YQ+DQ:XQ=DQ*M+XQ
4790 IF YQ<YB THEN RETURN ELSE GOTO 4750
4800 '
5000 'CRASH
5010 FOR I=1 TO 3:CLS(I):PRINT @234,"CRASH";:
     PLAY"T255;O1;V31;L1;3;L255;3;P60;V15;
     L10;2;L255;2;P40;V2;L100;1;L255;1;":NEXT I
5020 CLS(1):PRINT @234,"CRASH";
5030 GOTO 5660
5040 CLS:PRINT @234,
     "OVER SHOOTING RUNWAY.                GO AROUND.";
5050 FOR I=1 TO 2000:NEXT I
5060 X=200:Y=40:K=2:DK=0:GOTO150
5070 CLS(0):PRINT @170,"SHUT DOWN";:FOR I=1 TO 250:
     NEXT I:SCREEN1,1:FOR I=1 TO 11:
     SOUND 25-I*2,INT((I+2)/3):NEXTI
5080 CLS(0):PRINT @170,"PERFECT LANDING";
5090 IF ABS(AT)<.11 THEN GOTO 5100 ELSE
     PRINT @170,"A BIT ROUGH !"
     +CHR$(128)+CHR$(128)+CHR$(128);:GOTO 5630
5100 CLS(0):PRINT @170,"PERFECT LANDING";
5110 GOTO 5630
5120 '
5500 'SPIN OUT'
5510 IF DK=0 THEN DK=2
5520 FOR IK=1 TO 10
5530 IF PG=1 THEN PG=3 ELSE PG=1
5540 PMODE 2,PG:PCLS
5550 K=K+DK:IF K>32 THEN K=2
5560 IF K<2 THEN K=32
5570 FOR YD=30 TO 80 STEP 10:
     PSET(148,YD,5):PSET(162,YD,5):NEXT YD
5580 GOSUB 2180
5590 SCREEN 1,1
5600 NEXT IK
5610 FOR I=1 TO 500:NEXT I
5620 CLS:PRINT @234,"OFF COURSE !";
5630 PRINT @304,"TOUCH ANY KEY";
5640 FOR I=1 TO 1000:NEXTI
5650 CLS:SCREEN1,1
5660 I$=INKEY$:IF I$="" THEN GOTO5660
5670 CLS(0):FORI=1TO11:POKE 1255+I,PK(I):NEXTI
5680 SCREEN0
5690 GOTO140
6000 END
```

Draw

Copyright (c) Colin Carter

This utility program will allow you to draw pictures on your DRAGON in graphics mode 1. You may specify the background colour you like then draw on a blank page in any of the four available colours in this mode. You draw by moving a cursor about the screen.

Your cursor is controlled by the arrow keys with the direction of the arrow being the direction the cursor moves. By pressing the 'Y' key the computer is instructed to draw in the current colour as you move the cursor. Pressing the 'N' key turns this off so moving the cursor has no effect on the screen. You may change the colour by pressing the 'C' key followed by a number key between 1 and 4.

Lastly you may paint an area by pressing the 'P' key, the area will be filled in the current colour.

Program structure

10 - 190	initialization
200 - 320	check keyboard for input
330 - 380	paint subroutine
390 - 490	vertical movement
500 - 600	horizontal movement
610 - 640	colour change

Variables

C	Current colour
NU	ASCII value of control key symbol
X,Y	Position of cursor

DRAW

```
 20 CLS
 30 PRINT @7,"COLORS AVAILABLE ARE:"
 40 PRINT @39,"1 - GREEN"
 50 PRINT @71,"2 - YELLOW"
 60 PRINT @103,"3 - BLUE"
 70 PRINT @135,"4 - RED"
 80 PRINT @195,"INSTRUCTION SET:"
 90 PRINT @231,"ARROWS FOR MOVEMENT"
100 PRINT @263,"C3-CHANGE TO COLOR 3"
110 PRINT @295,"N-NO TRACE"
120 PRINT @327,"Y-YES, TRACE A LINE"
130 PRINT @487,"WHAT COLOR BACKGROUND ?";
140 I$=INKEY$:IF I$="" GOTO 140
150 I=VAL(I$):IF I=0 GOTO 140
160 IF I>4 GOTO 140
170 B=I:C=B:X=128:Y=96:ST=-1:NU=32
180 F=B+1:IF F>4 THEN F=1
190 CLS:PMODE 1,1:COLOR F,B:SCREEN 1,0:PCLS
200 I$=INKEY$:PSET(X,Y,1):PSET(X,Y,2):
      PSET(X,Y,3):PSET(X,Y,4):PSET(X,Y,C)
210 IF I$="" GOTO 200
220 DE=+2
230 NU=ASC(I$)
240 IF NU=94 GOTO  400
250 IF NU=10 GOTO 410
260 IF NU= 8 GOTO 510
270 IF NU= 9 GOTO 520
280 IF NU=80 GOTO  330
290 IF NU=67 GOTO 610
300 IF NU=78 THEN ST=-1:GOTO200
310 IF NU=89 THEN ST=+1:GOTO200
320 GOTO 200
330 REM: PAINT
340 C2=C+1:IF C>4 THEN C=1
350 PSET(X,Y,C2)
360 PAINT(X,Y),C,C
370 NU=32
380 GOTO 200
390 DE=+2:GOTO 410
400 DE=-2
410 Y=Y+DE
420 IF Y<1 THEN Y=1:GOTO 200
430 IF Y>196 THEN Y=196:GOTO 200
440 C2=PPOINT(X,Y)
450 PSET(X,Y,1):PSET(X,Y,2):PSET(X,Y,3):
      PSET(X,Y,4):PSET(X,Y,C)
460 IF ST<0 THEN C=C2:PSET(X,Y,C)
470 IF PEEK(341)=223 GOTO 400
480 IF PEEK(342)=223 GOTO 390
490 GOTO 200
500 DE=+2:GOTO520
510 DE=-2
520 X=X+DE
```

```
530 IF X<0 THEN X=0:GOTO 200
540 IF X>256 THEN X=256:GOTO 200
550 C2=PPOINT(X,Y)
560 PSET(X,Y,1):PSET(X,Y,2):PSET(X,Y,3):
      PSET(X,Y,4):PSET(X,Y,C)
570 IF ST<0 THEN C=C2:PSET(X,Y,C)
580 IF PEEK(343)=223 GOTO 510
590 IF PEEK(344)=223 GOTO 500
600 GOTO 200
610 I$=INKEY$:IF I$="" GOTO 610
620 C=VAL(I$):IF C=0 GOTO 610
630 IF C>4 GOTO 610
640 GOTO 200
650 END
```

Dragon Clock

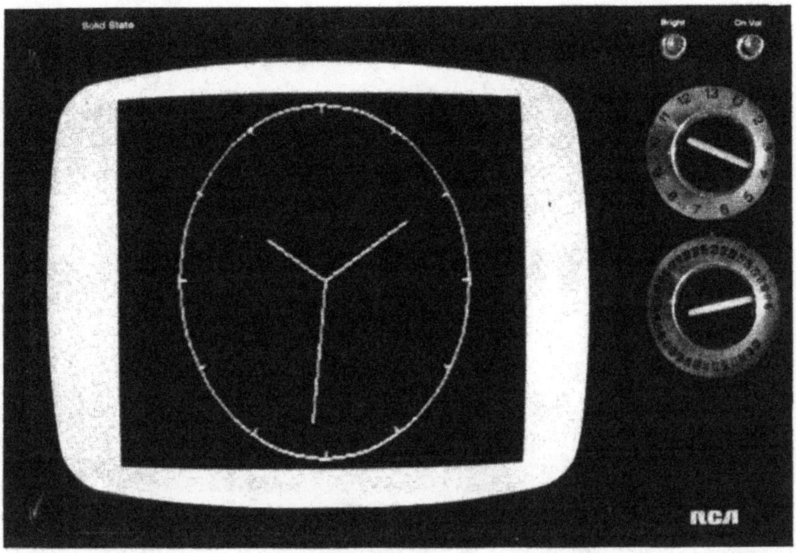

Copyright (c) Beam Software

DESCRIPTION

This program is a simulation of a REAL-TIME CLOCK; both normal clock and digital clock are implemented and displayed on different screens. You will be amazed at the accuracy of the DRAGON CLOCK; not only that, you can also set the ALARM and the DRAGON CLOCK will remind you by generating an alarm tone that is enough to drive you mad.

HOW TO RUN THE PROGRAM

Type RUN followed by (ENTER) to start the program.

You will need to enter the HOUR, MINUTE, at SECOND atwhich you want the clock to start. Note that HOUR is entered in a 24 hour basis; it means that you have to type in 13th hour instead of 1 PM.

The program checks the validity of the input, so you can't type a negative number or any number greater than 24 for hour, 60 for minutes and seconds; they won't be accepted.

You will have to input in a similar way if you want to set the alarm.

PROGRAM STRUCTURE

The program uses the DRAGON TIMER function as its internal counter. The TIMER function returns a count which varies depending on the frequency of the AC power supply. Normally it will be either 60 or 50 counts per second depending upon the country in which you live. In other words, if the TIMER is initialised as zero, it will return a value of 50 one second later in the UK.

The structure of the program is as follow :

INITIALISATION

```
    INPUT HOUR MINUTE and SECOND
    IF SET-ALARM
        INPUT ALARM HOUR MINUTE and SECOND
        DISPLAY ALARM TIME
    DRAW CLOCK FACE

     INITIALISE STARTING TIME
```

MAIN LOOP

```
H:  DETERMINE HOUR HAND POSITION
M:  DETERMINE MINUTE HAND POSITION
S:  DETERMINE SECOND HAND POSITION
    DRAW SECOND HAND
    DRAW MINUTE HAND
    DRAW HOUR HAND
    IF ALARM IS SET
        UPDATE INFORMATION ON DIGITAL SCREEN
    IF LEFT ARROW PRESSED
        DISPLAY CLOCK SCREEN
    ELSE
        DISPLAY DIGITAL SCREEN
    IF ALARM TIME MATCHES WITH DIGITS
            FLASH CLOCK and GENERATE ALARM
    FETCH TIMER COUNTER UNTIL ONE SECOND HAS PASSED
    REINITIALISE TIMER TO ZERO
    DRAW OVER SECOND HAND
    IF SAME MINUTE THEN GO TO S:
```

```
DRAW OVER MINUTE HAND
IF SAME HOUR THEN GO TO M:
DRAW OVER HOUR HAND
GO TO H:
```

SPECIAL FEATURES

The screen paging feature of the DRAGON is used to display the digital and the clock screen. This is because of the fact that there is no access to the text character shapes in the high resolution mode (in this case, mode 4). The alternative is what was adopted in this program, to prepare both screen and display them one at a time depending on which key is pressed.

SIN and COS functions are used to draw clock hands. The SECOND hand is moved every second; the MINUTE hand is moved every minute; and the HOUR hand is moved every 12 minutes.

Checking is built into the program to ensure validity of time input.

SPECIAL NOTES

The DRAGON CLOCK can be very accurate after you tune the clock by varying the value of FR in line 3030. An increase of its value will slow down the clock and vice versa.

Note that the TIMER counter is no longer an accurate count once any input/output is performed because the TIMER counter is not incremented during that time. Therefore once the alarm is sounded the clock is no longer accurate.

In this program, once the alarm is sounded the clock freezes to the time of the alarm and it will need to be reset; that is, if you want to use the clock again you will need press (SPACEBAR) to RUN the program again .

DRAGON CLOCK

```
  10 'DRAGON CLOCK
  20 GOTO3000
1000 'CLOCK MOVE
1010 TIMER=0:T1=0
1020 IFHI=60THENHI=0
1040 H=HI*C
1050 HX=128+40*SIN(H):HY=96-40*COS(H)
1060 IFMI=60THENMI=0:HT=HT+1
1065 IFHT=24THENHT=0
1070 M=MI*C
1080 MX=128+60*SIN(M):MY=96-60*COS(M)
1090 A=SI*C'ANGLE OF SECOND HAND
1100 SX=128+72*SIN(A):SY=96-72*COS(A)
1110 'DRAW HANDS
1120 LINE(128,96)-(SX,SY),PSET
1130 LINE(128,96)-(MX,MY),PSET
1140 LINE(128,96)-(HX,HY),PSET
1150 IFMM=0THENPRINT @144,HT:PRINT @147,":":
        PRINT @149,MI:PRINT @152,":":PRINT @154,SI
1155 IF(AL=1ANDHT=AH ANDMI=AM ANDSI=AS)THEN2000
1160 IFINT(TIMER/FR)<=0 THEN1160'WAIT UNTIL NEXT HAND
1170 TIMER=0
1180 IFPEEK(343)=223THENSCREEN1,1:MM=1
1190 IFPEEK(344)=223THENSCREEN0,1:MM=0
1210 SI=SI+1:LINE(128,96)-(SX,SY),PRESET
        'ERASE SECOND HANDS
1220 IFSI=60THENSI=0ELSE1090
1230 MI=MI+1:LINE(128,96)-(MX,MY),PRESET
        'ERASE MINUTE HANDS
1240 IF(MI-INT(MI/12)*12)=0THENHI=HI+1ELSE1060
1250 LINE(128,96)-(HX,HY),PRESET'ERASE HOUR HANDS
1260 GOTO1020
2000 'ALARM
2010 SCREEN1,0:SOUND200,5
2020 SCREEN1,1:SOUND130,5
2030 IFPEEK(345)<>223THEN2010
3000 'SET CLOCK
3010 CLS:PRINT @234,"[illegible]"
3020 PMODE4,1
3030 PI=3.141592654:C=PI/30:FR=50'FREQUENCY
3040 PCLS:CIRCLE(128,96),90
3050 FORI=1TO12
3060 Q=I/6*PI
3070 LINE(128+86*SIN(Q),96-86*COS(Q))
        -(128+90*SIN(Q),96-90*COS(Q)),PSET
3080 NEXTI
4000 CLS:INPUT"HOUR";HT
4010 IFHT<0ORHT>24THEN4000
4020 INPUT"MINUTE";MI
4030 IFMI<0ORMI>60THEN4020ELSEMI=INT(MI)
4040 INPUT"SECOND";SI
4050 IFSI<0ORSI>60THEN4040ELSESI=INT(SI)
4060 IF HT>12THENHI=HT-12ELSEHI=HT
```

```
4070 HI=HI*5+INT(MI/12)
4080 CLS:PRINT"DO YOU WANT TO SET THE ALARM?":
     PRINT"(Y OR N)"
4090 INPUTA$
4100 IFA$<>"Y"ANDA$<>"N"THEN4090
4110 IF A$="N"THENAL=0:GOTO4190
4120 AL=1:CLS
4130 INPUT"ALARM HOUR";AH
4140 IFAH<0ORAH>24THEN4130
4150 INPUT"ALARM MINUTE";AM
4160 IFAM<0ORAM>60THEN4150
4170 INPUT"ALARM SECOND";AS
4180 IFAS<0ORAS>60THEN4170
4190 'DISPLAY TIME
4200 FORI=1TO10:NEXTI
4210 CLS:PRINT @137,"TIME:"
4220 IFAL=1THENPRINT @201,"ALARM: ":PRINT @208,AH:
     PRINT @211,":":PRINT @213,AM:PRINT @216,":":
     PRINT @218,AS
4230 PRINT @421,"LEFTARROW:  NORMAL CLOCK"
4240 PRINT @453,"RIGHTARROW: DIGITAL CLOCK"
4250 PRINT @494,"TO START CLOCK";
4260 PRINT @144,HT:PRINT @147,":":PRINT @149,MI:
     PRINT @152,":":PRINT @154,SI
4270 PRINT @483,"<SPACEBAR>";
4280 FORI=1TO150:NEXTI
4290 PRINT @144,"          "
4300 PRINT @483,"          ";
4310 FORI=1TO150:NEXTI
4320 IFPEEK(345)<>223THEN4260
4330 PRINT @494,"                    ";
4340 MM=1:SCREEN1,1:GOTO1000
```

The Talking Dragon

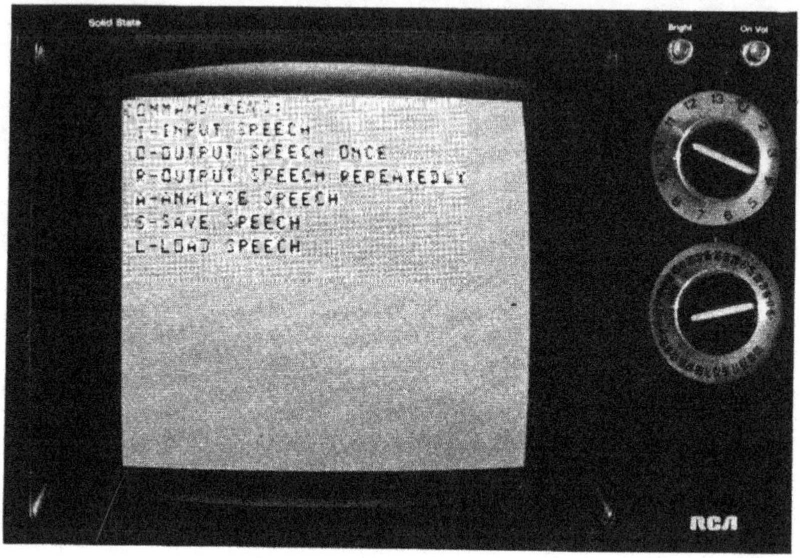

This program lets you talk to your DRAGON and have it talk back to you (no it can't really talk it just repeats what you say). You can include the talking section in your other programs and have talking games etc. The heart of this program is a small machine language section that performs the tasks of listening to the speech and storing it and later replaying it. Don't be worried though if you don't know machine language, you can still use this program - just be careful when typing in the data statements.

The speech is input through your cassette recorder and output to your television set so you do not need any special equipment.

Since the cassette port can have only one of two values (a high level or 1 and a low level or 0) the speech is stored as a series of values between 0 and 255 (this range is used because it is the range of values that can be stored in a single byte of the computers memory). Each value is simply the length of time between changes of the level of the cassette port, i.e suppose the cassette port is low (0) then we start counting until it goes high (1) at this stage we save the count in memory and reset the counter to zero. We then start counting again until the port goes low again save the count, reset it to zero etc, etc, etc. This process is continued until the available memory is filled up.

The stored speech takes up 6K of memory and will last about 1 to 4 seconds depending upon the content.

HOW TO RUN THE PROGRAM

When the program is run there will be a short pause while the machine code is put into memory. It is placed at the top of the available memory (at locations 28672 onwards) and protected with a clear statement. When this is done a menu of options will be displayed and pressing one of the keys I,O,R,A,S,L will select the option you desire.

I-Input speech

The speech is input from the cassette port using one of two methods described below.

When the I key is pressed the computer will display the message "PRESS ANY KEY TO START", at this point the cassette should be readied to send the speech to the computer. When all is ready press any key and the computer will start to store the speech. The computer will display a graphic screen which will fill up with what looks like rubbish but is actually the values that make up the input speech. When the screen is full the computer will return you to the menu.

Actually getting the speech to the computer is very simple and can be done in one of two ways, both using your cassette recorder.

Method 1:

Prepare a cassette with the speech you want the computer to record using either the built in microphone or an external microphone (note the better the sound of this recording the better the results will be when the computer plays back the speech, so it is usually best to use an external microphone).

Once the cassette is ready it is simply played into the computer just like a program cassette. Note that since the program will not start the cassette motor you should unplug the remote jack from the cassette recorder.

Method 2:

This is similar to the above except that you don't need to record what you want to say you just say it directly to the computer. Firstly your cassette recorder must be able to send what it is recording to the external speaker jack (this is where you plug the computer in to load a program from tape). If it can do this then all you need to do is put the machine into record mode and talk into the microphone when the computer is inputting speech.

To put the cassette recorder into record mode without a cassette in it you must open the cassette door and look inside. You should see a small switch at the back left hand side. If this is pressed in then the RECORD and PLAY buttons pressed the cassette will be in record mode.

O-Output speech

This will call the machine language subroutine to send the recorded speech to the speaker in the television set. The graphic screen containing the speech is displayed while it is talking and if you look carefully you will see a small white line moving around the screen. This line is tracing the speech on the screen as it is sent to the speaker.

R-Repeated speech output

This is similar to O except that it will repeat the same speech over and over until a key is pressed.

A-Analyse speech

Since the sound is stored as a sequence of numbers we can draw a graph of them and see the distribution of frequencies in what was said to the computer. The graph is drawn on the highest resolution graphics screen with the vertical scale being the total count that each number occurs (i.e the higher the line the more times that number occured), while the horizontal scale is the numbers (from 0 to 255, see above for how these numbers are calculated).

When this graph is finished the screen will change colour and the computer will wait until you hit a key. You will probably notice on this graph that the left side of the screen is full of tall lines while the right side is fairly empty. This is because in a given time interval you can fit more short counts (hence small numbers) than long ones. To try and correct this problem a new graph is drawn, after you press a key, in which the vertical scale is the total time used by each interval length. When this graph is finished the computer will again wait for a key to be pressed at which time it will return to the menu.

S-Save speech (to cassette)

This gives you the option to save the speech in the digital form the computers uses to store it.

The computer will ask you for a name to use when it saves your speech to cassette. After you press ENTER it will save the speech in digital form on the cassette so make sure your recorder is ready and that the microphone and remote plugs are back in.

L-Load speech (from cassette)

This will load a previously saved block of data representing speech from the cassette. The computer will prompt you for a name (optional). Note this can only be used to load blocks previously saved with the S command.

TIPS

To get the best results you will need to experiment with the volume levels on your cassette recorder. Since it may take a number of tries to find the optimum setting we suggest that you make a recording of some speech first and use method 1 to input the speech initially. Remember the better the sound on the casstte the better the results will be.

On some cassette recorders the silences between words will have enough background noise in them so that the computer will record the noise. Since the computer is only using two levels when the speech is output this background noise will be reproduced at the same volume level as the speech. This can be overcome somewhat by adjusting the volume level but if you have a noisy cassette recorder you will have to live with it. If your recorder does produce silent gaps between words you will notice that no matter how long the gap between two words when the speech is played back the gap will have been cut to a much shorter value. This is caused by having only values between 1 and 255 for the lengths between changes.

PROGRAM STRUCTURE

```
10-70  : initialise variables etc.
80-90  : store machine code
100-230: command section
       Print command screeen
       Enter command
       Execute command
All commands end with GOTO 120
240-310: Speech input
320-360: Speech output
370-410: Repeated speech output
420-460: Save speech to cassette
470-510: Load speech from cassette
520-710: Analyse speech
       Clear & display graph screen
       Clear count array
       For each byte in memory:
        plot an extra point
        increment the count for that value
       Change screen colour, wait for key press
       Correct the counts to make them times
       Scale and plot the times
       Wait for key press
730-760: Subroutine to wait for key press and return the
         key in A$. If BREAK it stops.
790    Speech routine offsets from the start of machine
        code
810    Start address of the machine code
830    Start of machine code: Memory start address
850    Memory length
870    Subroutines
```

MAKING OTHER PROGRAMS TALK

To use the machine code routines in your own programs it would be easiest to save the machine code together with the speech that you want to use on tape.

RUN the above program then press BREAK when at the command menu.

Prepare your cassette recorder for saving a program and type in:

```
CSAVEM "SCODE",&H7000,&H705D,&H7029
```

This will save the machine code to tape.

RUN the program again. Input the speech you wish to use and save it to tape - note that you can save as many blocks as you like and include them all in your program.

Now suppose you have saved the machine code and two blocks of speech to tape, and you wish to have a program that puts these two blocks at memory locations &H4000 and &H5800 respectively then in your program you will need the following.

```
10 CLEAR 200,&H4000 'PROTECT MEMORY
20 CLOADM "SCODE"   'LOAD MACHINE CODE
30 CLOADM "name1",&H4000-&H0600
```

This line loads the first block of speech (with name name1) at location &H4000 onward (the normal location is &H0600 so the offset to put it at &H4000 is &H4000-&H0600)

```
40 CLOADM "name2",&H5800-&H0600
```

Similarly for the second block.

When you want to output the first block of speech you should use

```
POKE &H7000,&H40: POKE &H7001,0
EXEC &H7029
```

To output the second block you need the lines

```
POKE &H7000,&H58: POKE &H7001,0
EXEC &H7029
```

For those of you who know something of machine language you may like to try moving the machine code higher in memory which will give you some more memory for your BASIC programs.

THE TALKING DRAGON

```
 10 ' SPEECH PROGRAM
 20 ' FOR THE DRAGON
 30 PCLEAR 8:CLEAR 200,&H7000
 40 CLS:PRINT" STORING MACHINE CODE"
 50 DIM A(255)
 60 SS=&H0600:SE=SS+&H17FF
      ' START & END OF SPEECH MEM
 70 READ IS,OS,I:IS=IS+I:OS=OS+I
 80 READ P
 90 IF P>=0 THEN POKE I,P:I=I+1:GOTO 80
100 '
110 ' COMMAND LOOP
120 SOUND 40,1:AUDIO OFF:CLS:SCREEN 1,0
130 PRINT"COMMAND KEYS:"
140 PRINT" I-INPUT SPEECH"
150 PRINT" O-OUTPUT SPEECH ONCE"
160 PRINT" R-OUTPUT SPEECH REPEATEDLY"
170 PRINT" A-ANALYSE SPEECH"
180 PRINT" S-SAVE SPEECH"
190 PRINT" L-LOAD SPEECH"
200 GOSUB 730
210 ON INSTR("IORSLA",A$)
      GOTO 260,340,390,440,490,540
220 PRINT" INVALID COMMAND"
230 GOTO 200
240 '
250 ' SPEECH INPUT
260 PRINT"PRESS ANY KEY TO START"
270 PMODE 4,1:PCLS
280 AUDIO ON:GOSUB 730
290 SCREEN 1,1
300 EXEC IS' INPUT SPEECH
310 GOTO 120
320 '
330 ' OUTPUT SPEECH ONCE
340 PMODE 4,1:SCREEN 1,1
350 AUDIO ON:EXEC OS' OUTPUT SPEECH
360 GOTO 120
370 '
380 ' OUTPUT SPEECH REPEATEDLY
390 PMODE 4,1:SCREEN 1,1:AUDIO ON
400 EXEC OS:IF INKEY$="" THEN 400
410 GOTO 120
420 '
430 ' SAVE SPEECH TO CASSETTE
440 INPUT"NAME";A$
450 CSAVEM A$,SS,SE,0
460 GOTO 120
470 '
480 ' LOAD SPEECH FROM CASSETTE
490 INPUT"NAME";A$
500 CLOADM A$
510 GOTO 120
```

```
520 '
530 ' ANALYSE SPEECH
540 PMODE4,5:PCLS:SCREEN 1,1
550 FOR I=0 TO 255:A(I)=0:NEXT I
560 FOR I=SS TO SE
570 P=PEEK(I)
580 IF A(P)<192 THEN PSET(P,192-A(P))
590 A(P)=A(P)+1
600 NEXT I
610 SCREEN 1,0:GOSUB 730
620 FOR I=1 TO 255
630 A(I)=A(I)*I'CORRECT VALUES
640 IF A(I)>P THEN P=A(I)
650 NEXT I
660 P=191/P
670 FOR I=1 TO 255
680 LINE(I,191)-(I,191-P*A(I)),PSET
690 NEXT I
700 GOSUB 730
710 GOTO 120
720 '
730 ' SUBROUTINE TO WAIT FOR KEY PRESS
740 A$=INKEY$:IF A$="" THEN 740
750 IF ASC(A$)=3 THEN STOP
760 RETURN
770 '
780 ' SPEECH ROUTINE OFFSETS FROM START OF CODE
790 DATA 4,41
800 ' CODE START ADDRESS
810 DATA &H7000
820 ' SPEECH MEMORY START HIGH&LOW BYTES
830 DATA 6,0
840 ' SPEECH MEMORY LENGTH HIGH&LOW BYTES
850 DATA 24,0
860 ' SPEECH SUBROUTINES
870 DATA 26,80,206,255,32,174,140,244,16,174,140,242
880 DATA 95,92,141,72,100,196,37,249,231,128,95,
        92,141,62,100,196
890 DATA 36,249,231,128,49,62,38,232,57,26,80,
        206,255,32,204,52
900 DATA 63,167,93,76,167,95,231,67,174,140,197,
        16,174,140,195,230
910 DATA 128,99,132,134,128,167,196,141,19,90,38,
        247,99,132,230,128
920 DATA 111,196,141,8,90,38,249,49,62,38,228,57,57
930 DATA -1
```

THE TALKING DRAGON MACHINE LANGUAGE ROUTINE

```
0E00                        NAM SPEECH
                    * SPEECH INPUT AND OUTPUT ROUTINES
                    * SUBROUTINE INPUT MONITORS THE
                    * CASSETTE INPUT LINE AND RECORDS
                    * THE LENGTHS OF THE HIGHS AND LOWS
                    *
                    * SUBROUTINE OUTPUT TAKES THESE
                    * LENGTHS AND OUTPUTS HIGHS AND
                    * LOWS TO THE TV SET
                    *
                    * THE SPEECH MEMORY LOCATION AND
                    * SIZE ARE SPECIFIED AT TSTART
                    * AND LENGTH RESPECTIVELY
                    *
                    * EACH LOOP IS 23 CYCLES LONG
                    *
FF20                PIA     EQU $FF20        PIA LOCATION
                    * BIT 0 IS THE CASSETTE INPUT LEVEL
                    * BITS 7-1 CONTROL THE D/A CONVERTER

0E00                        ORG $7000        START PROGRAM AT 7000 HEX
7000 0600           TSTART FDB $0600         START OF TEXT
7002 1800           LENGTH FDB $1800         LENGTH OF SPEECH
                    * INPUT SPEECH SUBROUTINE
7004                INPUT
7004 1A50                   ORCC #$50        DISABLE INTERRUPTS
7006 CEFF20                 LDU #PIA         POINTER TO PIA
7009 AE8CF4                 LDX TSTART,PCR   POINTER TO START OF MEMORY
700C 10AE8CF2               LDY LENGTH,PCR   MEMORY LEFT FOR SPEECH
7010                ILOOP
                    * TIME HIGH SIGNAL
7010 5F                     CLRB              RESET TIME COUNTER
7011                IH
7011 5C                     INCB              INCREMENT TIME COUNTER
7012 8D48                   BSR DELAY        DELAY
7014 64C4                   LSR ,U           TEST BIT0 OF PIA
7016 25F9                   BCS IH           LOOP IF STILL SET

7018 E780                   STB ,X+          SAVE TIME COUNT
                    * TIME LOW SIGNAL
701A 5F                     CLRB              RESET TIME COUNTER
701B                IL
701B 5C                     INCB              INCREMENT TIME COUNTER
701C 8D3E                   BSR DELAY        DELAY
701E 64C4                   LSR ,U           TEST BIT0 OF PIA
7020 24F9                   BCC IL           LOOP IF STILL CLEAR

7022 E780                   STB ,X+          SAVE TIME COUNT
7024 313E                   LEAY -2,Y        2 BYTES OF MEMORY USED
7026 26E8                   BNE ILOOP        LOOP IF NOT OUT OF MEMORY
7028 39                     RTS

                    * OUTPUT SPEECH
```

```
7029              OUTPUT
7029 1A50                 ORCC #$50        DISABLE INTERRUPTS
702B CEFF20               LDU #PIA         POINTER TO PIA
702E CC343F               LDD #$343F
7031 A75D                 STA -3,U         SELECT DAC
7033 4C                   INCA              BEING CAREFULL ABOUT
7034 A75F                 STA -1,U         MODIFYING INTERRUPTS
7036 E743                 STB 3,U          SOUND ENABLE
7038 AE8CC5               LDX TSTART,PCR   POINTER TO START OF MEMORY
703B 10AE8CC3             LDY LENGTH,PCR   MEMORY FREE FOR SPEECH
703F              OLOOP
                  * OUPUT HIGH SIGNAL
703F E680                 LDB ,X+          GET TIME COUNT
7041 6384                 COM ,X           FLASH NEXT BYTE(TO SEE IT)
7043              OH
7043 8680                 LDA #$80         OUTPUT LEVEL
7045 A7C4                 STA ,U           SEND TO PIA
7047 8D13                 BSR DELAY        DELAY
7049 5A                   DECB              DECREMENT TIME COUNTER
704A 26F7                 BNE OH           LOOP UNTIL 0

704C 6384                 COM ,X           RESTORE NEXT BYTE
                  * OUTPUT LOW SIGNAL
704E E680                 LDB ,X+          GET TIME COUNT
7050              OL
7050 6FC4                 CLR ,U           SET OUTPUT LEVEL TO 0
7052 8D08                 BSR DELAY        DELAY
7054 5A                   DECB              DECREMENT TIME COUNTER
7055 26F9                 BNE OL           LOOP UNTIL 0

7057 313E                 LEAY -2,Y        2 BYTES OF MEMORY USED
7059 26E4                 BNE OLOOP        LOOP IF MEMORY LEFT
705B 39                   RTS               RETURN TO BASIC

705C 39           DELAY   RTS               DELAY 12 CLOCK CYCLES

705D                      END
```

Draughts

Copyright (c) Beam Software

This program is a combination of BASIC and machine language that plays a pretty fair game of draughts.

The computer displays a graphic draughts board, with your pieces (yellow)at the bottom and its pieces (red) at the top. You always move first and is done by placing the flashing 'cursor' over the piece to be moved, pressing enter, then placing the cursor on the square to move the piece to and hitting enter again. You move the cursor with the following keys:

	UP LEFT	UP	UP RIGHT	
	Q	W	E	
LEFT	A		D	RIGHT
	Z	X	C	
	DOWN LEFT	DOWN	DOWN RIGHT	

The computer will only allow you to place the cursor over light coloured squares and will also check to make sure that your move is legal

The squares are identified by a letter and a number. The letters range from 'A' to 'H' and are the columns of the board. The numbers go from '1' to '8' and are the rows. The computer uses these letters and numbers to tell you where your cursor is (displayed on the right side of the screen) and also to tell you where its moves are made.

If you should happen to lose the game or wish to quit just hit 'K' as the first key when the computer asks you for your move.

All your moves are checked for legality so you can't cheat; but captures are not compulsory (for you), and multiple jumps are not allowed. The computer always captures if it can.

You make a king by getting a piece to the last line. Kings move only one square and can only make single captures but may move forwards or backwards.

How it works:

The BASIC part of the program performs the housekeeping functions. It sets up the board, accepts and executes the player's moves and graphically displays all moves on the screen. A short machine language program is used to make the computer's move. This was done to allow the game to be played without having to wait forever for the computer to make its move. For those with an understanding of machine language, a listing of this part of the program is included.

If you do not understand machine language do not worry as this part of the program is typed in as data statements at lines 9000 - 9450. Just be careful when typing them in.

As part of the machine language section the computer has a representation of the board in memory as a series of bytes. This is why PEEKs and POKEs are used to make changes rather than using an array. It is easier for the machine language program to access this board in memory than in an array.

The program

LINES	DESCRIPTION
1 - 8	These lines set aside room for the strings in the program and load in machine language program. The machine language is placed in an unused page of graphics memory.
10 - 90	This section sets the colors

to be used, the graphics mode
and builds the strings that draw the
pieces. It then dimensions the arrays
used and draws the board

100 - 160 Draws the pieces on the screen

200 - 220 Main loop

```
1  get players move
   get computers move
   goto 1
```

1000 - 1060 Draws a piece on the board at position X,Y with color C. The piece is determined by P : 0 = blank
1 = normal man
2 = king

2000 - 2540 Inputs the player's move
It can be broken down as follows:

- 2000 - 2020 displays message
- 2030 - 2050 displays from message and calls the subroutine (2500) to allow the player to move the cursor to the desired position. Also checks this position entered for being legal.
- 2060 - 2110 displays the to message and calls the subroutine at 2500 to allow the player to pick the position to move to.
- 2120 - 2200 makes the player's move if it was a capture
- 2300 - 2340 makes a normal move for the player
- 2500 - 2630 displays a flashing cursor and allows the user to move it to the desired square.

3000 - 3110 Calls the machine language program for the computer's move and does that move on the board

3900 - 3904 The program jumps to here if the computer has lost

9000 - 9040 builds the strings that are used to display characters and numbers on the screen in the graphics mode

10000 - 10390 Reads the data staements that make up the machine language program (10100 - 10240) and the initial board position (10300 - 10390) and puts them in memory

DRAUGHTS

```
    1 CLEAR 500
    5 PCLEAR 4: GOSUB 10000: GOSUB 9000
    8 DEF USR0=6672
   10 BS=3:WS=1:BP=4:WP=2
   20 PMODE 1,1: SCREEN 1,0: COLOR BS,WS: PCLS
   25 DIM Z(150): GET (194,0)-(255,191),Z,G
   30 P$="BM+10,0R2E2R2L10H2R14E2L18U2R18E2L22
        U2R22H2L18U2R18H2L14E2R10L2H2L2"
   32 K$="BM+4,-4E14H2L2H2L2G2L2G2F14E2U2E2U2H2
        U2H2H2L2H2L2G2L2G2G2D2G2D2F2D2F2F2R2F2
        R2E2R2E2"
   40 DIM BQ(30),WQ(30),CQ(30)
   45 KX=5: KY=6
   50 LINE(0,0)-(23,0),PSET
   51 LINE -(23,23),PSET
   52 LINE -(0,23),PSET
   53 LINE -(0,0),PSET: PAINT (8,8),BS
   55 GET (24,0)-(47,23),WQ,G
   56 GET (0,0)-(23,23),BQ,G
   60 O=0: FOR Y=0 TO 168 STEP 24
   70 FOR X=0 TO 168 STEP 48
   80 PUT (X+O,Y)-(X+O+23,Y+23),BQ,PSET
   90 NEXT X: O=24-O: NEXT Y
  100 P=1
  110 FOR X=1 TO 7 STEP 2
  120 C=BP: Y=1: GOSUB 1000: Y=3: GOSUB 1000
  130 C=WP: Y=7: GOSUB 1000: NEXT X
  140 FOR X=0 TO 6 STEP 2
  150 C=WP: Y=6: GOSUB 1000: Y=8: GOSUB 1000
  160 C=BP: Y=2: GOSUB 1000: NEXT X
  200 GOSUB 2000
  210 GOSUB 3000
  220 GOTO 200
 1000 X$=STR$(X*24):Y$=STR$(Y*24-1)
 1002 IF X-2*INT(X/2)<>Y-2*INT(Y/2) THEN
        PUT(X*24,Y*24-24)-(X*24+23,Y*24-1),BQ,PSET
        ELSE PUT(X*24,Y*24-24)-
        (X*24+23,Y*24-1),WQ,PSET
 1005 COLOR C,BS: DRAW "BM"+X$+","+Y$
 1010 IF P=1 THEN DRAW P$ ELSE IF P=2 THEN DRAW K$
 1020 COLOR BS,WS
 1030 RETURN
 2000 PUT(194,0)-(255,191),Z,PSET:
        DRAW "BM194,0"+XY$+ZO$+ZU$+P$(4)
 2010 DRAW "BM194,16"+XM$+ZO$+ZV$+ZE$
 2015 SOUND 100,10
 2020 DRAW "BM194,64"+X$(6)+ZR$+ZO$+ZM$+"BM210,80":
        GOSUB 2500
 2030 FX=X-1: FY=Y
 2040 FP=6912+9*FY+FX: F=PEEK(FP)
 2050 IF F<>2 AND F<> 130 THEN 2000
 2060 DRAW"BM194,96"+XT$+ZO$+"BM210,112": GOSUB 2510:
        TX=X-1: TY=Y
```

```
2070 TP=6912+9*TY+TX: T=PEEK(TP)
2080 DX=TX-FX: DY=TY-FY
2090 IF (ABS(DX)<>1 AND ABS(DX)<>2) OR
     ABS(DX)<>ABS(DY) THEN 2000
2100 IF DY>0 AND F=2 THEN 2000
2110 IF ABS(DX)=1 THEN 2300
2120 IF T<>0 THEN 2000
2130 JX=FX+DX/2: JY=FY+DY/2
2140 JP=6912+9*JY+JX: J=PEEK(JP)
2150 IF J<>1 AND J<>129 THEN 2000
2160 C=WP: P=0: X=FX: Y=FY: GOSUB 1000: POKE FP,0
2170 P=1: IF F=130 OR TY=1 THEN P=2
2180 X=TX: Y=TY: GOSUB 1000: POKE TP,F: IF TY=1 THEN
     POKE TP,130
2190 P=0: X=JX: Y=JY: GOSUB 1000: POKE JP,0
2200 RETURN
2300 IF T<>0 THEN 2000
2310 P=0: C=WP: X=FX: Y=FY: GOSUB 1000: POKE FP,0
2320 P=1: IF F=130 OR TY=1 THEN P=2
2330 X=TX: Y=TY: GOSUB 1000: POKE TP,F: IF Y=1 THEN
     POKE TP,130
2340 RETURN
2500 X=1: Y=8
2510 X2=(X-1)*24: Y2=(Y-1)*24:
     GET(X2,Y2)-(X2+23,Y2+23),CQ,G
2520 COLOR WS,WS: DRAW Z$+Z$+"BM-24,0": COLOR BS,WS
2530 DRAW X$(X)+Y$(Y)+"BM-24,0"
2540 PUT(X2,Y2)-(X2+23,Y2+23),CQ,NOT
2550 A$=INKEY$: IF A$<>"" THEN 2580
2560 PUT(X2,Y2)-(X2+23,Y2+23),CQ,NOT
2570 A$=INKEY$: IF A$="" THEN 2540
2580 PUT (X2,Y2)-(X2+23,Y2+23),CQ,PSET:
     IF ASC(A$)=13 THEN RETURN
2590 IF A$="K" THEN 5000
2600 NY=Y+(A$="Q")+2*(A$="W")+(A$="E")-
     (A$="Z")-2*(A$="X")-(A$="C")
2610 NX=X+(A$="Q")+2*(A$="A")+(A$="Z")-
     (A$="E")-2*(A$="D")-(A$="C")
2620 IF NX>=1 AND NX<=8 AND NY>=1 AND NY<=8 THEN
     X=NX: Y=NY
2630 GOTO 2510
3000 MP=USR0(0): IF MP=0 THEN 3900
3005 IF MP<0 THEN MP=65536+MP
3010 PUT (194,0)-(255,191),Z,PSET
3020 DRAW "BM194,0"+XM$+ZY$+"BM194,16"+XM$+ZO$+ZV$+ZE$
3030 DRAW "BM194,64"+X$(6)+ZR$+ZO$+ZM$+"BM210,80"
     +X$(XB)+Y$(YB)
3040 DRAW "BM194,96"+XT$+ZO$+"BM210,112"+X$(X1)+Y$(Y1)
3050 FY=INT(MP/256): TY=MP-256*FY
3060 FX=INT(FY/16): FY=FY-16*FX
3070 TX=INT(TY/16): TY=TY-16*TX
3080 DRAW "BM210,80"+X$(FX)+Y$(FY):
     DRAW "BM210,112"+X$(TX)+Y$(TY)
3090 P=0: X=FX-1: Y=FY: GOSUB 1000
3100 TP=6912+9*TY+TX-1: T=PEEK(TP)
3110 P=1: IF T=129 THEN P=2
```

```
3120 C=BP: X=TX-1: Y=TY: GOSUB 1000
3130 IF ABS(TX-FX)<>2 THEN RETURN
3140 X=FX+(TX-FX)/2-1: Y=FY+(TY-FY)/2
3150 P=0: GOSUB 1000: RETURN
3900 CLS: PRINT @224, "I HAVE NO MOVE -- YOU WIN"
3901 PRINT @288, "ANOTHER GAME ?"
3902 A$=INKEY$: IF A$="" THEN 3902
3903 IF A$="Y" THEN RUN
3904 STOP
5000 CLS: PRINT @224, "BAD LUCK -- I WON": GOTO 3901
9000 DIM X$(8):
        X$(1)="BM+0,4D8U8E2E2F2F2D8U6L8BM+12,-6"
9001 X$(2)="R6F2D2G2F2D2G2L6E2U2E2R2L4U4BM+10,-2"
9002 X$(3)="BM+8,2H2L4G2D8F2R4E2BM+4,-10"
9003 X$(4)="R6F2D8G2L6E2U8BM+10,-2"
9004 X$(5)="R8L8D6R6L6D6R8BM+4,-12"
9005 X$(6)="R8L8D6R6L6D6BM+12,-12"
9006 X$(7)="BM+8,2H2L4G2D8F2R4E2U4L4BM+8,-6"
9007 X$(8)="D12U6R8D6U12BM+4,0"
9008 DIM Y$(8): Y$(1)="BM+2,2E2D12L2R4BM+6,-12"
9009 Y$(2)="BM+0,2E2R4F2D2G2L2G4D2R8BM+4,-12"
9010 Y$(3)="BM+0,2E2R4F2D2G2F2D2G2L4H2BM+12,-10"
9011 Y$(4)="BM+6,0D12U12G6D2R8BM+4,-8"
9012 Y$(5)="R8L8D4F2R4F2D2G2L4H2BM+12,-10"
9013 Y$(6)="BM+8,2H2L4G2D8F2R4E2U2H2L4BM+10,-6"
9014 Y$(7)="D2U2R8D2G4D6BM+8,-12"
9015 Y$(8)="BM+2,0R4F2D2G2L4G2D2F2R4E2U2H2L4H2U2
        BM+12,-2"
9016 XM$="D12U12F4D2U2E4D12BM+4,-12"
9017 XT$="R8L4D12BM+8,-12"
9018 XY$="D2F4D6U6E4U2BM+4,0"
9019 ZE$="BM+6,+12L4H2U4E2R4F2D2L6BM+10,-8"
9020 ZM$="BM+0,+12U8R2F2D6U6E2F2D6BM+4,-12"
9021 ZO$="BM+2,4R4F2D4G2L4H2U4BM+12,-6"
9022 ZU$="BM+0,4D6F2R2E2F2U8BM+4,-4"
9023 ZV$="BM+0,4D2F2D2F2E2U2E2U2BM+4,-4"
9024 ZY$="BM+0,4D6F2R2E4U4D10G2L4BM+10,-16"
9025 Z$="D12R2U12R2D12R2U12R2D12BM+4,-12"
9026 ZR$="BM+0,12U8F2E2R2F2BM+4,-6"
9027 RETURN
10000 RESTORE: FOR X=6656 TO 6882
10010 READ A: POKE X,A: NEXT X
10020 FOR X=6912 TO 7001
10030 READ A: POKE X,A: NEXT X
10040 RETURN
10050 DATA 207,166,136,32,167,128,32,245,158,152,
        156,158,35,194,166,130
10060 DATA 52,8,31,80,31,139,127,26,1,127,26,5,
        134,35,183,26
10070 DATA 0,48,141,0,229,166,132,129,1,39,12,129,
        129,38,16,198
10080 DATA 246,141,95,198,248,141,91,198,8,141,87,
        198,10,141,83,48
10090 DATA 2,122,26,0,38,223,246,26,5,39
        ,8,190,26,6,111,133
10100 DATA 88,32,8,246,26,1,39,54,190,26,2,49,
```

```
        133,166,132,111
10110 DATA 132,167,164,31,32,141,21,52,2,133,8,39,
        4,134,129,167
10120 DATA 164,31,16,141,7,53,4,53,8,126,140,55,
        134,255,76,192
10130 DATA 9,42,251,203,10,88,88,88,88,52,4,171,
        224,57,79,95
10140 DATA 32,229,49,133,166,164,129,255,39,45,132,
        127,129,1,39,39
10150 DATA 129,2,39,36,127,26,4,134,246,141,46,134,
        248,141,42,134
10160 DATA 8,141,32,134,10,141,28,125,26,4,
        39,5,125,26,1,38
10170 DATA 6,247,26,1,191,26,2,57,166,165,38,251,
        247,26,5,191
10180 DATA 26,6,57,166,166,138,128,32,2,166,166,129,
        130,38,232,124
10190 DATA 26,4,57
10200 DATA 255,255,255,255,255,255,255,255,255
10210 DATA 0,1,0,1,0,1,0,1,255
10220 DATA 1,0,1,0,1,0,1,0,255
10230 DATA 0,1,0,1,0,1,0,1,255
10240 DATA 0,0,0,0,0,0,0,0,255
10250 DATA 0,0,0,0,0,0,0,0,255
10260 DATA 2,0,2,0,2,0,2,0,255
10270 DATA 0,2,0,2,0,2,0,2,255
10280 DATA 2,0,2,0,2,0,2,0,255
10290 DATA 255,255,255,255,255,255,255,255,255
```

```
                      * DRAUGHTS PROGRAM
                      * FOR THE DRAGON

0000                  BLANK  EQU 0            EMPTY SQUARE
FFFF                  NULL   EQU -1           BOARD EDGE
0001                  BLACK  EQU 1            BLACK PIECE
0002                  WHITE  EQU 2            WHITE PIECE
0080                  KING   EQU 128          ADD 128 FOR KING

1A00                  CSTART EQU $1A00        CODE START
1B00                  BOARD  EQU CSTART+256   BOARD IN NEXT PAGE
8C37                  GIVABF EQU $8C37        RETURN ADDRESS

0E00                         ORG CSTART
                      * DATA AREA
1A00                  COUNT  RMB 1
                      * DATA AREA FOR NORMAL MOVE
1A01                  MOVE   RMB 1            MOVE DIRECTION/FLAG
1A02                  MOVEFR RMB 2            MOVE FROM ADDRESS
1A04                  TRAPFL RMB 1            TRAP FLAG
                      * DATA AREA FOR CAPTURES
1A05                  CAPT   RMB 1            CAPTURE DIRECTION/FLAG
1A06                  CAPTFR RMB 2            CAPTURE FROM ADDRESS

1A08                         ORG CSTART+$10
1A10                  START
1A10 3408                    PSHS DP          SAVE DIRECT PAGE REG
1A12 1F50                    TFR PC,D         SET DIRECT PAGE REG
1A14 1F8B                    TFR A,DP
1A16 7F1A01                  CLR MOVE         CANCEL OLD MOVE
1A19 7F1A05                  CLR CAPT         "      " CAPTURE

1A1C 8623                    LDA #35          35 POSITIONS TO CHECK
1A1E B71A00                  STA COUNT
1A21 308D00E5                LEAX BOARD+10,PCR X=BOARD POSITION

                      * CHECK ALL POSITIONS
1A25                  NEXT
1A25 A684                    LDA ,X           GET PIECE
1A27 8101                    CMPA #BLACK      NORMAL BLACK PIECE?
1A29 270C                    BEQ MANFND       YES=>CHECK IT
1A2B 8181                    CMPA #BLACK+KING  BLACK KING?
1A2D 2610                    BNE ENDSCH       NO=>NEXT PIECE
1A2F C6F6                    LDB #-10         TEST BACKWARD MOVES
1A31 8D5F                    BSR TEST
1A33 C6F8                    LDB #-8
1A35 8D5B                    BSR TEST
1A37                  MANFND
1A37 C608                    LDB #8           TEST FORWARD MOVES
1A39 8D57                    BSR TEST
1A3B C60A                    LDB #10
1A3D 8D53                    BSR TEST
1A3F                  ENDSCH
1A3F 3002                    LEAX 2,X         NEXT PIECE
1A41 7A1A00                  DEC COUNT        FINISHED?
```

```
1A44 26DF             BNE NEXT        YES=>LOOP

                * ALL POSITIONS NOW CHECKED

1A46 F61A05           LDB CAPT        CAPTURE FOUND ?
1A49 2708             BEQ NORMOV      NO=> NORMAL MOVE
1A4B BE1A06           LDX CAPTFR      FROM ADDRESS
1A4E 6F85             CLR B,X         REMOVE PIECE JUMPED
1A50 58               ASLB            MOVE DOUBLE DISTANCE
1A51 2008             BRA GOTMOV
1A53            NORMOV
1A53 F61A01           LDB MOVE        MOVE FOUND?
1A56 2736             BEQ NOMOVE      NO=>COMPUTER LOSES
1A58 BE1A02           LDX MOVEFR      FROM ADDRESS
1A5B            GOTMOV
1A5B 3185             LEAY B,X        Y=NEW POS.
1A5D A684             LDA ,X          GET PIECE
1A5F 6F84             CLR ,X          MOVE IT
1A61 A7A4             STA ,Y
1A63 1F20             TFR Y,D         CONVERT NEW POS.
1A65 8D15             BSR CONVIT
1A67 3402             PSHS A          SAVE COL,ROW
1A69 8508             BITA #8         IS IT NOW A KING ?
1A6B 2704             BEQ NOTKNG
1A6D 8681             LDA #KING+BLACK  YES=>CONVERT IT
1A6F A7A4             STA ,Y
1A71            NOTKNG
1A71 1F10             TFR X,D         CONVERT OLD POS.
1A73 8D07             BSR CONVIT
1A75 3504             PULS B          GET NEW POS. COL,ROW
1A77            CEND
1A77 3508             PULS DP         RESTORE DIRECT PAGE REG
1A79 7E8C37           JMP GIVABF      RETURN A,B TO BASIC

                * CONVERT ADDRESS IN D TO COL,ROW COORDINATES
                * COL IN HIGH NIBBLE OF A
                * ROW IN LOW NIBBLE OF A
1A7C            CONVIT
                * OFFSET INTO BOARD=B REG
1A7C 86FF             LDA #-1
1A7E            CLOOP
1A7E 4C               INCA
1A7F C009             SUBB #9         SUBTRACT 9
1A81 2AFB             BPL CLOOP       UNTIL NEGATIVE
1A83 CB0A             ADDB #10        FIRST COLUMN IS NUMBER 1
1A85 58               ASLB            SHIFT TO HIGH NIBBLE
1A86 58               ASLB
1A87 58               ASLB
1A88 58               ASLB
1A89 3404             PSHS B          MERGE WITH ROW
1A8B ABE0             ADDA ,S+
1A8D 39               RTS

1A8E            NOMOVE
1A8E 4F               CLRA            RETURN 0 TO BASIC
1A8F 5F               CLRB
```

```
1A90 20E5              BRA CEND

                  *
                  * TEST TYPE OF MOVE POSSIBLE FOR
                  *  PIECE AT POS X MOVING TO B+X
                  * IF LEGAL MOVE POSSIBLE SAVE IT
                  * IF CAPTURE POSSIBLE SAVE IT
                  * NORMAL MOVES WHICH RESULT IN
                  *  POSSIBLE TRAPS(IMMEDIATE CAPTURE)
                  *  ARE SAVED ONLY IF THERE ARE
                  *  NO OTHER MOVES FOUND YET
1A92              TEST
1A92 3185              LEAY B,X         Y=TO POSITION
1A94 A6A4              LDA ,Y           TEST TO POSITION
1A96 81FF              CMPA #NULL
1A98 272D              BEQ RET          NULL=>RETURN
1A9A 847F              ANDA #$7F
1A9C 8101              CMPA #BLACK
1A9E 2727              BEQ RET          BLACK=>RETURN
1AA0 8102              CMPA #WHITE
1AA2 2724              BEQ EVALCP       WHITE=>EVALUATE CAPTURE
                  * EVALUATE NORMAL MOVE
1AA4 7F1A04            CLR TRAPFL       CLEAR TRAP FLAG
1AA7 86F6              LDA #-10         TEST TRAPS FROM BEHIND
1AA9 8D2E              BSR CHKKNG
1AAB 86F8              LDA #-8
1AAD 8D2A              BSR CHKKNG
1AAF 8608              LDA #8           TEST TRAPS FROM AHEAD
1AB1 8D20              BSR CHKANY
1AB3 860A              LDA #10
1AB5 8D1C              BSR CHKANY
1AB7 7D1A04            TST TRAPFL       ANY TRAPS ?
1ABA 2705              BEQ SAVEM        NO=>SAVE MOVE
1ABC 7D1A01            TST MOVE         ANY OTHER MOVE ?
1ABF 2606              BNE RET          YES=>RETURN
1AC1              SAVEM
1AC1 F71A01            STB MOVE         SAVE MOVE
1AC4 BF1A02            STX MOVEFR
1AC7              RET
1AC7 39                RTS

                  * EVALUATE CAPTURE
1AC8              EVALCP
1AC8 A6A5              LDA B,Y          EMPTY SPACE ON OTHER SIDE?
1ACA 26FB              BNE RET          NO=>RETURN
1ACC F71A05            STB CAPT         SAVE CAPTURE
1ACF BF1A06            STX CAPTFR
1AD2 39                RTS

                  * TEST POS Y+A FOR WHITE PIECE
                  * ( LOOKING FOR TRAPS )
1AD3              CHKANY
1AD3 A6A6              LDA A,Y
1AD5 8A80              ORA #KING        CAN BE KING OR NORMAL
1AD7 2002              BRA CHK
                  * TEST POS Y+A FOR WHITE KING
```

```
1AD9             CHKKNG
1AD9 A6A6                 LDA A,Y          CAN ONLY BE KING
1ADB             CHK
1ADB 8182                 CMPA #WHITE+KING
1ADD 26E8                 BNE RET          NO TRAP=>RETURN
1ADF 7C1A04               INC TRAPFL       SET TRAP FLAG
1AE2 39                   RTS

1AE3                      END
```

Chess

This program will allow you to challenge the computer to a game of chess. But be warned the computer is a terrible player and it is very very slow.

Hovever this program does have some nice graphics and for anyone who is a keen chess player it should not be too hard to turn the computer into a better player. Alternatively the program could be changed to allow two human players to have a game. The choice is yours.

This program is an excellent example of what is possible on the DRAGON. Chess is generally considered a game that is difficult for computers to play. While this program in no way pretends to play well it does show just what can be done in DRAGON BASIC with a little effort.

When the program is run the computer will set up the variables used, draw the board and pieces and then ask you for a move. You are white (at the top although your pieces are yellow in colour). Your move is made by moving a flashing 'cursor' over the piece that you want to move then pressing enter. You then move the cursor to the place that you want to move the piece to and press enter again. You move the cursor using the following keys:

	UP LEFT	UP	UP RIGHT	
	Q	W	E	
LEFT	A		D	RIGHT
	Z	X	C	
	DOWN LEFT	DOWN	DOWN RIGHT	

The computer does not check to see if your move is a legal one so be careful, (unless you are unscrupulous and want to cheat).

Should you wish to give up (or if you lose) press the 'K' key when it is your turn to move.

How the program works

The following is a breakdown of the program

lines	description
5	Jump to the main program. The main subroutines are placed close to the the start of the program to speed up execution
10 - 100	Takes the move that the computer is thinking about and checks to see if the piece will be threatened once the move is made.
200 - 640	makes the computers move. All the computers pieces are checked and each possible move that they can make is looked at. Finally the best move is chosen. Note since many moves will be of equal value a random factor is included so that the computer plays a little differently each time.
800 - 950	Puts the flashing cursor on the screen and allows the player to move it. When the enter key is pressed it returns the position that the cursor last occupied.

1000 - 1150	Draws the piece P with colour C at the board position X,Y
2000 - 2050	Puts all the pieces on the initial board.
3000 - 3150	inputs and makes the players move
4000 - 4400	performs program initialisation and sets up the arrays and strings used. Then draws the board and places the pieces on the screen.
4410 - 4450	main control loop 4410 get players move display computers move message get computers move goto 4410
6000 - 6010	control jumps here if the player gives up
9000 - 9040	defines the strings that are used to print letters and numbers on the screen.

```
  5 GOTO 4000
 10 PC=B(X+DX*C1,Y+DY*C1):
      B(X+DX*C1,Y+DY*C1)=B(X,Y): B(X,Y)=0
 20 F$="": FOR R=1 TO 6: FOR J=1 TO 8: D1=D(R,J,1):
      D2=D(R,J,2): L=1
 30 IF AX+D1*L<1 OR AX+D1*L>8 OR AY+D2*L<1 OR
      AY+D2*L>8 THEN 70
 40 IF R=1 AND D2<1 AND Q=0 THEN 70
 50 IF B(AX+D1*L,AY+D2*L)=-R THEN F$="1": GOTO 80
 60 IF R>2 AND R<6 AND B(AX+D1*L,AY+D2*L)=0 THEN
      L=L+1: GOTO 30
 70 NEXT J: NEXT R
 80 IF X>8 THEN 100
 90 B(X,Y)=B(X+DX*C1,Y+DY*C1): B(X+DX*C1,Y+DY*C1)=PC
100 RETURN
200 XB=0: YB=0: DB=0: CL=1: BP=0: X=9
210 AX=KX: AY=KY: G$="": GOSUB 20: G$=F$
220 FOR Y=1 TO 8: FOR X=1 TO 8
230 TB=0: CZ=1: TY=0: TX=0: D=0
240 IF B(X,Y)<1 THEN 580
250 P=B(X,Y): FOR I=1 TO 8: DY=D(P,I,2):
      DX=D(P,I,1): AX=KX: AY=KY: C1=1: PO=0
260 IF X+DX<1 OR X+DX>8 THEN 510
270 IF Y+DY<1 OR Y+DY>8 THEN 510
280 IF P>2 AND P<6 THEN 420
290 IF DY>-1 AND P=1 THEN 510
340 IF DX<>0 AND B(X+DX,Y+DY)>-1 THEN 510
350 IF P=6 THEN KX=X: KY=Y:: AX=X+DX: AY=Y+DY:
      GOSUB 10: IF F$="1" THEN 510
360 IF DX=0 AND B(X,Y+DY)<>0 THEN 510
370 PO=8-P-B(X+DX,Y+DY)*3
380 IF Y<>7 OR DX<>0 OR B(X,5)<> 0 OR P>1 THEN 510
390 IF G$="1" THEN GOSUB 10: IF F$="" THEN 510
400 IF G$="1" OR RND(0)>.3 THEN C1=2
410 GOTO 510
420 X1=X: Y1=Y
430 IF P=3 AND INT(I/2)*2<I THEN 510
440 IF P=4 AND INT(I/2)*2=I THEN 510
450 IF X1+DX<1 OR X1+DX>8 OR Y1+DY<1 OR Y1+DY>8 THEN
      C1=C1-1: GOTO 510
460 IF B(X1+DX,Y1+DY)>0 THEN C1=C1-1: GOTO 510
470 PO=8-P+RND(3)-B(X1+DX,Y1+DY)*3
480 IF G$="1" THEN GOSUB 10: IF F$="" THEN PO=PO+50:
      GOTO 510
490 IF B(X1+DX,Y1+DY)<>0 THEN 510
500 C1=C1+1: X1=X1+DX: Y1=Y1+DY: GOTO 450
510 IF PO=0 THEN 550
520 IF G$="1" THEN GOSUB 10: IF F$="" THEN PO=PO+50:
      GOTO 550
530 IF G$="" THEN GOSUB 10: IF F$="1" THEN PO=0:
      GOTO 550
540 IF PO>=TB THEN AX=X+DX*C1: AY=Y+DY*C1: GOSUB 10:
      IF F$="1" THEN PO=PO-P*2
```

```
550 IF PO>TB THEN TB=PO: TX=X: TY=Y: D=I: CZ=C1
560 NEXT I
570 IF TB>BP OR (TB=BP AND (RND(0)>.9 OR (TY<YB AND
     RND(0)>.5))) THEN BP=TB: XB=TX: YB=TY: CL=CZ:
     DB=D
580 NEXT X: NEXT Y: P=B(XB,YB): X1=XB+D(P,DB,1)*CL:
     Y1=YB+D(P,DB,2)*CL: IF P=6 THEN KX=X1: KY=Y1
585 IF Y1=1 AND P=1 THEN P(5)=P(5)+1: B(XB,YB)=5
590 AX=KX: AY=KY: B(X1,Y1)=B(XB,YB): B(XB,YB)=0:
     Q=1: GOSUB 20: Q=0
600 DRAW "BM194,64"+X$(6)+P$(4)+ZO$+ZM$+"BM210,80"
     +X$(XB)+Y$(YB)
610 DRAW "BM194,96"+XT$+ZO$+"BM210,112"+X$(X1)+Y$(Y1)
620 X=XB: Y=YB: P=0: C=BL: GOSUB 1000
630 P=B(X1,Y1): X=X1: Y=Y1: GOSUB 1000
640 RETURN
800 X1=1:Y1=1
805 X2=(X1-1)*24: Y2=(Y1-1)*24:
     GET(X2,Y2)-(X2+23,Y2+23),CQ,G
808 COLOR WS,WS: DRAW Z$+Z$+"BM-24,0": COLOR BS,WS
810 DRAW X$(X1)+Y$(Y1)+"BM-24,0"
820 PUT(X2,Y2)-(X2+23,Y2+23),CQ,NOT
830 A$=INKEY$: IF A$<>"" THEN 900
840 PUT(X2,Y2)-(X2+23,Y2+23),CQ,NOT
850 A$=INKEY$: IF A$="" THEN 820
900 PUT (X2,Y2)-(X2+23,Y2+23),CQ,PSET: IF ASC(A$)=13
     THEN RETURN
910 IF A$="K" THEN X1=999: RETURN
920 Y1=Y1+(A$="Q" OR A$="W" OR A$="E")-(A$="Z" OR
     A$="X" OR A$="C")
930 X1=X1+(A$="Q" OR A$="A" OR A$="Z")-(A$="E" OR
     A$="D" OR A$="C")
940 IF X1<1 THEN X1=1
941 IF X1>8 THEN X1=8
942 IF Y1<1 THEN Y1=1
943 IF Y1>8 THEN Y1=8
950 GOTO 805
1000 X$=STR$(X*24-24):Y$=STR$(Y*24-1)
1002 IF X-2*INT(X/2)<>Y-2*INT(Y/2) THEN
     PUT(X*24-24,Y*24-24)-(X*24-1,Y*24-1),BQ,PSET
     ELSE PUT(X*24-24,Y*24-24)-
     (X*24-1,Y*24-1),WQ,PSET
1005 COLOR C,WS: DRAW "BM"+X$+","+Y$
1010 ON P GOSUB 1100,1110,1120,1130,1140,1150
1020 COLOR BS,WS
1030 RETURN
1100 DRAW P$: RETURN
1110 DRAW KN$: RETURN
1120 DRAW B$: RETURN
1130 DRAW R$: RETURN
1140 DRAW Q$: RETURN
1150 DRAW KI$: RETURN
2000 FOR Y=1 TO 8: FOR X=1 TO 8
2010 IF B(X,Y)=0 THEN 2040
2020 C=BL: IF B(X,Y)<0 THEN C=WH
2030 P=ABS(B(X,Y)): GOSUB 1000
```

```
2040 NEXT X: NEXT Y
2050 RETURN
3000 IF F$<>"1" THEN 3010
      ELSE PUT (194,0)-(255,191),Z
3002 DRAW "BM194,50"+X$(3)+X$(8)+X$(5)+X$(3)+XK$:
      DRAW "BM200,66"+XM$+X$(1)+XT$+X$(5)
3004 DRAW "BM200,100"+XY$+ZO$+ZU$:
      DRAW "BM200,116"+XW$+ZI$+P$(2)
3005 SOUND 100,20
3006 IF INKEY$="" THEN 3006 ELSE STOP
3010 PUT(194,0)-(255,191),Z,PSET:
      DRAW "BM194,0"+XY$+ZO$+ZU$+P$(4)
3011 DRAW "BM194,16"+XM$+ZO$+ZV$+ZE$
3012 DRAW "BM194,64"+X$(6)+P$(4)+ZO$+ZM$+"BM210,80":
      GOSUB 800: IF X1=999 THEN STOP
3020 X=X1: Y=Y1
3030 DRAW"BM194,96"+XT$+ZO$+"BM210,112": GOSUB 805:
      IF X1=999 THEN 6000
3035 XB=X1:YB=Y1
3040 IF B(XB,YB)>0 THEN P(B(XB,YB))=P(B(XB,YB))-1
3050 B(XB,YB)=B(X,Y)
3060 B(X,Y)=0: C=WH
3070 IF B(XB,YB)<-1 OR YB<8 THEN 3120
3080 DRAW "BM194,150"+P$(1)+ZI$+ZE$+ZC$+ZE$
3090 A$=INKEY$
3100 A=0: FOR Z=1 TO 5: IF A$=C$(Z) THEN A=-Z
3110 NEXT Z: IF A=0 THEN 3090
3115 DRAW "BM230,170"+P$(-A):B(XB,YB)=A
3120 P=0: GOSUB 1000
3130 P=-B(XB,YB): X=XB: Y=YB: GOSUB 1000
3150 RETURN
4000 CLEAR 1000
4010 BS=3:WS=1:BL=4:WH=2
4020 PMODE 1,1: SCREEN 1,0: COLOR BS,WS: PCLS
4030 GOSUB 9000: F$="": DIM Z(150):
      GET (194,0)-(255,191),Z,G
4040 P$="BM+6,0R10H2L6E2R2E2L6H2R10U2L10E2R6H2L2"
4050 KI$="BM+2,0R18BM-4,-2L10BM+4,-2R2E2L6
      U2R6E2L10H2R14U2L2BM-4,0L2BM-4,0L2BM+6,-2
      R2BM-6,-2R10U2L10BM+4,-2R2"
4060 Q$="BM+4,0R14BM-4,-2L6E2R2U2L2H2R6E2L10
      U2R10U2L10E2R6H2L2H4F2E2R2F2E2"
4070 B$="BM+4,0R14BM-4,-2L6E2R2U2L2H2R6E2L10
      H2R2BM+4,0R6E2L6BM-4,0L4E2R4BM+4,0R4
      H2BM-4,0L6E2R6H2L2"
4080 R$="BM+6,0R10H2L6E2R2E2L6H2R10U2L10
      U2R10U4BM-4,0D4H2U2BM-4,0D4"
4090 KN$="BM+18,0L14E2R10U2L10E2R6H2L2U2R2U2L4H2
      R12D2R2U2H2L12E2R8H2L4E2"
4100 DIM BQ(30),WQ(30),CQ(30)
4110 KX=5: KY=6
4120 LINE(24,0)-(47,0),PSET
4130 LINE -(47,23),PSET
4140 LINE -(24,23),PSET
4150 LINE -(24,0),PSET: PAINT (28,8),BS
4160 GET (24,0)-(47,23),BQ,G
```

```
4170 GET (0,0)-(23,23),WQ,G
4180 O=24: FOR Y=0 TO 168 STEP 24
4190 FOR X=0 TO 168 STEP 48
4200 PUT (X+O,Y)-(X+O+23,Y+23),BQ,PSET
4210 NEXT X: O=24-O: NEXT Y
4220 DIM B(8,8): FOR Y=1 TO 8: FOR X=1 TO 8
4230 Z= (Y=8)*B(X,1)+(Y=2)-(Y=7)
4240 IF Y=1 THEN READ Z
4250 B(X,Y)=Z: NEXT X: NEXT Y
4260 DATA -4,-2,-3,-6,-5,-3,-2,-4
4270 GOSUB 2000
4280 DIM D(6,8,2), P(6)
4290 FOR X=1 TO 6: P(X)=2: FOR Y=1 TO 8
4300 D(X,Y,2)=-((Y<3) OR (Y=8))+((Y>3) AND (Y<7))
4310 D(X,Y,1)=-((Y>1) AND (Y<5))+(Y>5)
4320 NEXT Y: IF X<>2 THEN 4360
4330 FOR Y=1 TO 4: READ D(X,Y,1), D(X,Y,2):
        D(X,Y+4,1)=-D(X,Y,1): D(X,Y+4,2)=-D(X,Y,2)
4340 NEXT Y
4350 DATA -2,1,-1,2,1,2,2,1
4360 IF X=1 THEN P(X)=8
4370 IF X>4 THEN P(X)=1
4380 NEXT X
4390 DIM C$(5): FOR X=1 TO 5: READ C$(X): NEXT X
4400 DATA P,N,B,R,Q
4410 GOSUB 3000
4420 PUT (194,0)-(255,191),Z,PSET
4430 DRAW "BM194,0"+XM$+ZY$+"BM194,16"+XM$+ZO$+ZV$+ZE$
4440 GOSUB 200
4450 GOTO 4410
6000 CLS: PRINT @64, "BAD LUCK — I WIN"
6010 STOP
9000 DIM X$(8):
        X$(1)="BM+0,4D8U8E2E2F2F2D8U6L8BM+12,-6"
9001 X$(2)="R6F2D2G2F2D2G2L6E2U2E2R2L4U4BM+10,-2"
9002 X$(3)="BM+8,2H2L4G2D8F2R4E2BM+4,-10"
9003 X$(4)="R6F2D8G2L6E2U8BM+10,-2"
9004 X$(5)="R8L8D6R6L6D6R8BM+4,-12"
9005 X$(6)="R8L8D6R6L6D6BM+12,-12"
9006 X$(7)="BM+8,2H2L4G2D8F2R4E2U4L4BM+8,-6"
9007 X$(8)="D12U6R8D6U12BM+4,0"
9008 DIM Y$(8): Y$(1)="BM+2,2E2D12L2R4BM+6,-12"
9009 Y$(2)="BM+0,2E2R4F2D2G2L2G4D2R8BM+4,-12"
9010 Y$(3)="BM+0,2E2R4F2D2G2F2D2G2L4H2BM+12,-10"
9011 Y$(4)="BM+6,0D12U12G6D2R8BM+4,-8"
9012 Y$(5)="R8L8D4F2R4F2D2G2L4H2BM+12,-10"
9013 Y$(6)="BM+8,2H2L4G2D8F2R4E2U2H2L4BM+10,-6"
9014 Y$(7)="D2U2R8D2G4D6BM+8,-12"
9015 Y$(8)="BM+2,0R4F2D2G2L4G2D2F2R4E2U2H2L4H2U2
        BM+12,-2"
9016 XK$="D12U4E8G6F6BM+4,-12"
9017 XM$="D12U12F4D2U2E4D12BM+4,-12"
9018 XT$="R8L4D12BM+8,-12"
9019 XY$="D2F4D6U6E4U2BM+4,0"
9020 ZE$="BM+6,+12L4H2U4E2R4F2D2L6BM+10,-8"
9021 ZM$="BM+0,+12U8R2F2D6U6E2F2D6BM+4,-12"
```

```
9022 ZO$="BM+2,4R4F2D4G2L4H2U4BM+12,-6"
9023 ZI$="BM+4,0D2BM-2,2R2D8L2R4BM+6,-12"
9024 ZU$="BM+0,4D6F2R2E2F2U8BM+4,-4"
9025 ZV$="BM+0,4D2F2D2F2E2U2E2U2BM+4,-4"
9026 ZY$="BM+0,4D6F2R2E4U4D10G2L4BM+10,-16"
9027 Z$="D12R2U12R2D12R2U12R2D12BM+4,-12"
9028 ZC$="BM+8,6H2L4G2D4F2R4E2BM+4,-10"
9029 DIM P$(5):
        P$(1)="BM+0,16U12F2E2R2F2D4G2L2H2BM+10,-10"
9030 P$(2)="BM+0,12U8F2E2R2F2D6BM+4,-12"
9031 P$(3)="D12E2F2R2E2U4H2L2G2BM+10,-10"
9032 P$(4)="BM+0,12U8F2E2R2F2BM+4,-6"
9033 P$(5)="BM+8,16U12G2H2L2G2D4F2R2E2BM+6,-10"
9034 XW$="D12E4U2D2F4U12BM+4,0"
9040 RETURN
```

Adventure

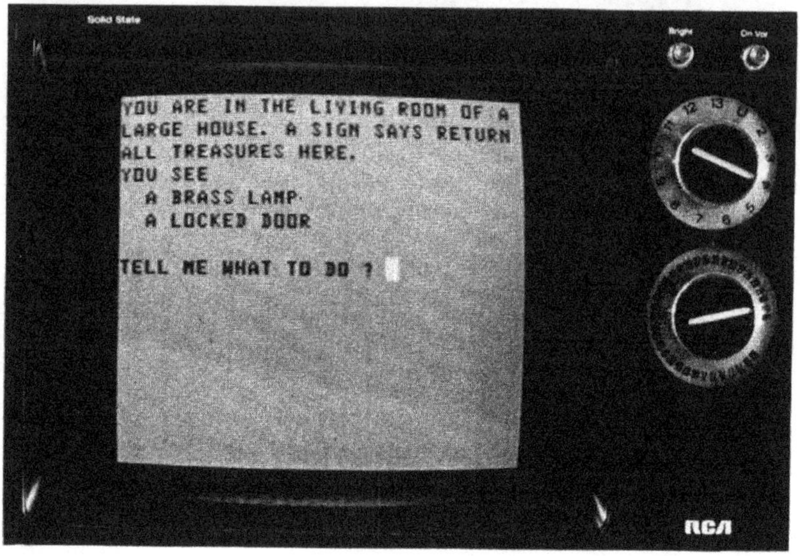

An adventure is a program that allows you to enter and explore strange new worlds, find treasures and battle fierce monsters. As an adventurer you must solve the riddles and problems of the world you will enter if you are ever to leave alive.

This program allows you to have an adventure on your DRAGON. The computer will describe the locations you will visit and the things you will see. Also it will prompt you to tell it what to do. The commands you may use consist of one or two words. You must always supply a verb (i.e the action you wish to do) and often you will need a noun (i.e the object you wish to perform the action on).

Some examples are :

'north' - move north and have a look around

'take axe' - if there is an axe where you are this will tell the computer to try and pick it up for you

In a few cases you will be asked for more information after you have given the computer a command.

For example if you say

'kill dragon' the computer will ask you what you wish to kill the dragon with. In this case just enter the name of the weapon you wish to use or nothing (just hit enter) if you wish to use your bare hands.

As well as giving you an adventure to play this program also allows you to easily create your own worlds for yourself or a friend to adventure in.

How to play

The computer will display a description of the location that you are in and it will describe any objects that you can see. It will then ask you what you want to do. You must then answer with a command as described above. The computer will try to perform your command and if all goes well it will go back and do this all over again. If however your command does not work - perhaps because of a spelling mistake - or if you are not able to do the command yet the computer will print an appropriate message, and ask you for a new command.

Some of the commands you can use are

north, south, east, west, up, down

These allow you to move around.

inventory - lists everything you are carrying

take - picks up objects

drop - drops objects

etc

If an object description has an adjective in it - e.g 'mean troll', then you cannot say 'kill troll'. You must use 'kill mean troll' or just 'kill mean'.

Note most words may be abbreviated to one or two letters; provided this does not cause any ambiguity between words. If an abbreviation would match more than one word the computer uses the first one it finds.

When playing an adventure it is usually a good idea to draw a map of the world you are exploring. Since many adventures contain mazes it is almost impossible to find your way around unless you have a good map showing you which way to go.

How the program works

This program consists of two distinct parts. Firstly there is the data base that is in effect the game. It contains all the descriptions, objects and actions that make up the game. Secondly there is the program needed to allow the player to interact with the data base. This consists of the initialization for the game, getting the user's input and performing the desired action.

The data base

The fundamental parts of this adventure are the locations that make up the world, a map describing how these locations are connected, the objects that exist in this world and all the actions that the player may perform. The way that each of these is built up will now be described in more detail.

Locations

For each location we need a description to give the player to tell him where he is and a list of the locations he can get to from where he is. As well as these it is often useful to have some sort of condition that can be applied upon entering a location. These can be anything from, making sure the player has a source of light before allowing him to enter, to performing some action when he enters (such as making monsters attack him if he is not carrying a particular object).

In this program each location has a unique number that the computer uses to access that location. The numbers start at one and increase in increments of one up to the last location. For example this adventure has 30 locations.

The locations exist in the program in a number of arrays. The array L$ contains the strings that describe the locationse i.e the element L$(1) is the description for location 1. The 2 dimensional array L contains the locations that the player will enter if he tries to move in one of the 6 directions N,S,E,W,U,D, i.e L(1,1) is the location north of location 1 L(1,2) is south of location 1 etc. A value of 0 means that there is no location in that direction. The array L contains another element for each location (e.g L(1,7)) that defines the CONDITION that must be applied for the player to ENTER THIS location. These conditions consist of short pieces of program that are located at lines 4000 - 4208 for this adventure.

Objects

The information we need for each object consists of its description, where it is, what type of object it is (i.e a treasure or a monster etc), how strong it is and to allow greater flexibility a condition to be performed if the player tries to pick up this object. These conditions may be one that always fails to stop people from taking things like tables, or one to kill the player if he tries to take a forbidden object.

The computer knows about each object by its number just like locations.

The data for the objects is contained in two arrays OD$ and OD. OD$ contains the object description as for the locations while OD is a two dimensional array that contains the following information:

First element	-	location of the object <0 if carried by the player, -1 if it is dead or destroyed)
Second element	-	type 0 for an ordinary object <0 for a monster

		>0 for a treasure and this is the score for the treasure
Third element	-	strength for a weapon this is added to the player's strength in a fight and for a monster it is the strength of the monster
Fourth element	-	the condition to be done if the player takes the object

Lastly we need a list of actions that the player can perform. These are stored in the array V$ so again each verb will have a number associated with it and in this case the number is used to find the subroutine that will perform the action for the player.

Clearly all these arrays need to be set up and this is done at the start of the program by reading in the strings and values contained in the large block of data statements at the end of the program. To make things more easily changed the number of actions, objects, and locations is also stored in the data statements and is read in first. These data statements will be explained in more detail later.

The following is a breakdown of the program

LINES	FUNCTION
10	clears the screen and calls the subroutine to set up the arrays
20 - 80	control loop for the program it consists of 1 print location description print any visible objects 2 get the players input command perform the action if the action failed goto 2 else goto 1
1000 - 1120	Inputs the players command the first two words of what the player typed are put into the variables A$ and N$ (a word is any sequence of characters ending in a space) The verb array is then searched for A$ and if it is found the subroutine returns the verb numner to the main program, otherwise the player is prompted to try again.

1300 - 1340	searches the object description array OD$ for the word N$ (actually searches for W$ so a call can be made to 1305 if W$ has been set to the required word). If the word is found it returns the description from the array, the object number and a flag indicating that the search was succesful, otherwise the flag is set to indicate failure.
1500 - 1862	comprises the subroutines to process all the actions that the player may perform. The appropriate subroutine is called from the ON GOSUB in line 60
1999	a jump to here is made if an action fails and the message YOU CAN'T is to be printed.
2000 - 2050	prints all the objects that are in location L, (if L=0 then prints all the objects carried by the player) If none are found then prints 'NOTHING'.
4000 - 4208	This subroutine performs the condition number in the variable C. For this adventure C can be in the ranges 0 - 8 or 50 or 60 0 always succeds, 1 always fails 2 - 8 are used for entering various locations and taking certain objects 50 and 60 are subroutines to be performed and not just simple tests.

The rest of the program comprises the data statments that are used to initialise the arrays and the program used to initialize them.

7000 - 7002	VERB data The first number is the number of actions the player may perform The rest is the words that define the actions
8000 - 8013	OBJECT data The first number is the number of the objects in the game.(call it O) Then there are O numbers that are the starting locations for each object The next O strings are the object's descriptions. Lastly there are O*3 numbers where each triple contains the type, strength and condition for an object.
8100 - 8130	LOCATION data

The first number is the number of locations in the adventure
There is then one line for each location containing the object description the locations that are connected to this one and the condition for this location.

9000 - 9120 reads all the data statements and fills the arrays

9980 - 9981 These lines are jumped to at the end of the game if the player has found all the treasures succesfully.

9990 - 9992 This section is used at the end of the game (either after the player has been killed or if he finished the game) it prints the score and asks if the game is to be replayed.

How to create your own adventure

Firstly you need a world to explore. This involves building into the data base the descriptions of all the locations to be visited along with the connections between then. Along with this you will need to decide what if any conditions will be applied to entering the location.

As an example let us build an adventure with two locations. These will be

A HALL STRETCHING AS FAR AS THE EYE CAN SEE.

and A SMALL CAVERN.

The hall is north of the cavern and going south from the hall ends up in the cavern. No other directions are allowed. As a condition there will be a door between the two locations that will be locked. The player can only pass between the two if the door has been unlocked.

So we have

```
8100 DATA 2                  (the number of locations)
8101 DATA IN A HALL STRETCHING AS FAR AS THE EYE
          CAN SEE.,0,2,0,0,0,0,0
8102 DATA IN A SMALL CAVERN.,1,0,0,0,0,0,1
```

Note doors are only one way so that entering the hall has no condition while entering the cavern requires that the door be unlocked

Since the hall is the first location this will be where the player starts and where treasures must be put.

Now we need some objects. We already need a locked door and an unlocked door (at the start the locked door will exist between the locations but when the door is unlocked we will put the locked door in location -1 to get rid of it and replace it with the unlocked one). Obviously we also need a key to unlock the door. For a treasure let us have an emerald in the cavern. As well there will be sword in the hall and a snake guarding the emerald.

So we have

object type, strength, condition, location

locked door	0	0	fail	1
unlocked door	0	0	fail	-1
key	0	0	0	1
sword	0	10	0	1
snake	-1	100	fail	2
emerald	30	0	2	2

This means that the player cannot take either the door or the snake, and the emerald can only be taken if condition 2 is met. We will write condition 2 as a test for the snake being alive.

The sword has a strength of 10 and the snake 100 so if the player starts with a strength of 100 the fight between them should be fairly matched with a slight advantage to the player.

The emerald has a score of 30, the snake is a monster and the rest are just objects.

In the program this would be

```
8000 DATA 6,1,-1,1,1,1,2,2
8001 DATA LOCKED DOOR,UNLOCKED DOOR,KEY,SWORD,SNAKE
8002 DATA SNAKE,EMERALD
8003 DATA 0,0,1,0,0,1,0,0,0,0,10,0
8004 DATA -1,100,1,30,0,2
```

Now we need the actions to perform. The movements and their subroutines as well as 'INVENTORY', 'TAKE', 'DROP' and 'KILL' are fairly standard and will probably be used in all your adventures so look at the program for these. The other action we will have will be 'UNLOCK' for the door, so the verb list will be

```
7000 DATA 11,NORTH,SOUTH,EAST,WEST,UP,DOWN
7001 DATA TAKE,DROP,KILL,INVENTORY,UNLOCK
```

As well line 60 of the program will need to be changed since this calls the subroutine to do the players action. You must decide where each subroutine will go and then fill in the addresses. (The first address is for the first verb, the second address is for the second verb etc).

The only routine we need to write is for unlock. This needs to check if the player is in the hall and is carrying the key and the door is still locked. We now need a variable to indicate if the door is locked or not say 'LU' (remember this must be initialized at the start or the door may be unlocked when we thought it was locked).

Unlocking, then will consist of

```
1700 IF LU=1 OR L<>1 OR OD(3,1)<>0 THEN 1999
1701 OD(1,1)=-1: OD(2,1)=1: LU=1
1702 F=1: RETURN
```

A note about the variable 'F', it is used to indicate success or failure in the following manner:

F = 0 - failure

F = 1   - success

We still have 2 conditions and they are

1 is the door unlocked

and 2 is the snake dead

The subroutine to test the right condition will be

```
4000 ON C GOTO 4101,4102
4001 F=1: RETURN
```

And the conditions themselves

```
4101 F = -(LU <> 0): RETURN
4102 F = -(OD(5,1) = -1): RETURN
```

These may need some explanation. Take the second, what it means is IF OD(5,1) = -1 THEN F=1

else IF OD(5,1) <> -1 THEN F=0

It works because the statement OD(5,1)<>-1 will be equal to 0 if if OD(5,1)=-1 and it will equal -1 otherwise.

So now we have an adventure even though it is pretty small. Good luck writing your own.

Hints for playing the ADVENTURE program

1). Lost in the desert ?

Do not despair the desert is not really endless and if you strategically drop objects in the desert you should be able to make a map of the desert. You will need this map to find the oasis.

2). Can't get through the living room door ?

You will need the key that is buried somewhere in the desert. To dig up the key you will of course need a shovel which is also outside the house - somewhere.

3). Stuck in HELL ?

Do what the devil says.

4). Can't get past the pirate ?

Try the rum.

5). Can't kill the dragon ?

Keep trying.

6). Can't find the key to the gate ?

Try the rope.

7). Can't cross the chasm ?

Maybe a magic wand would be of assistance.

8). Can't find the last treasure ?

Go swimming.

```
  10 CLS: L=1: GOSUB 9000
  20 PRINT "YOU ARE "; L$(L): Q$="YOU SEE":
        GOSUB 2000
  30 SOUND 100,2:PRINT
  40 GOSUB 1000: PRINT
  50 PRINT V$; " ";
  60 ON VN GOSUB 1500,1520,1540,1560,1580,1600,1620,
        1640,1660,1680,1700,1720,1740,1760,1780,
        1800,1820,1840,1860
  70 IF F=1 THEN 20
  80 PRINT: GOTO 40
1000 INPUT "TELL ME WHAT TO DO ";S$:
        IF LEN(S$)=0 THEN 1000
1010 A$="": N$=""
1020 X=0: FOR I=1 TO LEN(S$)
1030 I$=MID$(S$,I,1)
1040 IF I$>="a" AND I$<="z" THEN I$=CHR$(ASC(I$)-32)
1050 IF I$=" " AND X=1 THEN I=LEN(S$): GOTO 1080
1060 IF I$=" " THEN X=1: GOTO 1080
1070 IF X=0 THEN A$=A$+I$ ELSE N$=N$+I$
1080 NEXT I: VN=0
1090 FOR I=1 TO VC: X=LEN(V$(I)):
        IF X>LEN(A$) THEN X=LEN(A$)
1100 IF LEFT$(A$,X)=LEFT$(V$(I),X) THEN VN=I:
        V$=V$(I): I=VC
1110 NEXT I: IF VN=0 THEN PRINT
        "I DON'T UNDERSTAND "; A$: GOTO 1000
1120 RETURN
1300 W$=N$: GOSUB 1305: IF F=0 THEN RETURN
        ELSE PRINT Y$: RETURN
1305 VN=0: IF LEN(W$)=0 THEN 1335
1310 FOR I=1 TO OC: X=LEN(OD$(I)):
        IF X>LEN(W$) THEN X=LEN(W$)
1320 IF LEFT$(W$,X)=LEFT$(OD$(I),X) THEN VN=I:
        Y$=OD$(I): I=OC
1330 NEXT I
1335 IF VN=0 THEN PRINT: PRINT "I DON'T UNDERSTAND ";
        W$: F=0: RETURN
1340 F=1: RETURN
1500 D=1: GOTO 1601
1520 D=2: GOTO 1601
1540 D=3: GOTO 1601
1560 D=4: GOTO 1601
1580 D=5: GOTO 1601
1600 D=6
1601 PRINT: IF L(L,D)=0 THEN PRINT
        "YOU CAN'T GO THAT WAY": F=0: RETURN
1603 C=L(L(L,D),7): GOSUB 4000
1605 IF F=0 THEN 1615
1610 IF OD(1,1)=0 THEN L=L(L,D): F=1: RETURN
1615 PRINT "SOMETHING STOPS YOU": F=0: RETURN
1620 GOSUB 1300: IF F=0 THEN RETURN
1621 IF OD(VN,1)<>L THEN PRINT "IT'S NOT HERE": F=0:
```

```
        RETURN
1622 IF OD(VN,2)<0 THEN 1999
1625 C=OD(VN,4): GOSUB 4000: IF F=0 THEN 1999
1630 IF CX<>0 THEN CX=CX-1: OD(VN,1)=0: RETURN
1631 PRINT "YOU ARE CARRYING TOO MUCH": F=0: RETURN
1640 GOSUB 1300: IF F=0 THEN RETURN
1641 IF OD(VN,1)<>0 THEN PRINT "YOU DON'T HAVE IT":
        F=0: RETURN
1642 OD(VN,1)=L: IF L=1 AND OD(VN,2)<>0 THEN
        SC=SC+OD(VN,2): OD(VN,1)=-1: PRINT
        "THE ";Y$;" VANISHES"
1644 CX=CX+1: IF SC=220 THEN 9980
1645 RETURN
1660 GOSUB 1300: IF F=0 THEN RETURN
1661 T$=Y$: MN=VN: IF OD(VN,2)>=0 THEN 1999
        ELSE MS=OD(VN,3)
1662 S=0: SOUND 150,4: PRINT: INPUT "KILL WITH WHAT "
        ;W$: IF W$="" THEN 1670
1663 GOSUB 1305: IF F=0 THEN 1662
1664 IF OD(VN,1)<>0 THEN PRINT "YOU DON'T HAVE IT":
        GOTO 1662
1665 IF OD(VN,3)=0 THEN PRINT "IT'S NOT A WEAPON":
        GOTO 1662
1666 S=OD(VN,3)
1670 PRINT: S=S+ST: IF MS>S+RND(20) THEN 1679
1671 IF S>MS+RND(15) THEN 1678
1672 PRINT "THE "; T$: PRINT
        "FIGHTS BACK. YOU FEEL WEAKER"
1673 ST=ST-RND(5): F=1: RETURN
1678 PRINT "YOU HAVE KILLED THE "; T$: PRINT
        "THE BODY VANISHES IN A CLOUD OF SMOKE.":
        OD(MN,1)=-1: F=1: RETURN
1679 PRINT "THE "; T$; " HAS KILLED YOU": GOTO 9990
1680 L1=L: L=0: PRINT: Q$="YOU ARE CARRYING":
        GOSUB 2000: L=L1: F=1: RETURN
1700 PRINT SC: F=1: RETURN
1720 GOSUB 1300: IF F=0 THEN RETURN
1721 IF VN<>20 OR OD(2,1)<>0 THEN 1999
1722 OD(14,1)=OD(VN,1): OD(VN,1)=-1: PRINT
        "AN IVORY KEY FALLS FROM THE CEILING": RETURN
1740 PRINT: IF L<>11 AND L<>29 THEN 1999
1741 IF L=11 AND OD(3,1)<>0 THEN PRINT
        "YOU SINK TO THE BOTTON OF THE LAKE AND DROWN"
        : GOTO 9990
1742 L=40-L: F=1: RETURN
1760 GOSUB 1300: IF F=0 THEN RETURN
1761 IF L=1 AND OD(4,1)=0 THEN OD(22,1)=-1:
        OD(23,1)=L: LU=1: RETURN
1762 IF L=13 AND OD(14,1)=0 THEN OD(24,1)=-1:
        OD(25,1)=L: GU=1: RETURN
1763 GOTO 1999
1780 IF OD(16,1)<>0 OR L<3 OR L>10 THEN 1999
1781 PRINT "YOU FIND ";
1782 IF L=6 AND OD(4,1)=-1 THEN OD(4,1)=L:
        PRINT "SOMETHING": F=1: RETURN
1783 PRINT "NOTHING": F=1: RETURN
```

```
1800 GOSUB 1300: IF F=0 THE RETURN
1801 IF OD(VN,2)<0 THEN 1999
1802 C=OD(VN,4): GOSUB 4000: IF F=0 THEN 1999
1803 PRINT "THAT HITS THE SPOT.": OD(VN,1)=-1: RETURN
1820 GOSUB 1300: IF F=0 THEN RETURN
1821 IF L<>24 OR VN<>7 THEN 1830
1822 PRINT "A BRIDGE APPEARS ACROSS  THE CHASM.":
     OD(15,1)=L: BE=1: F=1: RETURN
1830 PRINT "NOTHING HAPPENS.": F=1: RETURN
1840 IF L=24 OR L=26 THEN PRINT
     "THE FALL HAS BROKEN YOUR NECK.": GOTO 9990
1841 GOTO 1830
1860 GOSUB 1300: IF F=0 THEN RETURN
1861 IF VN<>18 THEN 1999
1862 PRINT "THAT WAS DELICIOUS.": OD(19,1)=OD(VN,1):
     OD(VN,1)=-1: RETURN
1999 PRINT "YOU CAN'T": F=0: RETURN
2000 X=0: PRINT Q$
2010 FOR I=1 TO OC: IF L<>OD(I,1) THEN 2030
2020 X=1: PRINT "  A";
2022 Z$=LEFT$(OD$(I),A): IF Z$="A" OR Z$="E"
     OR Z$="I" OR Z$="O" OR Z$="U" THEN PRINT "N";
2024 PRINT " ";OD$(I)
2030 NEXT I
2040 IF X=0 THEN PRINT "  NOTHING"
2050 RETURN
4000 IF C>=50 THEN ON C/10-4 GOTO 4100,4110
4010 ON C GOTO 4201,4202,4203,4204,4205,4206,4207,4208
4020 F=1: RETURN
4100 IF OD(18,1)<>0 THEN F=1: RETURN
4101 OD(18,1)=-1: OD(12,1)=-1: PRINT
     "AS YOU ENTER A PIRATE STEALS    YOUR RUM AND
     RUNS OFF LAUGHING.": F=1: RETURN
4110 PRINT "THE DEVIL KILLS YOU": GOTO 9990
4201 F=0: RETURN
4202 F=-(LU<>0): RETURN
4203 F=-(GU<>0): RETURN
4204 F=-(BE<>0): RETURN
4205 F=-(OD(3,1)=0): RETURN
4206 F=-(OD(11,1)=-1): RETURN
4207 F=-(OD(12,1)=-1): RETURN
4208 F=-(OD(10,1)=-1): RETURN
7000 DATA 19,NORTH,SOUTH,EAST,WEST,UP,DOWN
7001 DATA TAKE,DROP,KILL,INVENTORY,SCORE,CUT,SWIM
7002 DATA UNLOCK,DIG,EAT,WAVE,JUMP,DRINK
8000 DATA 25,1,12,27,-1,14,17,21,25,29,12,14,17,20,
     -1,-1,11,2,2,-1,19,11,1,-1,13,-1
8001 DATA BRASS LAMP,SWORD,SNORKEL,LARGE KEY,
     PERSIAN RUG,GOLD COIN
8002 DATA SILVER WAND,RUBY,DIAMOND,MEAN TROLL,
     GREEN DRAGON,PIRATE
8003 DATA DEVIL,IVORY KEY,CRYSTAL BRIDGE,SHOVEL,
     KITCHEN TABLE,BOTTLE OF RUM,EMPTY BOTTLE
8004 DATA ROPE TIED BETWEEN THE FLOOR AND CEILING,
     SMALL LAKE,LOCKED DOOR
8005 DATA DOOR,PADLOCKED GATE, GATE
```

```
8010 DATA 0,0,0,0,20,8,0,0,0,0,0,0,10,0,6,
     50,0,7,20,0,0
8011 DATA 30,0,0,100,0,0,-1,87,0,-1,110,0,-1,200,0,
     -1,200,0,10,0,0
8012 DATA 0,0,0,0,0,0,0,0,1,0,0,0,0,0,0,0,1,0,0,1
8013 DATA 0,0,1,0,0,1,0,0,1,0,0,1
8100 DATA 30
8101 DATA IN THE LIVING ROOM OF A LARGE HOUSE.
     A SIGN SAYS RETURN ALL TREASURES HERE.
     ,2,0,0,0,0,12,0
8102 DATA IN THE KITCHEN.,0,1,3,0,0,0,0
8103 DATA IN AN ENDLESS DESERT.,0,4,5,2,0,0,0
8104 DATA IN AN ENDLESS DESERT.,3,7,6,0,0,0,0
8105 DATA IN AN ENDLESS DESERT.,0,6,7,3,0,0,0
8106 DATA IN AN ENDLESS DESERT.,5,8,0,4,0,0,0
8107 DATA IN AN ENDLESS DESERT.,0,0,0,4,0,0,0
8108 DATA IN AN ENDLESS DESERT.,6,9,0,0,0,0,0
8109 DATA IN AN ENDLESS DESERT.,8,0,10,0,0,0,0
8110 DATA IN AN ENDLESS DESERT.,11,0,0,9,0,0,0
8111 DATA AT AN OASIS.,0,10,0,0,0,0,0
8112 DATA IN AN CELLAR.,0,16,13,0,1,0,2
8113 DATA AT THE GATES OF HELL.,0,0,0,12,0,20,0
8114 DATA IN A BLACKENED CAVERN.,0,15,0,0,0,0,0
8115 DATA IN A PASSAGE.,14,18,0,16,0,0,0
8116 DATA IN A PASSAGE.,12,0,15,0,0,17,0
8117 DATA IN THE PIRATES LAIR.,0,0,0,0,16,0,50
8118 DATA IN A PASSAGE.,15,19,0,0,0,0,0
8119 DATA IN A PASSAGE.,18,0,0,0,0,0,0
8120 DATA IN HELL... A DEVIL SAYS 'FIND THE RIGHT
     DIRECTION AND  LIVE ELSE DIE.
     ,30,30,30,21,30,30,3
8121 DATA IN A PASSAGE.,0,24,22,20,0,0,0
8122 DATA IN A DEAD END.,0,0,0,21,0,0,0
8123 DATA DEAD IN HELL.,0,0,0,0,0,0,0
8124 DATA AT THE BRINK OF A DEEP  CHASM.
     ,21,25,0,0,0,0,0
8125 DATA IN A BEAUTIFUL JEWELLED HALL.
     ,24,0,27,0,0,0,4
8126 DATA AT THE BRINK OF A DEEP  PIT. THERE ARE
     TRACES OF FIRE   AND BRIMSTONE HERE.
     ,26,0,0,25,0,28,0
8127 DATA IN A PASSAGE.,26,0,0,25,0,28,0
8128 DATA IN A PASSAGE.,0,0,0,0,27,18,0
8129 DATA SWIMMING IN A SMALL LAKE,0,0,0,0,0,0,5
8130 DATA ,0,0,0,0,0,0,60
9000 RESTORE: READ VC
9010 DIM V$(VC)
9020 FOR I=1 TO VC: READ V$(I): NEXT I
9030 READ OC: DIM OD(OC,4): DIM OD$(OC)
9040 FOR I=1 TO OC: READ OD(I,1): NEXT I
9050 FOR I=1 TO OC: READ OD$(I): NEXT I
9060 FOR I=1 TO OC: FOR J=2 TO 4
9070 READ OD(I,J): NEXT J: NEXT I
9080 READ LC: DIM L$(LC),L(LC,7)
9090 FOR I=1 TO LC: READ L$(I)
9100 FOR J=1 TO 7: READ L(I,J): NEXT J: NEXT I
```

```
9110 SC=0: BE=0: LU=0: GU=0: CX=6: ST=100
9120 RETURN
9980 PRINT: PRINT: PRINT: PRINT
9981 PRINT "CONGRATULATIONS  THIS ADVENTURE IS OVER
       AND YOU HAVE RETURNED   SAFELY WITH ALL THE
       TREASURES."
9990 PRINT: PRINT "SCORE "; SC: PRINT
       "DO YOU WISH TO PLAY AGAIN ?"
9991 M$=INKEY$: IF M$="" THEN 9991
9992 IF M$="Y" THEN RUN
```

Also Available

CPSIA information can be obtained
at www.ICGtesting.com
Printed in the USA
LVHW102343250722
724375LV00002B/11

9 781789 829457